running strong

CANDICE WARNER

running strong

HarperCollins*Publishers*

If this book raises any issues for you or someone you love, you can contact Lifeline Crisis Support Line (13 11 14) or Beyond Blue Support Service (1300 22 4636).

HarperCollins*Publishers*
Australia • Brazil • Canada • France • Germany • Holland • India
Italy • Japan • Mexico • New Zealand • Poland • Spain • Sweden
Switzerland • United Kingdom • United States of America

HarperCollins acknowledges the Traditional Custodians
of the land upon which we live and work, and pays respect
to Elders past and present.

First published in Australia in 2023
by HarperCollins*Publishers* Australia Pty Limited
Gadigal Country
Level 13, 201 Elizabeth Street, Sydney NSW 2000
ABN 36 009 913 517
harpercollins.com.au

A catalogue record for this book is available from the National Library of Australia

ISBN 978 1 4607 6363 6 (hardback)
ISBN 978 1 4607 1600 7 (ebook)
ISBN 978 1 4607 4788 9 (audiobook)

Cover design by Hazel Lam, HarperCollins Design Studio
Cover and endpapers photography © Alana Landsberry
Internal photographs are courtesy of the author's family archives unless otherwise specified.
All reasonable attempts have been made to trace the copyright holders and obtain permission to reproduce this material. The publisher would be grateful to be notified of any omissions that should be incorporated in future reprints.
Typeset in Bembo Std by Kirby Jones
Printed and bound in Australia by McPherson's Printing Group

FSC
www.fsc.org
MIX
Paper | Supporting
responsible forestry
FSC® C001695

For Mum, Dad, Tim and Patty,
and for Dave, Ivy, Indi and Isla

CONTENTS

PROLOGUE

Arrival

If I were to say there were a hundred people waiting for us at Sydney Airport, it might sound like an exaggeration, but I think perhaps there were more. There may have been two hundred, two thousand, the whole country. It *felt* like the whole country. Every person in every city and town in every state, who all wanted to come and get a piece of the biggest news story around.

Today it was ball tampering, and tomorrow there'd be something else. Today it was me and Dave and our family, and tomorrow, who knows? For us it was our lives, however. For them it was for today, tomorrow and maybe next week. For us it was forever.

Yelling, questions, flashes and clicks. There was nothing to do but put our heads down and keep going. I knew that. I'd learned that. I had one of our girls in my arms. Dave had the other. We'd just flown from South Africa to Dubai, Dubai to Sydney, and they were exhausted. We were exhausted too. But they would sleep, and go to daycare or to Mum's place, and they'd bounce back; we'd make sure of that.

I knew Dave and I would bounce back also, but it would take time.

There were policemen around us, and also ill-will. I felt like a criminal, returning for justice to be served. Dave stopped and spoke briefly to the cameras and to every person wanting their little piece. He was hurting. I could hear it in his voice, and that hurt me deeply.

It's all my fault. I heard that in my head as he spoke. *It's all my fault.* When he stopped speaking, I knew we'd just have to put our heads down again and keep going. *Just keep going.*

He finished and I put my arm around him and he put his around me. We had a car waiting for us ahead. *Just keep going.*

I'd been at the centre of a media firestorm that had begun eleven years before: a night out that became a conversation the entire country wanted to have. I was a kid having a pash with a boy at the pub, but the newspapers called it a toilet tryst. They put sex in the story – never explicitly, because they couldn't prove something that didn't happen, but it was between and behind the words that they used. Sex, technology and misogyny.

That story was a fire that raged longer than anyone would have expected, but it died eventually. Back then, I put my head down and pushed forward. I tried to avoid the flames and the toxic smoke, and I survived. I didn't seem to be burned, but these things affect you, inside. Parts of you become raw and others become hardened. Tough times create tough people, as they say. For better or for worse.

Some things end up being unspoken, and some ideas fester. Old wounds are there to be opened. This was all my fault.

I hadn't told anyone, but throughout the nightmare tour of South Africa, as that country's players and fans and officials tried to use my past to pierce through Dave's armour, I felt that somehow I was to blame. I pushed that idea down though. It was an idea that didn't need to be named or spoken out loud. Success would come, the tour would end. The old wounds would heal again. They didn't, though.

We were bustled from the airport and into the waiting car, and were driven to a hotel suite in the city. From there, crisis management. It seemed the whole country was baying for blood, with even the prime minister weighing in, calling the incident a 'disgrace'. It was all too much. People were calling for Dave's blood, but I knew that ire was misplaced.

I've never spoken to Dave about the ball-tampering incident: not then, not now. I don't ask him about it now because I don't want to know more. I love him and I know enough to know that he's taken much more than his share of the blame. I don't ask him now, because I don't care. He's the best husband, the best father, and the best man any woman could ever dream to spend their life with.

I didn't ask him then because I knew where the weight of blame should be placed.

It was all my fault.

The ball-tampering incident tapped into a wellspring of guilt in me that I didn't even know still existed. Guilt and shame I thought I'd come to terms with coursed through me, and amplified as I felt more shame and more guilt – even when I knew those feelings were affecting my ability to support

Dave and be a good mum for our girls in a bizarre time in their young lives.

The weight became heavy and while my shoulders are strong, I eventually buckled.

I look tough, like Dave, but we feel and want and hurt like anyone else. Scars split open in the wake of South Africa, and old wounds were aggravated. In this life where there is so much goodness; so much sun and sea and growth and family, there have been dark moments. But after every night comes a dawn, after every drought comes rain. This life isn't always easy, but it's always good.

You have to breathe through it. You have to keep running.

I

The Dream

I was the product of a dream, a dream that became a home. That home is still there, a two-storey piece of Australiana just a couple of blocks from the beach. The dream is still there too, expanding, as family does.

The dream and the house was, and still is, owned by Mickey and Kerry Falzon, my dad and mum. That house isn't where I live anymore, but I still call it home. It'll always be home as long as Mum and Dad are there. That house is in the coastal suburb of Maroubra, in Sydney's east, south of Bondi and north of the mouth of Botany Bay, adjacent to Matraville, the suburb where my husband, David, grew up.

I, my husband and kids, my mum and dad, and my past, present and future, live in this area. When Dave, the kids and I travel – something we do a lot – the coastline, the beaches and the ocean go with us. This area will always be a part of me and I can imagine I'll always be here, living what is now my dream, but was first my dad's dream.

Mickey Falzon first came to Maroubra more than sixty years ago. He came on a pushbike when he wasn't much more than a boy. Looking out at the sand and ocean and the little outer-suburban beach community, as it was then, he said to himself: 'This will be where I will live and make a family.'

My dad was born of immigrant parents from Malta, a tiny island country sitting in the Mediterranean Sea about eighty kilometres south of the Sicilian coast. Maltese immigration to Australia was widespread at the time my grandparents settled here. Before independence in 1964, Malta had the strongest of post-war bonds with the United Kingdom, with the colony having fought bitterly during the Siege of Malta against Axis forces. In fact, the entire country was awarded a George Cross – equal in stature to the Victoria Cross – after the war, and that cross is now on the Maltese flag. Australia considered the Maltese 'white British subjects' after the war, meaning there was no barrier to emigration.

With a seriously depressed economy, a tenth of the Maltese population decided to emigrate to Australia in the two decades after World War II. Mickey was born in Australia and was raised almost wholly by his formidable mum, after my paternal grandfather disappeared. There were sporadic attempts by my grandfather to reconnect with my dad throughout his life, but for the most part it was just Mickey and his mum living in the light-industrial inner-city suburb of Waterloo, and then Rosebery.

My dad first came to Maroubra one Christmas Day in the sixties. He was given the pushbike as a present, and he and his uncle, his mother's brother Dicky, decided to head to the nearest piece of coast. When Mickey arrived at Maroubra Beach, he stood on the sand and saw his whole ideal life ahead of him. He saw a house that was touched by sea-spray, scents of dinner mixed with a salty breeze, and he saw a wife and children in his imagination.

My father has taught me a lot of things that have been useful in my life, but I'm not sure anything has been as useful as his showing me that dreams and fantasies are not the same thing, and that the difference between a dream and a fantasy is hard work.

Hard work is something that Mickey has never, ever been fearful of. It's something he still embraces to this day. For my entire childhood, Dad worked his arse off, every day, in so many ways.

For fifty years Dad worked at Randwick Council, a local government entity that extends from Sydney's Centennial Park in the north, down south to the cliffs of La Perouse, and east–west from the ocean to a line of golf courses extending from Moore Park south to Eastlakes. In that half-century, I believe he took two sick days. Maybe it was three.

He would always get out there, in sickness and in health, because he loved his work at the council, which basically involved anything and everything that the residents needed. One day he'd be picking up rubbish and gardening, the next he might be finding lost dogs or mediating disputes between neighbours. Sometimes his job even had him lifeguarding on Maroubra and Coogee beaches, a task he particularly loved and something one of his sons, my brother Patty, does to this day.

My dad didn't only work in his council role. When he could pick up extra work, Mickey earned money on weekends and at nights, mowing lawns for the schools, or marking lines for the local rugby club, and working as a doorman at the Bexley North Hotel, now an inoffensive suburban pub with a TAB, bistro and clean motel rooms, but back then a grungy, fun destination for live music, with bands like AC/DC, Cold Chisel and Mental As Anything gracing the stage.

My dad was working at that hotel when he met my mum, Kerry, in 1977. They were very much kindred spirits. They both lived in strong, matriarchal homes. My mum hadn't grown up without a father as my dad had, but her mother exerted a powerful influence on the family. My grandad was a pastry chef and usually out of the house well before dawn and then often in bed before the rest of the family had dinner. The mantle of responsibility was something my grandmother wore easily. A strict Catholic, my maternal grandmother went to church every Sunday and, every night, prayed the Holy Rosary. She adhered to the tenets of her faith and ran her house with an iron will.

When Mum met Dad, she'd just returned from Europe and the expectation from her family was that she meet a nice, normal fella and settle down. There was probably a little part of Mum that believed that Europe was the peak of her life's excitement, and life was going to be a little more settled and predictable after her travels, whether she liked it or not.

I wouldn't call Dad settled and predictable, and he's far lovelier because of it.

Mum says she was attracted to Dad when she first met him. He was tanned and muscular and very outgoing, but the thing that set him apart was that he wasn't full of Dutch courage like the other men she knew. When they first met, Mum thought Dad was gregarious because he was drunk, like almost every other man in the pub, but he actually wasn't. He was never drunk. It wasn't that he had a moral or religious objection to alcohol – he'd have a sip of beer or wine sometimes – it was just that he didn't need alcohol to be the life of the party.

Mum says Dad really made her laugh, and that was what started their relationship, but she says the reason their partnership has endured is because they have always shared the same values, ethics and dreams. They have always wanted to enjoy themselves, at the beach, together and with a big, close family. That has been their love; that has been their marriage. Theirs is a marriage that worked and still works. Theirs is a partnership worth studying.

It only took a few weeks after their first meeting for my mum and dad to know that they would be together for their whole lives.

One night after a nice meal at Dimitri's Restaurant on Cleveland Street in Surry Hills, Dad asked Mum, 'What d'ya reckon – we might get married?' If you knew my dad, that style of proposal is in no way surprising. If you knew my mum, it's in no way surprising that she told him she reckoned they should.

They were married in 1978 in a little Catholic church called St Patrick's in Guildford, with all of the bells and whistles attended to, before moving to my maternal grandparents' backyard in Guildford for a reception that Grandad catered.

Shortly afterwards, Mum and Dad moved together to Maroubra. Dad had been saving money for a handful of years and, without any family help, he and Mum managed to buy a semi-detached home a stone's throw away from Maroubra Beach, and within walking distance from Dad's little council offices.

This is where they live now. This is where I lived and left, and then came back to with Dave and our girls.

It's worth noting that the path to ownership of a beachside family home in Sydney in the seventies was quite different to the one that exists now. Now a family home in Maroubra costs forty to fifty times the average yearly Australian salary, but back then it was only four or five times — attainable to a young man with little education, very limited reading and writing abilities, but the ability to work his arse off.

My parents' plan was always to fill their beachside home with kids, and the first to arrive was my eldest brother, Timothy, or Timmy. Eighteen months later, Patrick — or as we know him, Patty — arrived. Roughly eighteen months after Patty's birth, Mum's prayers for a girl were finally answered and I came into the world, Candice Ann Falzon, born 13 March 1985.

With three extra mouths to feed, Dad didn't slow down but worked as hard as he ever had. In fact, some of my first memories are of seeing Dad from the window or the front yard returning from work, wandering up the street towards his house, his family and his lunch. I also can see him at Souths Juniors Leagues Club at Kingsford, where he picked up glasses after hours, and the Randwick Rugby Club, where he marked the lines before games and training.

Mum was just as hard a worker. She worked at Souths Juniors, too, at the front desk, and the managers knew to give

Mum and Dad alternating shifts so there was always someone for us kids. Eventually Mum took a job selling Nutrimetics make-up and skin care products, and she poured herself into that job. I watched her work at all hours and give seminars in such an authoritative way, I was in awe along with my brothers, especially when she came home with a company car and the title of director. We weren't surprised though.

But I can perhaps most vividly remember seeing my young Mum and Dad at the Maroubra Surf Life Saving Club, where Dad worked and we all played. Those memories are especially fond, because in the surf club we found a second beachside home.

*

Dad used to say: 'Why would anyone want a pool when you have the beach?' That sounded like wisdom to me. It still does. That's the mantra of a beach person, and all of us in our family were and are beach people. The beach is a big reason as to why we all love Maroubra so much: surfing, swimming, running, fishing, the shimmering sunrises over the water and the blue becoming purple at sunset. It's a beach and an ocean that never fails to give. Of course, there are a lot of places in the world fringed with a bit of beach and ocean that aren't Maroubra. But Maroubra is what it is because of its people and places, and they're something very special to our family.

Maroubra is unique. It's part of Sydney's beachside east but it sure as hell ain't Vaucluse, or even Bondi. Maroubra is working class, and it's also multicultural, with Indigenous roots that are yet to be uprooted. Maroubra can be confrontational, but never without cause. Tough but fair, that's a way you could describe the mood of Maroubra. That's also how you may describe my Dad. And that's how you may describe me, too.

Dad was a member of the Maroubra Surf Life Saving Club before I was born. An inauspicious and cheaply built low-slung structure squeezed between Marine Parade and the beach, the club building itself is nothing to write home about, but the community and history is another thing altogether. One of the original fourteen surf lifesaving clubs that were established after bathing in the ocean was made legal in New South Wales in 1906 (the ban, often ignored, had existed since the 1830s), the club has a strong, enduring and generationally replenishing history, with that history being hung, in black and white, on pictures on its walls.

Dennis Green OAM, bearer of the Australian flag at the 1972 Munich Olympics opening ceremony, is one of the more well-known characters pictured. A pioneer of surf-ski paddling, he won an Olympic bronze medal with another Maroubra lifesaver, and then competed in the next four Olympic Games. His athletic career started at the surf club and he actually lived in the surf club when he was fifteen.

There's also Olympic sprint canoeist Graham 'Johno' Johnson and Dennis Heussner, a legend of Australian surf lifesaving who, after a career as an Olympic sprint canoeist, became one of the most successful competitors in the history of the Australian Surf Life Saving Championships, the annual national carnival competition featuring the essential elements of surf lifesaving, such as Malibu board riding, beach running and ocean swimming.

Heussner wasn't only a champion of the sport, he was an originator. Alongside Barry Rodgers, another Maroubra champion and the man who taught me how to swim, Heussner travelled to the United States and, seeing a combined event in a surf carnival there, Rodgers and Heussner petitioned for a new event to be included in the Australian Surf Life Saving Championships.

This event that they were calling for would combine the major individual surf lifesaving disciplines that a lifesaver must master, namely swimming, running, paddling and board riding. These events were to be rolled into one multi-discipline super event, to be called the Ironman. This event would end up dominating and growing surf lifesaving as a sport, with the title 'Ironman', and later 'Ironwoman', becoming uniquely powerful in the Australian sporting lexicon.

The Ironman was first introduced into the 1966 Australian Surf Life Saving Championships, with the second, third and fourth Australian Ironman competitions won by Barry Rodgers. The first was won by a Queensland competitor named Hayden Kenny, whose son Grant pushed the sport to places it hadn't been before – and, frankly, hasn't been since.

In 1980, only fourteen years after his father had won the first Australian Ironman, sixteen-year-old Grant Kenny won the junior and open Australian Ironman titles on the same day, thrusting himself into the public consciousness.

As Grant matured throughout the eighties, so too did the sport. Through a sponsorship with the Kellogg's cereal brand

Nutri-Grain, an Ironman-centred film named *The Coolangatta Gold* was produced, about two brothers who are competing for their father's love, who is determined that one of his sons should win the competition, with Grant Kenny playing himself as an emerging semi-professional Ironman.

When the film came out, Kenny's broad smile, broader shoulders and his tan and blond-flecked hair were known to pretty much every Aussie, and so too did the Coolangatta Gold, the fictional race from the film, which then became an actual race and one of the nation's blue-ribbon surf lifesaving competitions. In another twist of life reflecting art and vice versa, two talented young brothers, Darren and Dean Mercer, would soon start competing in the Gold only a few years after its inception, competing strongly into the early 2000s with podium finishes. The race would also herald the arrival of a superstar competitor, Guy Leech, who took out first place in the first two years of the competition.

When I was a young girl, this new sport was exploding in popularity across the country and one of my very early and hazy memories is of being at the surf club watching the televised Ironman events with Dad. At the time, I didn't really understand how these events worked, but I knew they were a big deal for everybody at the surf club. I knew they were a big deal for Dad. I understood also that there was a link between the people in those races and the photos of the men on the walls of the club, and I wanted my photograph on the wall.

That wasn't a dream for girls back then, it seemed. There were no Ironwomen then: not at our club, anyway. For a long time Maroubra Surf Club didn't allow female members, as it was one of the last clubs in the country, if not the last, to provide facilities for women.

Fortunately I was too young to be so easily disheartened. My dreams thankfully persisted, until role models could arrive.

2

A Maroubra Girl

It was a Sunday morning. I was six, and Dad and I were up early. He asked me if I wanted to walk the length of the beach with him to the southern end of Maroubra, where the Malabar headland largely cuts off much of the wind and waves. And there, in front of Maroubra's second club, the South Maroubra Surf Life Saving Club, I saw a group of kids my age having the time of their lives, running and wading and jumping in a jumble of semi-organised fun.

Back then, our club, Maroubra, didn't have a Nippers program, and this was the first time I'd ever seen kids competing and training in modified surf lifesaving events.

I was instantly jealous, and the green streak in my belly spread even more when I saw that a girl from kindergarten was one of them. That girl's name was Llara, and I sat next to her at school. In the common way in which girls bond at that age, we said we were going to be best friends forever. What is uncommon, however, is that it actually turned out that way. Llara and I are still best friends.

I asked Dad what exactly was going on in front of us when I saw those other girls racing around. Dad told me that this was called Nippers, the kids' version of the training that all the teens and adults did at the surf club.

My eyes were saucers. It looked like so much fun. I told Dad I wanted to join in, but he told me that I couldn't because our surf club didn't have a program. After much pouting and perhaps complaining, Dad told me that if I really wanted to join the other kids in Nippers, he'd sign us up at the rival South Maroubra club, where Llara and the other kids were members.

My experience of that first year was one big ball of laughter and competition and running. It was there at Nippers that I found that I *loved* running. Even as a six-year-old, it made sense to me: the mechanics of it, the feeling, the glorious exertion. I was good at it, too. At that age, everything you do at Nippers is a based around running – when you're that young you don't really swim or board; you mostly just run around, sometimes on the sand, in beach sprints and flag races, and sometimes through the water in wading races, but then no deeper than your waist.

I loved running, I loved wading and I loved winning, even at that age. There was something transcendent about it. It made me more than what I had been before I'd raced. It was Dad's smile. It made me feel good. I liked to win.

At the end of the season our family was invited to the South Maroubra presentation night. I had one of the best feelings of my young life, when it was my name that was called out as the best performer in my Nippers group. There's a photo I still have of that night and in it you can see that my body is about to burst out of my skin, it's swelling so much with pride.

The next year Maroubra Surf Club started offering a Nippers program of their own, so I moved over, and that next year was quite a different experience. I still had all the fun, perhaps even more fun, but after moving north 400 metres or so up the beach, and progressing to a different age group, I was exposed to much different conditions. Further north at Maroubra Surf Club we didn't have the protection from the Malabar headland and the surf would sometimes roar through the middle of the beach. We were also expected to venture further into the waves.

I can strongly remember what those big days would feel like as a little girl. I was never thinking about the surf as we started the day, because we always ran before we swam, and I was always concentrating on trying to beat my main competitor in my age group, John Sutton, who went on to become a South Sydney Rabbitohs legend. Even then I was very focused when I was racing, and doing everything I could to win.

Then after the running, my mind would turn eastward to the water. Anxiety would flood in. I wasn't a strong swimmer and I wasn't comfortable in the waves. I loved the beach, but preferred to be on the sand. I'd have to force myself to push through the foamy threshold between sand and ocean.

That worry got worse when, at about the age of nine, we started to train on the board, which meant lying down on foam boards and paddling out to buoys and then back onto the beach, through the waves. This was when I realised there was a crucial part of surf lifesaving that I would struggle with for my whole career: the surf. Waves would tip me over, sending me and the board into the briny mess. I'd find it hard to be calm underneath the surface. Anxiety would surge through me, my thoughts only about what it would mean if I couldn't get back to the surface. Then I'd burst back into the air gasping, my hair matted, trying to find the board that I knew could smash into me at any second. God, I hated it. The surf scared me. Sometimes it still scares me. I really wished that I could be one of the girls in the group who just flatly refused to get in the water and stood on the beach, the coaches trying to coax them in.

That wasn't me though. The fear of the waves and water was always a lesser fear. The big fear was being considered a chicken, or somehow less than the boys, who would always get into the water due to bravery or a sense of masculine pride.

I wanted to be one of the boys. I wanted to be better than the boys. I bloody loved beating the boys.

*

There are some suburbs in Sydney that are defined by food, or by nightlife, but Maroubra is defined by sport and surfing, and when I was growing up, sport and surfing were predominantly male endeavours.

Out on the break you'd see some female surfers, but not that many. It was the same at the epic Friday social touch footy game that took place every week in the field out the back of the Maroubra Surf Club during the summer months.

That game was a staple of my childhood. Everyone from the neighbourhood – mainly surfers and members of the surf club – would collect at the field and play informal games of touch until they lost the light.

Dad played each week, and my brothers as well. I did too sometimes, and when I did I was so bloody proud. Touch, backyard footy, backyard basketball: it all made me want to be one of the boys. This was an enduring element of my childhood, not because I wanted to be masculine, but because it looked like the boys were allowed to have more fun.

Why? It became a persistent question. Why did I have to wear a skirt and make sure I didn't accidentally flash my undies? Why couldn't I wear shorts? Why wasn't there a local girls soccer team, just netball? Why weren't there any pictures of women on the walls of the surf club? Why, why, why?

There weren't any answers to those questions, and perhaps I didn't really want them. I just wanted to be included in the fun. And for the most part, I was – Mum and Dad never stopped me from doing the things I wanted to do, because that wasn't their way. If I wanted to play soccer, they'd argue to the local football club that I should be allowed to play in the boys' team. If I wanted to play touch footy with the boys and men, they'd tell me to just get out there and play, and they'd cheer as I competed.

Tim and Pat grumbled a bit when Mum and Dad forced them to include me in what had otherwise been one-on-one games, but my brothers were always good to me. They are still good to me. They're kind and loving and, in many ways, two super-charged versions of Dad, with Tim incredibly driven and absolute, and Pat more laid-back, humorous, and perhaps, considered. Both are very family oriented and both became protective of me as I got older. I can't imagine loving my brothers any more than I do.

There were other boys I hung out with who were part of the surf club, and this was a group who were driven to succeed in fields they chose, including UFC fighter Richie Vaculik, filmmaker Macario De Souza, big-wave surfer Mark Mathews, and NRL players Reni Maitua and John Sutton. And there were, of course, the Bra Boys.

If you're not familiar with the local group of surfers and friends known notoriously as the Bra Boys, they were a group – a gang, if you like – of mates who lived in Maroubra, liked to surf, and rejected any other external criminal influence trying to enter the area. At the core of the group were four brothers who were raised by a troubled mother: Sunny, Jai, Koby and Dakota Abberton. All were, and still are, excellent surfers, especially Koby, who is a world-renowned big-wave surfer.

The Bra Boys and the Abberton brothers cop a bad rap in no small part due to Jai and Koby's highly publicised role in the killing of an underworld standover man, but growing up I never saw the dark side, only the positive influence.

As I grew up, I could see the brothers were doing something with their lives. They were surfing all over the world and earning a living from what they loved, and doing it on their own terms. There was a perception about the Bra Boys and about people from Maroubra in general, then; a perception of criminality, theft, violence and drugs, but that's not what I saw. Maybe it was happening elsewhere, but I just saw these guys working hard to become surfers, or filmmakers, or MMA fighters, or professional sportspeople. I only saw them as exemplars: they were local boys who, by way of hard work, were out there fulfilling their goals and dreams.

*

I really enjoyed school, all the way up until Year Five. Until then I attended St Mary–St Joseph Catholic Primary School, which was less than 200 metres from both the surf club and our home.

It was a place that was very easily incorporated into my life, not only geographically but socially too. School was fun. My friends were there, and it was just a seamless part of my life. On the weekend, Llara and I would make treehouses and put on little concerts, and find junk for the garage sales we held where nobody would buy anything except our dads. And of course there was Nippers, which we did together. During the week Llara and I would be playing sport, or painting or learning about geography, and escaping to the beach when the school bell rang. It was a happy time.

Then, in Year Five, my enjoyment of school started to die. My parents had decided that, for the duration of high school, I would study at St Catherine's School, a very old, very august Anglican private girls school in Waverley, only a fifteen-minute drive from home, but another economic world away. In preparation for high school, it was recommended that girls move over in Year Five so they could make the transition from primary to high school more seamlessly.

I didn't fear the move as it was one that was made by a number of my friends and, besides, it was a school that was familiar to me.

St Catherine's had a swimming pool and the primary coach of the swimming program was Barry Rodgers, the Maroubra

SLSC legend and original Ironman himself. Before I moved to the school, I'd learned to swim in the St Catherine's pool with Barry, and because I'd already spent time around the campus, I thought I knew what school might be like there, what the social life might be like. But I had no idea – the transition was a shock for me.

When I moved to St Catherine's, teachers identified that I had an issue with English comprehension. I was doing well in every other subject, but I simply couldn't keep up with my reading. Auxiliary classes were arranged to give me the opportunity to improve, but that just put me in more of a funk. I wanted fewer hours staring at pages of text, not more.

No matter how long I spent staring at those pages, things never seemed to get any better. I could never get things straight – which characters in which settings, the significance of places in the story. Later, my comprehension improved vastly but in Year Five, at age ten, reading felt like torture to me, and when I was forced to sit down inside with a book, I'd invariably end up staring out the window thinking about all the sport that was happening without me. I really wanted to improve my reading but there were so many other things I wanted to be doing more, especially when it was so hard to make my mind understand what was happening on the page. In the end, I think the fact that my reading had been singled out as poor may have been a contributing factor to me being 'othered' and, ultimately, bullied.

There was one very influential girl who was behind the bullying and she identified something other than my reading that she homed in on as a weapon against me. Writing what that thing is now with an adult perspective seems so ridiculous or absurd that it almost makes me laugh, but it almost makes me cry, too, because I can still remember the pain of it.

This girl had decided that I had unusually large thumbs, and teased me about them constantly. Not fingers, not hands, just thumbs. If only the internet was then what it is now, I'd have documentary evidence that I had normal-sized thumbs, but back then it made me embarrassed to show my hands.

It affected me, probably not because I really believed my thumbs *were* any different to anyone else's, but because this girl and her friends, many of whom were girls I had been and still wanted to be friends with, had decided that they wanted to create distance between me and their social group.

It was an isolating time in my young life. The thumbs thing wasn't the most painful aspect of the bullying either. That, at least, I kind of knew was ridiculous, and I think they were aware I knew that, so instead they started mocking Dad and his car, a relatively recent Toyota Lexcen. It was a perfectly normal and functional family sedan, but I suppose not the Land Rover or Lexus that some of the girls were being picked up in. I used to cry sometimes when they taunted me about my dad. Those words against him were daggers that reached deeply inside of me.

I used to wonder why – why were they being so mean, and why were they attacking my father?

I'd always put Dad on a huge pedestal, working as hard as he did. I admired every aspect about him, including his car. Dad had worked hard to buy that car, which did a great job ferrying us all here and there. I simply couldn't understand what was wrong with it. Of course, there was nothing wrong with it; it was an honestly earned vehicle that did everything it should. But I wondered whether there was something I was missing; that perhaps there was something lesser about Dad's car, and perhaps even something lesser about him – but I didn't want to think that. I refused to think that. My dad was a champion, and still is a champion, and no mean girls at school were going to steer me away from that immovable fact.

Even though it was foremost in my mind, I didn't tell anyone about the isolation or bullying I felt at my new school. Sitting down and pouring out the minutiae of emotions wasn't what we did in our family. In the context of a loving supportive family in a loving supportive community, we didn't have to – there were no darker motivations to consider, so I just didn't have the skills in my emotional toolbox to talk about the problems I was having at school.

In response, I retreated into myself, and I think this was a dubious skill that I learned well and put in the emotional toolbox I still own to this day. I became reluctant to speak at all in some school situations, fearful of saying something that might trigger jokes and derision. I avoided certain people, even friends who I feared might join in the bullying. For the first time in my life I became something of a loner.

In that period, sport massively helped me stay sane. When I was competing, I knew exactly what was expected of me. Sport was a place where the rules and goals and your own ambitions were starkly obvious. It was also a place where you were judged on merit. If you ran faster than another girl, you were better than that girl. If you ran slower, worse. No snide comments could change those facts.

It also helped that I was very good at sport, and only improved when I arrived at St Catherine's. I think even as such a young person, I used all that hurt and anger I was feeling as fuel. It probably wasn't healthy, but it was better than staying inside myself, or eating my feelings, or thinking ever darker thoughts.

When I was playing sport, whether I was training or competing, I had drive. I wanted to show the other girls what I could do, what our family could do. I wanted to have proof that we were tougher than they were, tougher than any of their barbs.

I became the school athletics champion and I became the school gymnastic champion. I became someone – and that was someone defined wholly as an athlete. I didn't care what anyone thought of me as a reader, or even as a friend. As an athlete, people had to respect me because, as the kids say now, I had the receipts.

In class, I developed something of a carefree attitude to school work. I was progressing decently in most of my classes, but made little effort to address my lack of English comprehension, and as the last days of my primary-school life were disappearing behind me, a fear of high school and the expectations around reading that I would be faced with started to rise in me.

The ocean would be calm sometimes, but of course, not always. Life would be easy sometimes, but of course, not always. There's always a way to keep your head above the surface, even though sometimes it doesn't feel that way.

3

The Mantra

I love to watch a storm roll in over the ocean. We live on a cliff now, and it's a wondrous thing to watch the sky darken and the bulbous rain clouds gathering on the horizon. It's movement and change; it's the world imposing itself on us, inescapable and absolute. You cannot be outside. You cannot be in the ocean. The waves rise and bring chaotic form. The ocean can be your friend and then, in a moment, your worst enemy.

As a girl I was scared of storms and scared of the waves. We sometimes forget what childhood fears are like, but I remember the fears I had as a girl. They were complete and overwhelming. I was scared of the surf, scared of the wash, scared of the roiling uncertainty of the ocean because it made me feel that I might disappear below it and never emerge.

Maroubra can be quite a rough beach compared to some in the east. It's far from calm and friendly, and as a little girl, I would be in awe of what the surfers could create on the waves, and of the ocean swimmers and board riders who confidently smashed their way through the break on the way out to the back, and then artfully used that break to glide back in.

When I was an older Nipper and competing in swimming and board events, there was no confident smash and there was no artful glide. I was all panic in and all panic out, sometimes screaming as I went.

Year after year I became an even better beach runner, though. Reluctantly I had to train in the other aspects of the sport, but primarily I did what I was good at, what I felt comfortable doing. When I was staring down a flat stretch of beach, ready to race with girls either side of me, I knew I could power through that sand faster than anyone.

Obviously I knew how to swim and I enjoyed swimming, but only as a means to an end. I swam to stay safe as I body-surfed or splashed around in the shallows, not for competition or fun. That wasn't my thing and a fear of storms and waves was a big part of that.

Dad always encouraged me to compete in ocean-swimming events at Maroubra as a Nipper and sometimes I'd enter them, but if I did line up, I'd end up screaming and complaining. Even if I did make it out to the marker, it was always fear that brought me back to the beach, always, and not even my competitive drive could overcome it.

I got better on the board which, for Nippers, is an event often raced in calmer conditions and where the surf is smallest on the beach. I just wasn't a natural swimmer or board rider; I was a beach runner – it was as though there was a line along the beach and on one side lay the area I could compete in and the other side in which I couldn't.

I had no problem with that, either. I was a really good beach runner, and usually won my races. Those wins gave me confidence, and getting praise from the people who Dad looked up to and respected, the older blokes, the officials and the club's best athletes, made me feel good. My cup was full already with validation after beach-running events. I didn't need the others.

But that all changed one day. Dad and I had driven over to Bondi for a Nippers branch carnival. Life had overtaken us a little bit that day and we were running late, so by the time we got to the beach the girls in my running event had already finished.

With the board event still to come, Dad told me I might as well get out there and have a go. The sea was as flat as a pancake, and the board race was happening in the protected northern part of Bondi Beach where any little waves that may come would largely be collected by Ben Buckler Point before they'd get to me and my board.

I didn't want to disappoint Dad, especially now after all the effort of getting there, so I lined up with precisely no expectations about what my results might be.

We were off, and I remember naturally wanting to keep up with the girls at the front, and managed to do it without too many problems. I kept my head down and the rest of my body flat on the board and was largely untested by wave and wake. I remember it being a long race, but I also remember thinking that was a good thing, something that could benefit me. All I needed to do was to keep going. That was easy. I might be out of breath and exhausted and my arms were hurting, but that was it. I wasn't going to be washed into the water and I wasn't going to drown; I just had to keep going.

I kept going and going and was very happy to find, as we headed back to the beach, that I couldn't see a pack of girls ahead of me, only a few. To my great delight and surprise, I ended up finishing second. I didn't even know that I'd got used to the gratification I felt from winning running races until I came second in this event – I was flushed from head to toe with happiness and endorphins.

From that day on I started to love board events, and quite often would choose them over running events in carnivals. 'Just keep going' was my board-event mantra, and it became my mantra at school, and later in life too.

Things do get better, if you just keep going, keep striving. This particular belief was embedded deeply in me, and I had Mum to thank for it. For Dad, hard work is a switch inside him that's stuck in the 'on' position. Maybe it was just the continuing momentum of the Maroubra dream, maybe it was always in Dad, but that's how it was and how it still is for him. Dad was the relentless worker, but Mum was the optimist. She was a hard worker too, but she believed in fate and affirmations as well. She believed in sunny skies inevitably following dark days.

As I was already a good runner and was now becoming a very decent competitor in the board events, I started talking to Mum and Dad about one day competing in multi-discipline Ironwoman events which were now being offered to girls. Women had finally been given their own Ironwoman competition in 1992, and the inaugural event at Collaroy, then sponsored by Ella Baché, was won by a Samantha O'Brien from South Maroubra Surf Club. It was exciting seeing the sport take off, especially with a local champion.

My parents were encouraging, but Dad's pragmatism intruded; he said that I'd have to seriously improve my swimming if I was going to be competitive.

He was absolutely right. While I could swim, I certainly wasn't speedy. If I was ever going to be competitive in an Ironwoman competition, I'd have to be a far, far better swimmer than I was, and far more confident in the surf.

I joined a local swim club to improve my stroke and speed, training with a squad under coach Angelo Basalo at the Des Renford Leisure Centre. Renford was another legend in surf lifesaving. He was an active member of the South Maroubra club, and then, at age thirty-nine, he started competing in marathon swimming events. He became famous for completing nineteen English Channel crossings and was known as the King of the Channel.

When I started with the squad I was painfully slow. One of the ways we trained was by using time cycles, meaning that we would swim a certain number of laps, with each lap starting after a certain amount of time had passed since we'd started the last lap. That time could be a minute, for instance, meaning for the very fast girls, they might spend thirty-five to forty seconds swimming and then have up to twenty seconds' rest before starting the next lap. But I needed every second of that time to complete my lap, which meant no rest at all before starting again.

As I swam, I could hear the other kids and parents in my head. I was out of my depth; I was just dragging the rest of the girls back. Sometimes I was physically in the way as I lumbered my way down the pool, having missed a time cycle.

I just kept going, though. I could hear the disparaging voices of the other kids and other parents as I swam, but I could also hear my encouraging mum, calling from the bleachers, 'Come on, Candice.' I knew if I kept working, kept concentrating on my form, kept moving forward, I would get to sunny skies.

For a long time – months, at least – it looked to everyone else as though I wasn't getting better. I was still in the wake of the other kids, still being lapped. I knew something was happening, though. My times were improving, and quite significantly. I knew I was on a steep learning curve, but I never once doubted that I'd improve even more, and I never once stopped enjoying it.

I always felt that I'd eventually catch the rest of the girls I was swimming with – to me, they seemed to train complacently, most likely because they were already good. They were there because it was what they and their families did; it was part of a routine. I was there because I wanted to be good, and wasn't.

Even though it was difficult, I ended every swimming training session champing at the bit for the next session, not because I enjoyed it but because I knew I'd be a little bit better the next time, and the time after that, and then the time after that. Soon there was no denying that if I kept improving, I was actually going to be good … or at least competitive.

I started to figure that competitive might just be good enough. In Ironman and Ironwoman competitions, every competitor had a leg that was their weakest, and could design their race strategy around that. And while my swim leg was never going to be my strongest, I knew there were ways that a lack of raw speed might be mitigated. For instance, a lot of the girls I did swimming training with were part of the surf club too, and I knew how much faster I was than them in the run. I knew that was an advantage that I'd always take into a race, an advantage that would always be represented in the final time, the final result.

That wouldn't necessarily be true of the swim leg, though. Getting through the break and coming back into the beach was where time could be won and lost. Knowing and understanding the surf was an integral part of racing, especially in the swim leg, and with a good feel for the surf, a great deal of time could be saved.

'Just have fun.' That was Dad's advice for learning how to master surf conditions. 'Get in there as often as you can with your friends – play, surf.' I did that as much as I could, down at Maroubra Beach, smashing myself into the waves and bodysurfing back in, over and over, and over again. That was just a fun thing to do, and it still is. I became much more confident in the water as I put myself in more and more situations and conditions that I knew I could get myself out of.

I suppose I was about twelve or thirteen when I started to realise that seeing my photo up on the wall of the surf club was a realistic goal. By now the Ironwoman series had really taken off, with superstars like Reen Corbett and Karla Gilbert competing against each other in the then-named Meadow Lea Ironwoman Series.

I could be an Ironwoman, I thought, as we all gathered at the surf club on Sunday afternoons to watch the Super Series and cheer on legends like Glenn Cowdrey, and Kane

Heussner, Dennis's son, who was now competing in the series and was representing our club.

People from our club were in the series. Women were in the series. Why couldn't I be in the series? I could. That belief really became cemented in me in 1997, after winning the under-14 New South Wales State Ironwoman Championships and the under-14 board event.

I wasn't surprised that I won the board race, as I'd been very good in that event for a long time by then, but I was in a state of delighted disbelief when I charged across the line first in the Ironwoman event. The first leg of the competition had been the swim leg, and I planned to stay in touch with the leaders, but it was to my immense surprise I came out of the water second. I knew I was home. I had my strongest leg, the board, next and I knew I'd take first position, and no one was going to take the win from me in the run leg. I wasn't going to allow that!

I ended up winning easily. I was the state champion, even though my swimming was still nowhere near what I knew it could soon be. I was improving in all three disciplines of the sport, and knew I was still on a steep learning curve with my swimming, with the capacity to get faster. Much faster.

At fourteen, I felt my Ironwoman dreams were within touching distance – a berth in the professional Ironwoman series wasn't years away, but perhaps only months. Joining the ranks of the professional series was an exciting prospect – the local, state and national surf lifesaving competitions were thrilling and you competed for the love of the sport and for your community, but the professional series came with prestige and television coverage, and the potential to earn decent prize money. If you qualified into the series, you were flown to all the events, and if you were a podium contender or one of the top ten, that opened you up to sponsorship too, which freed you up to concentrate on your training.

The state championships in Maroubra were conducted in March. Each September a qualifying race for the women's professional series was held in Mooloolaba on Queensland's Sunshine Coast to decide who would compete in the prestigious competition. With no age limit to qualification, I felt I was ready. I'd have to transfer from the smaller Nippers board, on which we'd lie flat, to the larger adult board, on which you paddle on your knees, but I had months to manage the change.

I honestly thought I was ready and asked Mum and Dad if they'd take me up to Queensland for the trials. They certainly didn't have the money to just throw away on what may have been an expensive whim, but as they could see how hard I'd been working and how realistic I usually was about my goals and aspirations they simply said: 'Okay, sweetheart.' I was so lucky to have such supportive parents – they truly never thought that anything was out of my reach.

*

Mum and Dad always put their emphasis on school over anything else in our lives, but it wasn't the hub around which my life and those of my two brothers revolved. Tim proved to be an excellent soccer player, and his life was built around that, often travelling overseas for some trial or training he'd been invited to. Pat was (and is) a very social animal, and the life of any party he decides to bless with his presence. Pat was also a very gifted swimmer – when he was younger he placed second in an open national title with Surf Life Saving, but he just didn't love it as much as I did.

Me, I had my Ironwoman dream almost immediately from the moment I started high school and it surpassed all other aspirations.

I have to say that my brothers better incorporated their other interests into school life than I did. I did okay in most classes, but I did so with a genuine disinterest, and in classes where I struggled, like English, I'm sorry to say I could sometimes be disruptive.

I was becoming aggressive in the way that I raced, and while I wasn't aggressive at school, I recognise that I could be absolute in my thinking: to me there was only sport. I chose not to play the social game at school, and had little interest in what a lot of other girls considered fun. I didn't want to go to what I saw as silly parties, or play games I considered pointless. I had friends at school, but it's safe to say that I wasn't inviting maximum social interaction. That wasn't what I wanted, anyway, especially not in the half-year between March and September of 1998.

I'm not sure anyone expected me to qualify for the professional series, not my coaches or my parents, and I'm not sure I thought I would be able to either, but that was an immaterial part of my efforts to realising my goal.

My goal was qualification and I knew the best way to achieve it was simply by hard work, and visualisation, which

Mum taught me. Whether it was a realistic goal or not, I'd be more likely to get there if I worked hard than if I didn't, so that's what I would do, regardless of the shifting numerical chances of success. That was my heuristic.

I had a couple of role models then. One was Trevor Hendy, the golden god of the sport, who had replaced Grant Kenny in the minds of Australians as the Ironman prototype after a record number of wins in televised races, and who had become the centrepiece of a Kellogg's advertising campaign. An unbelievable athlete with true name recognition, Hendy had even guest starred in an episode of *Baywatch*, in which he narrowly beat David Hasselhoff in an Ironman race.

The other role model was a girl named Linda Halfweeg. She was also a stellar competitor, and one of the best Ironwomen around, but it wasn't only her athletic abilities that I respected and wanted to emulate. She'd kind of transcended her position in the sport, known as much for her looks and the way she carried herself as she was for her racing ability. Perhaps she wasn't as well respected as Trevor Hendy in the sport, but she'd managed to arrange many opportunities for herself, including an offer to join the cast of *Baywatch* after the success of the episode in which Trevor Hendy appeared. Linda was only a few years older than me, so that was another reason why I idolised her. She was young, she was successful, she was a master of the surf and she was glamorous – living what looked to me to be a charmed life.

I thought a lot about Linda and Trevor when I was training in the lead-up to the Ironwoman trials in Mooloolaba.

I remained dedicated to my swimming training, but also added extra board sessions as moving from the Nippers board to the full adult board required different muscles and different movements, not only when entering and exiting the surf but also while powering through open ocean. I trained incredibly hard, and have strong, happy memories of finishing board training exhausted but exhilarated, blood and seawater beading down my shins.

In life, choices have to be made; I knew that even then. There are only so many hours in the day, and so much energy in each person each day. As a young teen, I was making my choice; I was choosing sport. I don't regret that decision at all, but I recognise now as an adult that there are social consequences of making a choice like that, at a time like that.

These consequences would only be exacerbated after Mooloolaba, and all of my hard work started to pay off.

*

There were about eighty women who had fronted up in Mooloolaba, with the fastest fifteen given entry into the professional series. All of the competitors would race on day one and then, on day two, the thirty fastest would gain entry into the final.

I felt the pressure on day one. This trip to Queensland was an investment in time and money for our family, and if I showed nothing for that investment, I'd feel like I'd let my parents down. If I could make it to the final, that would be something we could hold up as a return. That would be enough for Mum and Dad, I thought, and it was enough for me, too.

I wasn't outclassed, outmuscled or overawed on day one. I wasn't in the front of any races, but I wasn't near the back either. I felt immense relief when I qualified for day two; in fact I felt ecstatic. I slept very well and arrived back at Mooloolaba the next day with no weight of expectation at all. I'd already done what I wanted to do. I planned to do the best I could, and whatever the result was then so be it.

That race was a long one: two swims out and back to a buoy, then a long run, then two trips on the board out to a buoy and then another long run. When I came out of the second swim at seventh place, I felt shocked, but also pretty good. I didn't feel exhausted or depleted; I felt as I should, a third of the way into a race.

During the run, I gained a couple of spots and went back into the water in fifth place. I was very happy where I was, so I decided just to sit in the wake of the girl in front of me for both legs. Using the excess energy she'd given me by cutting through my surf, I passed her and took her spot.

From there I kept my place in the run and crossed the line in fourth place. I was fourteen years of age and I had easily qualified for the professional Ironwoman series. That made me the youngest female competitor at the time ever to do so.

I couldn't quite believe it. It was such a strange feeling, replicating and amplifying how I felt when I started winning running races on the beach with Mum watching on. I was so happy, not knowing that every event in life, even this, had benefits, but also pitfalls.

What I did know, though, was that I'd made my mark and was on a path of achievement that I'd been working so hard to get to. Previously, the youngest Ironwoman had been Linda Halfweeg, and now it was me. There was so much more ahead of me, but back then I didn't completely understand what this qualification meant. It was an invitation to more work and not yet really an outcome. I would do the work, but while I was gaining skills, fitness and strength, I was missing out on time as a child and as a schoolgirl.

I was going to be an Ironwoman when I wasn't even yet a woman.

I had already started to distance myself from the academic and social life of school, and this result wasn't going to get me any closer to either. But now I had an Ironwoman series ahead of me and, as far as I was concerned, there wasn't anything at school that was more important.

4
A Girl Among Women

Before I started Year Nine, I heard about Endeavour Sports High School, a New South Wales government school in Caringbah, in Sydney's Sutherland Shire, which primarily selects students for their sporting aptitude. Endeavour provides students with an education but it also prepares them for a sporting career, or supports them in their existing sporting career.

A few of the girls I swam with went to Endeavour and had told me about the extra training sessions they were getting, with their school allowing them, twice a week, to finish school at midday and then go for afternoon training sessions at Sutherland Pool. That didn't sound like any school I'd ever heard of, but I was keenly attentive, as these girls were consistently the highest performers of the group.

I pressed them eagerly for more information on this school of theirs. It sounded like heaven, with everyone competing in one or more sports at a high level, sport filling every conversational gap, and every lunchtime spent in the gym or competing informally on the school's expansive soccer or footy pitches.

I was sold. I was miserable at St Catherine's and was sure I could improve my grades, or at least not fall behind any further, at this new high school, while also enjoying my life and getting more swimming sessions in to boot.

I spoke to Mum and Dad about it, and they weren't as keen on the idea. They were spending a lot of their limited income for me to attend a very expensive private school because they thought that's what was best for my academic and spiritual future and welfare. The return on investment, however, was clearly a little shaky, and eventually they said that I could apply, and we'd see what happened after that. Apply I did, and I was excited to be accepted and would start at the beginning of Year Nine, and so, after qualifying for the Ironwoman series, I prepared to start at Endeavour.

The school had not been oversold. I absolutely loved it there. The only drawback was how far it was from home – Endeavour was more than half an hour away from Maroubra by car on the days I got a lift from one of the teachers who lived in Bondi, and more than an hour on the bus – but as far as I was concerned, it was time well spent.

There were like-minded people at Endeavour, and for almost all of the students, their school days and social lives were oriented around sport. There were students who would undoubtedly one day play soccer or rugby league professionally, and others who were sure to compete in the Olympics in a variety of sports. Everyone shared tips on training and diet, and when someone was performing well in their sport, it was the talk of the school.

I was much better suited to being at a co-ed school than

the girls-only school St Catherine's. I was yet to have my first boyfriend, but I loved the company of boys and always had, ever since I was a little girl. I had a very feminine streak in me too, but I grew up with the camaraderie, competitiveness and light-hearted confrontational nature of boys and men of the surf lifesaving culture I was born into, and it was such a joy to be immersed totally in sport at school with similarly minded people.

I found the all-girls culture of quiet exclusion and bitchiness unbearable, and felt a noticeable release when I left. And not only that — my swimming improved markedly over that first year at Endeavour.

I certainly wasn't a swimming star at school, but I was solid in the pool and getting faster every day in the ocean. I didn't know whether I was ready to be a professional Ironwoman, but I was happier all round, and that was certainly something.

*

My first professional Ironwoman event took place in 1999 at North Cronulla Beach, almost walking distance from Endeavour High. It wasn't a beach that I'd spent much time at growing up, but it was close enough to home for friends and family to watch me compete.

I'd like to tell you that I made their trip worthwhile, but I didn't. Still only fourteen, I was very much a girl among women. I was just happy to be there, my usually aggressive competition stance on hold as I was so in awe of my competition.

I'd brought a small camera along with me so I could get photos of the athletes in the races I'd be competing in. I couldn't believe I was in the competitors' tent with people like Reen Corbett and Karla Gilbert. These girls were my idols, the champions who stared down at me from posters in my bedroom.

But awe wasn't the only reason I underperformed, however. I still wasn't a very fast swimmer, nor someone who was particularly comfortable in large surf – and large surf was what I was confronted with at North Cronulla. It was a huge shore break, which took me back to the fear I'd felt as a Nipper. That first race was a baptism of fire, and I quickly fell to the back of the pack when we entered the water and stayed there until I crossed the finish line. I had come dead last, and yet I didn't really care. I'd had an amazing time, meeting and competing – if you can call it that! – with my heroes.

That was the only race that season that I came dead last in, but in fact, all my performances were pretty unremarkable. Throughout that season the surf really only pumped at North Cronulla, and at Glenelg, Coolangatta, Elwood and Manly there was only negligible surf. But it turned out those flat conditions weren't ideal for me either. As a relatively poor swimmer, I wasn't fast in that leg, so could only perform well when I could get through the surf more quickly than the other competitors and surf into the beach faster than they could, using the lifetime I'd spent at the beach to intuit when and where the waves were going to come and when they were going to break.

When the surf was really big, that intuition was lost, though, and gave way to pure fear. It seemed to me the only way I could really compete was when there were Goldilocks conditions, with some surf, but not too much surf, and those conditions didn't present themselves in any of the races of that first season. It probably wouldn't have made a difference anyway. I was flirting with the wooden spoon constantly and, being the grommet that I was, I didn't really care. I was so far away from competing with the top competitors in my races that failure was baked into the experience, so I just didn't give it too much thought. For the events where there were heats, I didn't care if I got knocked out before the final – it just meant that I'd get to watch my heroes from the comfort of the competitors' tent, cheering on girls I'd been shoulder to shoulder with just a few hours before.

The top ten competitors from the season automatically qualified and I fell short by some measure. I was going to have to go back to Mooloolaba, but I didn't yet feel the pressure that would build when a young career full of promise didn't materialise in the way I and everyone assumed it would.

*

The next year, the Uncle Toby's Super Series was held alongside three other series: the Australian Beach Volleyball series, a triathlon series and a professional short-course swimming series. All of it rolled up together was being called the One Summer Series.

There was a time when the Uncle Toby's series wouldn't have considered throwing itself in with less popular Olympic sports like beach volleyball or triathlon, but the sport had hit a few financial waves in recent years. Australia had just hosted an Olympic Games that was widely loved by almost every Australian and a huge amount of government funding had been pumped into Olympic sports, including a few that had previously held only marginal interest in Australia.

Interest in those particular sports peaked, after the Olympic triathlon had been held at the Sydney Opera House and the beach volleyball at a stadium built right in the middle of Bondi Beach. Both events had been played out under the bluest of skies, and were a marketers' dream, as were the results with Australian Michellie Jones winning a silver in the triathlon and the Australian team of Natalie Cook and Kerri Pottharst winning gold in the beach volleyball. That gold was one of sixteen won by Australia at the 2000 Games, with five others being won by the swim team.

In the zero-sum game of interest in professional sports sponsorship and coverage in Australia, Olympic sports were now at their zenith in Australia, and non-Olympic sports, like Ironman racing, were not. So it seemed to make sense to fold the other sports into the Super Series, with Channel Ten televising it all. It didn't work ultimately, and was only put on for that one summer, but for a kid like me, it was certainly fun while it lasted.

*

After two wonderful years at Endeavour, I was forced to move to another school. Endeavour was changing their hours, starting the school day at 7.30am so that all students could finish their day at lunchtime. The change was to help the student athletes, so that they could train each afternoon, but it just wasn't going to work for me, as I lived twenty kilometres away and had essential and immovable swimming training sessions in the morning either with my swim team or in the ocean.

I was going to have to move schools for Years Eleven and Twelve. My parents' preference was that I move to Brigidine College at Randwick, a Catholic day school for girls. I wasn't happy that I had to move, but if I had to, I was happy for that move to be to Brigidine as it was relatively close to home, close to the beach and was a place where I still had friends.

Soon I'd be back at school with Llara again, someone who I hadn't been at school with since Year Five. I hoped that the transition from Endeavour to Brigidine would be easier than the one from St Mary–St Joseph to St Catherine's ... but it proved not to be. Brigidine was very academically focused, with ATAR results of great importance to the marketing of the school. I found the social life at school didn't suit me either.

Brigidine was a concrete jungle, and the social life of students at that school was drastically different to Endeavour. No one played sport at lunchtime, especially not the Year Eleven girls who were preparing for a more adult life. Gossip was how the girls passed the time at Brigidine, social hierarchy discussed and arranged, and talk was of parties gone and to come.

One aspect of school life I had looked forward to when moving to Brigidine was being reunited with Llara. I thought we would be best buddies, and that I'd wedge myself into the social group that she was part of, which included girls we'd been to primary school with. It didn't work out that way, and it's only now that I realise that it was an unrealistic and unfair thing to hope for. Llara had her own life, in her own way, and I was asking her to amend her life for mine, without amending my life at all.

I wasn't interested in many of the things that she and her school friends were, and I didn't even try to be interested. I was pretty unyielding in my ways – I was only at school because I had to be, and spent most of my day wishing the minutes away and for the final bell to ring so that I could race down to the beach and train.

I had no interest in weekend parties or social gatherings. I judged girls who had started drinking or taking drugs, and silently scolded them for not having goals that were similar to mine. In short, I don't think I was a lot of fun. On the weekends Llara spent time with her school friends instead of me, and I unfairly maligned her for that, but I only realise that now, later in life.

I struggled socially at Brigidine, and also academically. I was adept at maths as I had always been, but English comprehension continued to be an issue, with my second most difficult subject being religious studies. As Brigidine is a Catholic school, religious studies were compulsory, and while I understood and adhered to the Catholic faith – after all, my dad's homeland was one of the true homes of Roman Catholicism – there were other elements of the curriculum that we were tested on too. Students weren't only graded on Catholicism, but on a swathe of religions from around the world – other sectarian Christian faiths and also Buddhism, Hinduism, Judaism and Islam. I can imagine I might have gained an appreciation and understanding of these religions if I'd been studying the subject for years, but from a standing start I was lost.

I tried to hold on in the first couple of terms at Brigidine, but as each week passed I moved further and further behind. Eventually a meeting was called between my parents, myself and some school administrators to talk about my future.

The upshot of the meeting was that the administrators thought that there'd be better ways for me to use my time than attending their school. They came armed with a suggestion: the TAFE in Ultimo in Sydney's inner city, was starting a new course in personal training and they suggested that perhaps that would be a better fit for me than Brigidine.

My parents were disappointed, but also forearmed with some experience that would help this bitter pill go down. Both of my brothers had wanted to leave school early and start trades and my parents had been staunchly against it. As someone who didn't finish school, Dad had always believed in his kids getting the education he never had, but after watching his sons matriculate and start trades that they would have benefited from one or two years earlier, his attitude changed somewhat.

I was happy to try the TAFE course, which I thought would work well with my training and interests, and Mum and Dad grudgingly accepted that. We all agreed that I'd stay in school until the Brigidine debutante ball, a social event that I thought would be a bit of fun, and then move over to TAFE.

If you haven't been to a debutante ball, it's quite an antiquated event. All of the girls wear long white dresses and white silk gloves and their dates are required to wear tuxedos. Historically the balls were designed as a marriage market, where the young women, having been trained in comportment and ethics, are introduced to aristocratic men and their families so that they may potentially be matched in marriage.

At Brigidine, we weren't obliged to train in comportment and ethics, but we were told we had to learn a series of waltzes and foxtrots each week after school with our dates.

My date was my brother Patty and we had a nice enough time, but both the dance and the school simply were not for me. I was very happy to leave school. While I was a hard worker, and someone who strived to achieve the goals I set for myself, the Catholic girls school system wasn't suited to me.

Although I seemed to have a lot going for me, I remember that year as a dark time. I had become a loner again without even knowing that it was happening. I just didn't care about what the kids around me were doing, really. I didn't have any really close friends, and didn't do much except go to school and train. Often on the weekends, if the weather was bad or after training, I'd end up with fallow hours. I was proud, and stubborn, and ended up on my own quite a lot.

It really affected Mum, how isolated I was. I could tell that. I felt the loneliness too, but didn't see it for what it was. I think I developed coping mechanisms that became part of my personality, and sometimes these mechanisms have been useful in my life, and sometimes they've been to my detriment.

*

I've always felt comfortable in a swimming costume. Always. Even as I got older and as my body changed. Of course it's due to the fact that it has been my uniform, competing in surf lifesaving events for so long. I think that's why I was happy, at only fifteen, to do my first professional photoshoots in swimwear.

One of the first, and the biggest, was in a popular local magazine called *Inside Sport*, which was a powerhouse of Australian publishing in the nineties and early 2000s. It combined some excellent short- and long-form sports journalism and some pretty suggestive shoots that were similar to men's magazines like *FHM* and *Ralph*.

My shoot wasn't as suggestive as others, but, looking back, it undoubtedly sexualised a minor. I was in a bikini, sitting on a car before I could even drive. I guess you could say it was fodder for creeps.

The questions for the interview that accompanied the shoot were probably modified, but I remember them being pretty intrusive and sexual. I walked away feeling a bit off afterwards. I was still only a kid, and knew I was being used in some way, but I didn't really understand exactly how. Despite this, I was excited when the piece came out. It was really the only way to get exposure for a sport like mine then, and with a raise in profile came some sponsorship money that I knew I'd need to focus on my training.

I was also treading a path that Karla Gilbert and Linda Halfweeg had walked before me, now also scoring a spot on the cover of lads magazine *FHM*. It wasn't the last shoot I'd do for a men's magazine, in fact, one of the final ones I did was for *Maxim*, just after I'd met Dave in 2013. For each one I did I was happy with the results, but in each instance there was a part of me that didn't love the transactional nature of such coverage.

On one hand, I was in my swimwear all the time, and I was always happy in swimwear, so it didn't mean much to me to be photographed in it. Later, as a grown adult, I was proud of my body, and proud of the hard work I'd poured into it. On the other hand, the context in which the photos were published meant something. Some of those shoots were demeaning, and the sexualisation of a child, as I think was the case with *Inside Sport*, just wasn't right.

Looking back, and raising three girls with the benefit of today's perception of sexualisation and exploitation, I recognise how precarious the ethics of the arrangement was as such a young person. But it was a different time then, and while I don't regret anything I did, I can also see what was happening now with fresh eyes.

5

Fear and a Trigger

In 1999, the National Rugby League, the NRL, contracted in size. In the wake of the Super-League expansion there had been twenty clubs playing in the rugby league premiership, but the Australian Rugby League had struck a deal with News Limited saying that by the year 2000, there'd only be fourteen teams, the fourteen most profitable out of the twenty teams. A number of clubs decided to amalgamate after being given cash incentives, and when this resulted in fifteen teams left in first-grade football, the decision was made to throw Souths – the South Sydney Rabbitohs – out of the competition.

Souths took the NRL and News Limited to court over the decision, and in November, 2000, in support of the club and the legal action, 80,000 Souths fans marched from the club headquarters to Town Hall, including all of my family. This was a big moment for the Falzons. We were a Souths family through and through. Going to the footy was our family outing for many, many years: going to a home game at the Sydney Football Stadium (SFS), listening to the 2GB

Continuous Call Team trying to hear the names of some of the local boys, guys from the surf club who were playing in the reserve grade or the Jersey Flegg Cup, a junior New South Wales competition, or even to away games at Kogarah or Shark Park at Cronulla.

I wasn't with them, however, because that day was the first race of my second Ironwoman series.

After successfully qualifying again in Mooloolaba, I trained my butt off and would have been stoked to have all my family at this first race of the season, but I completely understood why they couldn't be. If you know the relationship between the South Sydney Rabbitohs and Maroubra, you'd understand too. That said, Mum made sure she was there on race day itself, driving up on the morning of the event.

My race was in Newcastle, two hours north of Sydney, and I'd travelled up with Jade Sutcliffe, a friend and competitor from North Bondi Surf Life Saving Club. Also travelling with me was a very different mindset to the one I'd had eight months earlier, when I'd finished the last race of my first season.

I'd worked so hard at my swimming, and my body and times were changing. I was much faster and much more confident that I wasn't going to be the grommet I'd been a year before. I was still only fifteen, but I told myself I was going to be a contender this season.

I'd been sacrificing a lot. Perhaps I didn't know exactly how much I had been sacrificing at the time but I knew I'd been missing out on things other girls my age were experiencing, and I wanted that to mean something.

Participation alone wasn't going to be enough for me this season. My goal was to be one of the permanent Ironwomen, one of the top ten who automatically qualify for the next year's season with a guaranteed contract for the series, so I went into that race with certain expectations. I knew I was going to be faster and stronger than ever. I knew my results were going to be improved. I knew I had it in me.

I was working hard in the calm surf, and through the swim and paddle sections I managed to keep most of the other competitors behind me. When I got out of the surf for the final run leg, I could see only three or four girls in front of me.

I was heading into my strongest leg now, so I decided to go hard and try to chase them down. It worked for a little bit. I was powering through my stride, as I had for my whole athletic life; my legs were gliding over the sand and I felt like a million bucks. Then the limits of training and ability and will hit me. There are limits to everything, and in that moment my legs became weighty then heavy, and then felt like stone. I pushed as best I could, but I'd gone out too hard, too strong. A few girls passed me close to the line, but I still managed to hang on for seventh place.

While I'd been in reach of a podium finish and it had disappeared like a mirage, I was still ecstatic. The season before I'd been the girl who couldn't hack it, who probably shouldn't have been out there, and I definitely wasn't that now. I'd threatened some of the top girls and had finished in a decent position, which told me and the rest of the competitors that I belonged, and not only that but that as a fifteen-year-old, I was going to be a problem for them very soon. I was coming for their spots on the podium. I knew it now, and they knew it now, too.

Going into that race my goal had been top ten, but now I reassessed. I wanted to finish the season in the top ten so I'd requalify for the next year, but I also wanted a top-five finish. And at an event in North Wollongong, I did it.

North Wollongong is only an hour or so from Sydney and my family decided to rent a bus so they and some of my friends could make a day of watching me compete. It was a glorious day for all of us. My brothers brought a slab of VB with them on the bus and had a grand old time drinking all day, Mum and Dad both got to watch me compete, and I got my top-five finish. The format of this event was that competitors accumulated points throughout a series of races during the day. Going into the last race, I was placed second. Again, I faded somewhat in the last race and ended up placing fourth overall, but once again I'd achieved what I'd set out to do and was very happy.

The surf had been just right, I'd been in just the right mindset and I think I actually got a little performance boost knowing that so many people had come to watch and support me. I felt great, and now I was ready for a top-three finish, then a race win.

It was coming, I could feel it. I was going to win a race before too long; I was going to be the best girl racing soon. It was going to happen. I could feel it in the very fibre of my being.

*

In the lead-up to .the season and indeed throughout the season, my coaches had a mantra that they'd repeat every time the surf was large, when storms were coming in and when I, accordingly, didn't want to train.

'You have to train, because of Portsea.'

Portsea Beach in Victoria was scheduled as the last race in the series, and the surf at that beach was known for its messiness and volume at times. I needed to practise in large surf, just in case Portsea was big when I competed there, or so my coaches told me. I never thought that much about it, but I would acquiesce to their wishes. I was always half-hearted when training in big surf, however. I was still a schoolgirl and not particularly big, physically. I was definitely becoming a good swimmer, but there was still a deep-seated fear in me whenever I threw myself into really big surf.

Portsea is a tiny but beautiful seaside town on Victoria's Mornington Peninsula, about 100 kilometres south of Melbourne, straddling a long, wide spit that separates Port Phillip Bay from the ocean. On the bay-facing side of the spit is a lovely pub, guesthouses and an idyllic historic pier, photographed to death each sunset, usually with small waves lapping the pier supports and rolling gently onto the rocky shore of Portsea Beach.

After checking into the pub, which was the official accommodation for the competitors, I checked out the bayside conditions.

'This is nothing!' I thought to myself, wondering why my coaches had made such a big deal of this race. I felt confident. I was within the top ten on the eve of the final race. As long as a couple of girls didn't place better than I did (and by some measure) I'd be on track to automatic qualification.

Little did I know there was a surprise waiting for me on the other side of the spit.

All of the competitors were told to meet at the pub where we'd be taken on buses to the competition course so we could do some pre-race training and warm-up. Once on the bus, we travelled about a kilometre south on the other side of the spit to Portsea's surf beach, also known as Mount Levy Beach.

The beach is part of a national park and is bare of any marks of civilisation, except for the surf lifesaving club, which was built in the 1940s after a number of adventurous locals had entered the surf and later washed up, drowned. When I arrived I was shocked at what I saw. It was a wall of waves as far as the eye could see, dumping hard on the shore and overlaying – as I found out later – a vicious rip.

Only one thought was dancing around in my brain, over and over and over.

I can't do this.

I can't do this.

I can't do this.

I'd never seen surf like this before, let alone attempted to compete in it. It was bigger than anything I'd seen at home, and certainly like nothing I'd ever trained or competed in. I had a physical reaction to the surf – something that I felt in every cell.

I just couldn't go in. That idea seeped into my bones. I just couldn't.

Some of the girls decided to try to warm up, wading into the ocean with their boards, but most stood with me on the beach, watching. We stared at the mountainous waves, listening to a roar that seemed to be saying something to us. After a while, it was clear though. It was saying, 'Go away.'

Not one girl who had gone into the water to warm up had been able to get through the break. Not one. Every single competitor had been thrown back onto the sand, collected her board, ran back into the ocean and was then thrown back onto the sand again. Honestly, I was so impressed and amazed that they'd even tried.

The race organiser of the Ironman series had collected all of us competitors on the beach to survey the conditions and decide whether or not we should compete. I thought that, surely, there was only one choice. The surf was messy, massive and, to my eye, verging on homicidal. I didn't think anyone would want to attempt to race when not a single person had made it out in warm-up.

Although I hadn't been there myself, I knew everyone's minds were at Piha Beach in the North Island of New Zealand. Two years earlier the series had travelled to Piha and the surf had been roughly the same size there, or so many of the girls had said. There the competitors had voted on whether the race would go on. Only one girl, Kirsty Holmes, had wanted to race and all of the others had voted to cancel. It was widely acknowledged that it had been the right decision. The boys had raced that day, and many wished they hadn't.

I thought that in this instance the same decision would be made. Sure, there might be one or two girls who would say they wanted to race, knowing full well that most would say no and the race wouldn't proceed anyway, but surely common sense would prevail.

It turned out that, for some of the bigger, stronger and more experienced girls, the size of the waves wasn't a warning; it was something else: it was a challenge. Two of the biggest stars of the sport and idols of mine, Reen Corbett and Karla Gilbert, said they wanted to race. And after they had committed to the race, more hands reluctantly edged up, and then more.

Eventually there were eleven hands in the air, indicating that they wanted to race. Ten hands stayed down, including mine of course.

With a slim majority established, there would at least be an attempt at starting the race. The race officials said we would all be lining up and from the start gun we had forty minutes to try to get through the surf. If someone managed to do that within forty minutes, the race was on. If no one managed it, we were all to come back in and the race would be null and void. No series points would be awarded.

I left the meeting completely terrified. I absolutely didn't want to race. Every fibre of my being was telling me to quit before even starting, but there was something else that wouldn't allow that. I'd fought so hard to gain acceptance and to no longer be seen as a little girl, just happy to be there. There was also the question of the following year's qualification, but in the hierarchy of considerations, that was a distant second place for two reasons. The first was that existential concerns usually trump everything else, and the second was my belief that no one was going to get out the back. The surf was enormous and I didn't believe any of the competitors had its measure. I thought we'd all simply be smashing ourselves against the ocean for forty minutes before, hopefully, returning to the beach exhausted, bedraggled and with just as many series points as we all had the previous week.

But I just couldn't bring myself not to line up. It was like being back at Nippers, fielding the same battle between fear and stubbornness.

Perhaps it was because of pride that I raced, perhaps it was the fact that my mum and Llara had both come down to Portsea to watch me compete in the last race of the season (and then join me for the season's end party). Perhaps it was just a young lifetime of never wanting to quit. Whatever it was, I found myself in my race costume and cap, on the beach, facing walls of tumbling water and a terrifying roar.

I was scared before the race and after the starter's gun fired, I remained scared. We all ran to the water, none of us particularly quickly. We were all thinking of our tactics, considering taking the break on the right-hand side of the beach, where the waves were perhaps a little smaller and a little cleaner, but further from the buoy.

The first leg was the board. I tried to fight my way out in a straight line, but quickly found myself in trouble. The surf was just too big and too strong. I tried every strategy I could – rolling with the board over the waves, sitting and attempting to go straight over them, popping through them. But every time a wave came, there was another monster in its wake.

I was being smashed. Sometimes the waves would seize my board and hurtle it back to the beach and I'd be back at square one – in fact, not even square one, but square *minus* one as the drag of the ocean wrenched my board hundreds of metres down the beach from the start line and I'd have to retrieve it.

After about ten minutes, I had blood pouring down into my swimmers from the board handles smashing into my hips, and also from increasing chafe in the wild conditions. I was picked up and tumbled down deep into the surf, and in those long, airless moments, as my lungs became tighter and my disorientation more extreme, I had the momentary clarity to consider the fact that I may die competing here, with my mum and best friend on the beach watching. Then I'd push back to the surface, back to the race. I'd grab as much air as I could, push forward if I could keep going, and then I'd be smashed again and again.

As ten minutes became fifteen and fifteen became twenty, we continued to be smashed. There were girls ahead of me, but none were punching through the waves and out to the back. Then, after twenty-five minutes in the surf, my limbs aching and my lungs burning, I saw a devastating sight. One of the girls had made it.

She was going to finish the race and make it official, and not only that, she was going to show the other bigger, stronger girls that it was possible. After this first girl, another followed her, and another and, in total, six competitors punched their way through the waves.

There were a few instances when perhaps I could have followed them: gaps in the surf that would have allowed me to expend the rest of the energy that I had, empty the tank and get out there. I never did though. If I had, I would have really been screwed. I would have had to surf back in, as I was completely exhausted. I honestly didn't think I'd survive getting both out and back.

I couldn't quit though. My mind and body wouldn't do it. I just kept throwing myself into that surf. After forty minutes, I came back onto the beach exhausted, defeated, fearful and, after the season's points had been tallied, behind ten other girls, two of whom had leapfrogged me in this final race. I wouldn't automatically qualify now, but as I'd discover, the series would soon take a financial blow that it would never really recover from.

After that event, Ironwoman racing would be different for me. I changed when I was under those waves, and not necessarily for the better. Sometimes exposure to pressure and stress is good, and sometimes it's bad. Often it's a mix of both.

My fear grew as I watched the men's race, which followed ours. At that time the men had one extra leg in their competitions, the ski-paddling leg, which involved propelling their craft through the surf, around a buoy and then back to the beach. Only some of them weren't making it out, being upended and tossed around like wet lettuce. Some of their surf skis were literally being smashed in half by the power of the waves. It was a terrifying sight, as the broken men and their now two-piece craft were coming back onto the beach like wounded soldiers from a failed cavalry charge.

After that Portsea event I think there was perhaps some more resilience built in me, but also a fear, and a trigger.

*

The first sponsor I ever signed with was Oakley, and I think I was attractive to them largely because of the potential I represented as a future possible Ironwoman champion. In that first season, they approached me with an offer that supplied me with free products – an array of different styles of sunglasses – and also two ways to earn cash. The first was through results, with a sliding scale of cash incentives, with a win in an Ironwoman competition paying the most, second place paying me the second-most, and so on. The other way to earn money was through exposure, wearing Oakley sunglasses. If I appeared on the television news or in the newspaper, or in a magazine wearing Oakley sunnies, then I'd be paid for that. I managed to attract a few other sponsors too, with Souths Juniors Leagues Club giving me financial support, and also a local real estate agency, NGFarah.

Then, at age sixteen, I signed with Running Bare and Rival, sportswear brands I loved, which were owned by the same company. I was sponsored by them after I wrote a letter to the company telling them who I was, what my accomplishments were and what I was planning to achieve in my sport. They already had a strong association with surf lifesaving, having been born out of North Bondi and worn by many of the North Bondi competitors, as well as having Linda Halfweeg as the face of their brands for a number of years.

Linda's career was the one I wanted to emulate, but unfortunately it was cut short. In 2000 she started battling chronic fatigue syndrome, a very serious disease with symptoms involving a significant loss of energy and strength. Linda removed herself from professional competition and, in some ways, I came through in her wake.

I had so much respect for Linda and for Running Bare, who had also sponsored other athletes in the sport, including my friend Jade Sutcliffe, and Ky Hurst. The brand brought me on board and I ended up doing a lot of modelling for them too, for advertisements, posters and catalogues. I found I really liked doing it, as the shoots were often with friends, and promoted the sport that I love.

As a teen I'd been managing these sponsorships and deals myself, but eventually I was approached by Max Markson, a big-time Sydney celebrity agent. It was good timing and seemed like a great fit. I wanted help navigating sponsorship and the growing media opportunities and requests so I could concentrate on my training and my Ironwoman goals. But in the wake of what was to happen to me in a few years' time on a night out at a pub, this would change.

6

Running Away

When I left school, I enrolled in the personal training course at TAFE, mainly to honour the agreement with Mum and Dad, but once I'd completed it, I decided I needed a job that would give me some regular income. To that end I talked to to Glenn Farah, one of the principals of the real estate agency NGFarah, which had been sponsoring me in my Ironwoman career. He told me he could give me some work, as long as I got my real estate certificate, which I obtained without any problems.

I worked at reception, job sharing with a woman who had just had a baby, and I loved it. Real estate is an industry built around relationships, not a job based around paperwork. Of course paperwork was required, but the work itself was more about creating rapport with a prospective buyer or seller, and I really respected how deftly the people around me created that sense of connection.

There was also big money to be earned. I was only on the reception desk but I'd hear about the commissions that the agents around me were earning – sometimes fifty, sixty, seventy thousand dollars on one sale. I went online and saw that many of the highest-earning real estate agents were women. It was a fun job, working in this industry, and one that I'd dip in and out of for years to come.

When I left school at sixteen, I opened up a little bit more socially. I was a bit more relaxed and confident, and started to make my own way with new friendships and relationships. At Maroubra Surf Club, I met an incredible ocean swimmer and Ironwoman competitor named Belinda Gladstone, at that time the premier female athlete at the club. She was an inspiration to me.

Alongside Kane Heussner and Glenn Cowdrey, Belinda and I represented the elite competitive group at the surf club, and we trained together daily. I really looked up to Belinda, who was around five years older than me, and I felt an immense sense of gratitude when she took me under her wing and helped me train. She was one of the high performers of the Ironwoman series, and in her I saw a vision of my future. The tips and techniques she gave me about ocean swimming helped me enormously.

The other relationship I developed was my first serious romantic one. Around the neighbourhood, I'd noticed a Greek-Australian boy who was a few years older than me called Braith Anasta. He and I were introduced by a mutual friend who went to school with Braith, and he was also a member of Maroubra Surf Club. He was athletic like me, and excelled at his chosen sport of rugby league. When we met there were sparks.

There was just so much that I liked about Braith; we both loved to train and be active, and were very dedicated to success in our athletic careers. He had just started his professional NRL career with the Canterbury Bulldogs, having played junior footy for the Maroubra Lions, and our weekends together flew by, watching sport, playing sport and spending time at the beach. During the week, we'd play tennis, grab lunch and just hang out together. It was a happy and easy relationship for both of us.

During my second season competing in the Ironwoman series I was starting to challenge Belinda, both in training and in competitions. I was now winning on the board and on the sand. She still had me in the swimming, but I was improving every day. I thought that our local rivalry was pretty healthy, pushing both of us to better results and ultimately making the club stronger. But I wanted to win – I was younger and had the advantage of time to improve. I could now see a future in which I could be number one, and I thought, naively perhaps, that ambition, friendship and love could co-exist happily alongside each other without any problems, but I was about to learn that life could get very complicated.

Belinda and I were fast friends, training and socialising together, until one Saturday night in the off season after my second professional series the wheels fell off our friendship spectacularly – and it was all over a boy.

Everyone else around me was out socialising at the pub but, underage as I was, I wasn't much of a drinker so I usually didn't go out when they did. Braith and Belinda were around the same age and had known each other since they were kids, and I thought nothing of it when they ended up in the same pub or bar with friends.

But when Braith told me he and Belinda had caught a taxi home together after a late night out, it made me deeply uncomfortable. Braith was my first serious romantic relationship and I reacted exactly like the hot-headed teenager I was and confronted Belinda. Very strong words were exchanged between us by text, including some volatile messages from me.

After a few days of more texts between us, there was a knock on our front door – it was the police informing me that there'd been an application for an apprehended violence order against me. I was horrified and shattered, and soon there was talk about me around the surf club; whenever I was out with Braith, whispers and gossip followed. I was at the end of my tether.

Things came to a head one night when I snuck into the Coogee Pavilion, otherwise known as 'The Palace', with some of-age friends. A friend of Belinda's made one too many comments about me, and regrettably I snapped and reacted badly. We were separated by bouncers, and I was thrown out of the hotel. Later that night, the friend's father came around to our house, and he and Dad ended up having a fight on the front lawn. Since then, Maroubra has changed a lot, but back then in the 'Bra, it wasn't uncommon to see people sorting things out in a physical way. In any case, the Falzon DNA is strong – family means everything, and we always have each other's back.

Looking back as I tell this story, I regret how toxic the situation became and how it all went so wrong, but it would also usher in something else that would become a devastating pattern in my life. Somehow the media had got onto the story, and I was shocked to find myself the subject of a tabloid gossip column, and more. There's an old saying that all publicity is good publicity, but I learned early on that is just not true. The application for the AVO also meant there would be a court hearing, where a judge would decide whether there was enough cause for it to be upheld. As I was under eighteen, I wasn't required to attend, but thankfully the judge dismissed the order with a long list of reasons why the AVO wouldn't be upheld against an aggrieved minor after an exchange of text messages.

After the hearing, we all hoped that would be the end of it, but then Dad and I were called in to the surf club to talk to the club captain and board members about how the incident could be put behind us. There had been bad press, and they didn't want the incident to linger, but it felt as though we were being hauled in like criminals to explain ourselves. Again, I was horrified – I resented the way they were treating me as I'd worked so hard for the club, but even more so, I resented the way they were treating Dad, who had given his adult life to Maroubra Surf Life Saving Club. I agreed that it wouldn't be easy for Belinda and me to train together, but I thought they could have had a little more concern for Dad. He loved the club, and all he was guilty of was supporting and defending his daughter. But it was the last straw for me. I told them in no uncertain terms what I thought of them, and left.

I already had friends and fellow elite competitors like Jade Sutcliffe at North Bondi Surf Life Saving Club, and was determined to take my hard work somewhere else – so I did.

Dad ended up remaining a member of Maroubra SLSC, but I was done with them, and along with a shoulder injury that would effectively take Belinda out of competition, our combined departure would shatter the club's elite women's ranks.

The Uncle Toby's Super Series was about to suffer a financial grounding, too, and the series that replaced it would look like another sport altogether.

*

In June 2001 a decision was made to discontinue the Uncle Toby's Super Series. After thirteen years the series, which had been the most lucrative and star-studded series in the sport, was over. Public interest and, more importantly, sponsorship dollars dried up in the lead-up to and the wake of the 2000 Sydney Olympic Games, and before the 2001/2002 season, the series was over.

However, my dreams of competing in a professional Ironwoman series weren't completely smashed. From 1989 until June 2001, another competition had been running concurrently, one with a different structure and a different sponsorship and organisational foundation. This was the Kellogg's Nutri-Grain Ironman Series, which was run by the Australian Surf Life Saving Association (SLSA). With a different and more confusing format, less money and without the bountiful television relationship that the Uncle Toby's series had enjoyed, the Kellogg's Series had never been the premier event while the Uncle Toby's Super Series was in operation. (At its peak, each Uncle Toby's event had four hours of coverage on commercial television, with three of those hours live during the day and the fourth hour a package show.) The Kellogg's Series, nevertheless, did have at least two things going for it: Darren and Dean Mercer, two incredible athletes from Wollongong.

Ever since they were juniors, the Mercer brothers were identified as premier athletes in the sport and from the time they were teenagers they'd been the faces (and broad, tanned shoulders) of the SLSA and Nutri-Grain and had distinguished themselves as stars in the Coolangatta Gold. Schweppes had the Solo Man and Kellogg's had the Mercer brothers, meaning that no matter what financial enticement Uncle Toby's offered them, they were never going to compete in the Super Series, and with the Mercer brothers in the Kellogg's Series, that series was never going to be completely irrelevant. For eleven of the first twelve years the competition ran, one of the Mercer brothers had won the Kellogg's series men's championship.

When the Uncle Toby's Super Series died, all the competitors from that series, men and women, had to make a decision as to whether they'd continue with the sport or retire. Many chose the latter, especially many of the women, who had to learn an entirely new discipline if they were going to continue competing, as the Kellogg's competition included a surf-ski leg on top of the swimming, running and board legs.

Many of us knew introducing that discipline into our repertoire was going to be incredibly difficult. I knew it was going to be especially difficult for me. I'd become a strong swimmer and was becoming even stronger, and was happy with my running and board legs, but I'd barely done any work on the ski as you could only compete in ski events in the professional series unless you were sixteen and over. I knew that ski racing was very much its own sport. In fact, it was its own Olympic sport that athletes spent entire careers perfecting.

Ski racing is now an integral part of Ironwoman racing, and is actually a breeding ground for women's Olympic kayaking, but when I started at Nippers and throughout my career up until this point, it just wasn't something that the girls did. We were just too weak, too small. We couldn't handle the ski. That was the perception, at least, and so I'd never really trained on it. None of us in the Uncle Toby's series had much.

Two or three of the top competitors managed to migrate to the Kellogg's Series, but many of the girls just retired. Belinda never raced in the Ironwoman series again, nor did Jade Sutcliffe. I wanted to give it a try, however. I'd only just turned eighteen and still had vivid aspirations.

There was only a couple of months between the announcement that the Uncle Toby's Super Series was ending and the qualification trials for the Kellogg's Series were beginning, and in those months I tried to pick up ski racing. I found it difficult. I was a cautious paddler, even in pretty flat conditions. It always felt unnatural. Part of that was the modified ski that I was using – when people are more adept and experienced, they usually have a larger, custom-made ski when racing rather than the one I was training in – but it wasn't only that. Ski racing was a whole new paradigm. Sure, it used muscles and cardiovascular capacity that I'd been developing, but the muscle memory was brand new, and so were the surf tactics.

The 2003 qualification trial was in Burleigh Heads on the Gold Coast. My plan was the only one available to me – to go as hard as I could in the swim, board and run legs and hope I was in qualification zone, and then hold on as best I could in the ski leg.

When I arrived, I saw most of the competitors carrying their professional skis with moulded scoop paddles. I had a modified ski and my dad's flat wave ski paddle, which he had loaned me for the race. I knew I was underprepared and I knew I was going to be up against it.

The race went as expected. I was quite fast for most of it, and stayed well inside the qualification zone, but when I started the ski leg I started to fall back in the pack, the other competitors moving ahead of me.

In the ski leg it never once felt as if I was racing, but struggling, fighting. I didn't feel like an elite athlete, I felt like an amateur. It felt bad; my performance was bad. I didn't qualify.

I was disappointed, but I figured with another year of paddling training, I'd start to feel far more comfortable on the ski and my results would reflect that.

*

Meanwhile, at the North Bondi club, I found a scene and social life that I loved. It was a very sociable club, with a large cohort of guys and girls who were a similar age to me. Every weekend was full, often ending with a barbecue at the club and attending a party with some friends, or going to the North

Bondi RSL with people from the club where a weddings-parties-anything–style covers band called The Shark Alarms played.

I was enjoying my work in real estate too, which was becoming more involved and time consuming. After an educational and fun time at NGFarah I was poached by a client of the agency who was starting his own real estate business in Double Bay. In my new role I was tasked with contacting people who were advertising in the newspaper to rent out their properties privately to see if they were interested in having our agency represent them.

It was a thrill, convincing people about the virtues and benefits of professional management. When I did sign people up, I felt a real sense of accomplishment.

I was living the start of a good, adult life. I had friends and work and a little bit of money. I was living at home still, but that worked out well for me, having my brothers and Mum and Dad around. I was still competing too, at state carnivals for North Bondi, with some success. I'd become the state board champion, alongside other accomplishments. I was happy, but when it came to my sport, I didn't feel complete yet. I felt like I needed the Ironwoman dream to be fulfilled, and I think perhaps I was holding on to that dream a little too tightly.

When I went back to Burleigh Heads in 2004 for the qualification race for the Kellogg's Series, I really felt the pressure. I'd qualified for the first time so many years ago, and expectations had built up: I was going to be a champion one day. I was going to get to the top of the mountain, the best in my sport. I defined myself by these expectations, and called myself an Ironwoman, as did others, and yet I hadn't achieved that title – unless I proved myself at Burleigh Heads.

My head was cluttered when I lined up for the qualification race. My shoulders felt heavy, my heart was pounding. This was a moment that athletes should yearn for. I'd done the work and should have appreciated the challenge, but I was fixating on failure and, like a motorcyclist staring at a tree they want to avoid, I ran myself straight into it.

Even though I'd worked hard all year on my ski training, when the time came I underperformed. I didn't qualify, and a dark cloud gathered around me. I'd had a recognised trajectory in my beloved sport and now it had been arrested. I was out for another year, a year in which I should be approaching my athletic peak. It was after that failure that I started to wonder if it was going to happen for me at all. In fact, it wasn't even wonder, it was fear.

Ever since I was a schoolgirl, I'd always felt strongly that something special was going to happen in my sporting career, and at this moment, I realised that perhaps it might not actually be the case. It was crushing. While doing my ski training I'd also developed a painful impingement in my shoulder. A cortisone injection had seemed to fix it, but a recurrence was one of the fears that swam in my head. Another was that I simply wouldn't ever be fast enough to compete. Perhaps I just wasn't good enough. Perhaps I just wasn't cut out for my dreams. After all, most people aren't, otherwise they wouldn't be dreams.

Every day people quit their childhood dreams, and nineteen-year-old me probably would have thought of those people as losers, which I'm embarrassed to admit now. I knew so little about life and what actually makes people happy and, indeed, what would have made me happy.

I could have enjoyed the first experiences of a colourful social life that really agreed with me. I could have balanced my work with training, and let the cards fall where they lay in competition. If my dreams migrated, then that would have been okay. I knew that happened to people every day and, in most instances, it was a blessing. Sometimes new dreams are even better than the old ones.

But at that age and stage, I had a myopic understanding of life. Training to win was my whole personality, my whole perspective. If I wasn't doing that, then who was I?

Now, I think it was a fear of failure that chased me away from surf lifesaving when I came away from that failure to qualify at Burleigh Heads. Instead of running towards friends and family, though, I ran away even further, towards an even loftier athletic goal, with even more training required.

*

In my heart of hearts, I saw myself as an Ironwoman, and had worked hard to become a capable swimmer in the surf in medium to long distances. But I'd found that I was actually faster over shorter distances in the pool. I did wonder whether, deep in my genes, I was a sprinter. I was still young at nineteen, and thought that perhaps there was time to pivot.

I spoke to Angelo Basalo, my swimming coach, about the possibility of competing in swim meets at the highest national levels, and he said it would be difficult, but not impossible. He asked what my goals would be and I told him: the Olympic Games. Starting in this sport in earnest so late, I knew an individual Olympic medal was too lofty a goal, but perhaps I could be part of the 4 x 100 metre Australian relay team.

The 2008 Beijing Games were only a few years away, and qualifying for that meet in the time I had was unlikely, but the 2012 Games in London was a more attainable goal. My coach told me that if I really wanted to do this, I'd have to start taking my training seriously now. Even for the London Games, I had no time to spare.

I'd already been training in the pool every morning, but all of my afternoon swim sessions had been in the ocean, and my coach told me I'd have to start exclusively swimming in the pool. At the time, competitive swimming had become an arms race of time and effort. Many of the best swimmers in the world were pacing through between fifty and eighty kilometres a week, training seven days a week in strictly regimented programs, and that was now the standard.

I threw myself into the paradigm, keeping a swim diary of every training session with every time recorded, and training twice a day. It was something that I enjoyed for a time.

Swimming had been something that I had to do so I could compete capably in my chosen sport, and now it was my chosen sport. I liked that fact, almost as though I'd wrestled control of my circumstances. I saw improvement too, pushing my times through the 27-second barrier and down towards 26 seconds for 50 metres freestyle.

At the time I was part of the Cranbrook Eastern Edge Swim Club, which operated out of the prestigious private boys school facilities in Bellevue Hill, but when the coaching of that club went out to tender and the coach left, I moved. I had international aspirations, so I wanted to train with athletes who had similar goals. One of the real estate agents I was working with at Double Bay had been a competitive swimmer and he recommended a club at Sydney Olympic Park Aquatic Centre at Homebush, so I started training there.

The training was great, but my life became exhausting. Most days I woke up at 4am and drove west to Homebush for training before coming back east for a day's work, and then I'd often be driving west again for another session in the pool in the evening. I often trained on the weekends too, and if I wasn't training I was a depleted zombie.

I was also trying to maintain a relationship. Through friends I had met a professional rugby union player named Matt Henjak. Canberra born and bred (well, Queanbeyan) Matt was a great guy and someone I thought doing the three-hours-plus drive down south to the nation's capital dozens of times was worth it for.

The relationship always seemed stuck in second gear, though. Some of it was the tyranny of distance, and some was that we were living discordant lives. He was an athlete too, but he was creating space outside of that life. Matt was a few years older than me and liked to party. I didn't like to drink, and barely went out at night, knowing that I'd have to be up at the crack of dawn for training.

Soon I was zeroed in on a goal and date: the Australian Swimming Championships in Melbourne at the start of 2006, which doubled as the Commonwealth Games trials, with my hope being that at that meet I might get my fifty metres sprint just under the 27-second mark.

Throughout the winter of 2005, training as hard as I did wasn't too difficult, but as the cold gave way and spring arrived, I felt some pangs of yearning for the beach, to be outside in the sun and surf. I trained constantly, I raced constantly. Many Sundays I spent driving out to the indoor pool at Homebush, doing a two-kilometre warm-up swim, thrashing out a 50-metre race in less than thirty seconds, doing it again and again, and then driving home. That was my day. As I drove back home east with the sun behind me, I'd be thinking about what was happening at Maroubra or North Bondi and who was there, carefree and happy, just enjoying each other's company.

I'd have dinner with my family and then go to bed early so I could start all over again. There were only so many hours in the day and days in the week, and I was dedicating the bulk of them to the inside of an aquatic centre. Whatever time that was spare, I dedicated to my new relationship.

That was my life. My whole life. I was getting faster. Yes, I was only getting faster in tiny increments, and I was still a very long way from being competitive in a national final or getting an Olympic berth, but those tiny increments kept me going. When my times gave me qualification into the Australian Swimming Championships I reset my goals. I wanted to get to the semi-finals of the championships, which, admittedly, was very ambitious, but it wasn't completely beyond the realm of possibility. I knew I wasn't yet one of the eight best sprinters in the country, but my times weren't too far away from being in the best sixteen. With a little bit of luck and a personal best, it wasn't just a dream.

It didn't go the way I wanted, though. I didn't get my personal best in Melbourne, as you want to in a big meet, nor did I get into the semi-final. But given what I'd already achieved, I wasn't upset, and tomorrow was always another day and another opportunity to train.

However, the cold hard reality of not cracking the Australian Swimming Championships meant I was out of contention for the 2008 Olympics and I'd now have to keep up the tempo and dedication of my swimming training for another six years if I was to have a chance of reaching my Olympic goals for 2012. I thought there was definitely a chance I could do it, but there was part of me that was wondering if that was what I really wanted. This lifestyle would account for most of my twenties.

This is the athlete's dilemma. It's madness to ever assume that you'll get to the top of the athletic pyramid, when you consider the dozens of other athletes in your race, the hundreds in your competition, the thousands in your age group and the masses in your sport. Why would you assume it might be you on that podium one day?

You don't assume anything, but you do dream. And that dream kept me training. I got straight back into it after Melbourne: back to Homebush, back to training, back to 4am starts. But there were some troubling echoes in the back of my mind. I couldn't get past the thought that perhaps I'd never break through.

I'd been competing against two incredible athletes, Libby Lenton (later Libby Trickett) and Jodie Henry, and in them I didn't see competitors I could beat. I'd never felt that way when I was racing in an Ironwoman competition. My confidence had certainly been affected by moving from one series to another and the introduction of the ski leg had rocked me, but I didn't look at any other Ironwomen and think that they were inherently better competitors than I was.

But in Libby and Jodie I saw athletes who had already done so much work that I hadn't, and I was sure their dedication wouldn't diminish any time soon. Ultimately Jodie wouldn't qualify for the 2008 Games after a serious injury, but Libby competed in the 2004, 2008 and 2012 Olympic Games, earning four gold medals.

I wondered whether the life that I'd been living, with all of its deliberate and organised hardships, wasn't the one that a young person should be living. But still I kept going. I pushed my friends away and became quite boring. Eventually, and possibly predictably, considering the amount of time I was spending training, I suspected that I wasn't the only woman in Matt's life, and our relationship ended.

I didn't have anyone to talk to either. The people I spent the most amount of time with were the swim team and that was either in the exhausted dawn or post-workout moments that bracketed training, or in the pool itself.

I was stuck in a vortex. I defined myself by my training, and had no idea who I was without it. Everyone in my life saw me in those terms, too. I just kept going, however, my internal mantra pitching me onward, endlessly. Down the black line, down the lane, lap after lap after lap, each day searching for microseconds that I could discard from my time.

And then, one day, I broke.

*

It happened in Waverley, near Bondi Junction, on a side street after an open-home inspection I was working at. I was driving my car back to the office, and the feeling just gripped me and overwhelmed me. I fought it as I had before; it wasn't the first time I'd had this dark, desperate feeling. There had been other times when loneliness and sadness and something verging on depression had risen in me, and here it was again. I tried to push it back, push it aside. *The feeling will leave*, I thought.

I pulled over so I could pull myself together. I couldn't. I was overwhelmed. I sat there and I just cried and cried and cried. I was deep in a hole of overwhelming *something*. Was it depression? Sadness? Anxiety? I didn't know, but I knew I was deep within it.

It was such unusual behaviour for me. If I did ever find myself starting to wallow in self-pity, I'd see myself from outside of my body. I'd feel a sense of disgust and tell myself: *Pull yourself together, Candice!* But not this time. There was no disembodiment, no self-criticism and no recuse. I was just overwhelmed. I did what I never thought I'd do. I called home and cried.

I love my parents more than almost anything in life, and Mum and Dad would do absolutely anything for me, and I for them, but we didn't have a relationship in which we leaned on one another emotionally. Or at least, we didn't do it overtly.

We cared for one another deeply, but we didn't talk about our feelings. We just kept going, always forwards, always onwards. We didn't wallow, as that wasn't the Falzon way, and yet here I was in my car crying and phoning home, desperate for help.

Mum answered and all she could hear were sobs. I couldn't articulate to her what was going on, because I didn't know what was going on myself and, besides, even if I did I'm not sure I had the language and capacity to share it.

'Stay right where you are,' said Mum, as she listened to me sobbing, realising that I was in no state to drive myself home. And within ten minutes she and Dad had arrived and had bundled me into their car.

Mum was worried. Dad was too. They didn't know what was happening to me, and they didn't like it. Their youngest child and their only daughter simply couldn't enjoy her life for reasons that weren't apparent to them, or even to her.

Mum got the Yellow Pages out and looked for services that could give me some psychological help. She settled on a counsellor in Randwick, whom I visited with some trepidation. I wasn't scared that she might uncover something; I was terrified that she might find something broken in the centre of me.

That fear was at the heart of what she discovered; what we discovered together. I really connected with this counsellor and shared what I knew that may have been affecting me. Over a series of sessions, we talked about why I had these bouts of blueness. I'm reluctant to call it depression, because I don't think it was that. It wasn't ever-present, the feeling I had, nor did it require medication, but it was just a sadness that was inside of me and profound. She found that inside of me there was a lack of deep, personal satisfaction and, regardless of what I did and what I was achieving, I wouldn't be able to find fulfilment without first addressing that lack.

She suggested that the reason I was having these feelings was because I was at an athletic nadir. For the last five years, I'd been known as an Ironwoman and notable for being the youngest-ever competitor to make the professional series. My most notable achievement had happened when I was barely a teenager and now, as a young adult, I felt as though I was nothing. Just another swimmer at just another meet, nothing more.

That was why this attack of sadness came when it had. She recognised that perhaps I would never be satisfied, regardless of what I did, unless I was achieving for the right reasons.

Achievement is a by-product of hard work, and therefore hard work can't only be in the service of achievement. Hard work has to be part of life; it can't be life itself. My counsellor asked me why I wanted the things I was working for, and for whom.

Then, after a number of sessions, she prescribed something that seemed completely counterintuitive to someone who appeared to be burning out from athletic training. She prescribed what looked like more training.

She suggested that I start running.

I was to do it for myself, though. I wasn't to run on the sand in an attempt to better my surf training, nor was I to time myself or work through a program, setting myself goals along the way. I was just to put my shoes on, walk out the door and run. When I'd run far enough for myself, I was to turn around and run back.

I was speechless. She had identified that inside of me, the thing that I loved, the thing that was the driving force in my life, my need to gain validation through athletics, was also the cause, the root, of my bouts of blueness. Inside of me was a restlessness, and achievement wasn't ever going to quell that. That restlessness was caused by the other parts of life that I wanted to be part of, and was striving to be expressed.

I couldn't recognise that need for those other parts of my life though, because it was being contained by my constant pursuit of athletic achievement. If I trained and maintained focus, I didn't have to worry about anything else because nothing else really mattered. If I wasn't having fun at social gatherings, it didn't matter, because I'd decided that wasn't who I was. If I wasn't invited to parties or the pub, that didn't matter either, because I'd be getting up early anyway. Who needed friends when you had training partners? Who needed a healthy relationship when you had certain places to be and things to do?

In those counselling sessions I discovered that I really wanted to do the very normal things that twenty-year-olds did. I wanted to be the kind of person who worked at Coles and who had a regular boyfriend and who hung out and got drunk on the weekends and lived a normal young person's life, but in reality I was fearful of what being that normal, decently adjusted person meant. Would I still be me?

My counsellor told me I didn't have to worry about that, I just needed to run. 'Just for you,' she said. 'Out and back, with no one but Candice alongside you. This is something you do with Candice, and for Candice. You do it to feel good – body and mind. No other reason. No expectations and no voices in your head.'

By now I had broken my swimming training regime, and although I hadn't completely accepted that the Olympic dream was over, I knew I wasn't the kind of swimmer who could half-arse their way to success. Running replaced swimming, and it changed my life.

When I started, running almost became a religion for me. From Mum and Dad's house I'd run to the beach and then up the hill towards the northern headland. I'd run along the cliffs with the ocean to my right and, after cresting the hill, I'd run down to Coogee Beach and then back up to another set of cliffs towards Clovelly Beach. Then I'd turn around and do the whole thing in reverse, having covered about fourteen or fifteen kilometres, and always feeling better finishing than I did when I started.

Often I listened to music; often I became lost in my own thoughts. Always I was running for me. Rain, hail or shine, I ran. When it was sunny, the ocean and beach and cliffs were beautiful. When it was overcast, the ocean, beach and cliffs were beautiful in a completely different way.

It was such a different way of exercising for me. The joy was there, but the pressure was gone. If I ran fast, that was great, but if I didn't, that was great too. I could run without thinking of running, without thinking of times, without thinking about getting better or faster. Running was a happy emptiness. It was a wooded park in a city. It was white space in a cluttered mind.

But even though I sometimes ran twice in a day, I never became fanatical. It was just part of my routine, and something that made me feel better about myself, and the rest of my day.

Running helped me immeasurably through this period and it has helped me through so many others since. It's one of the best coping mechanism I have ever found and looking back now, I think it may have even saved my life when I ended up at the centre of a vicious and confusing media firestorm that took me completely unawares.

7

The Incident

I had known Sonny Bill Williams before the fateful incident. He'd lived in the area and he and I knew each other enough to say hello. We had a lot of friends in common, so we'd sometimes end up in the same room at parties, albeit usually talking to other people.

We'd even flirted a little bit before. Nothing serious, but we had each other's numbers and we had texted a few times, like guys and girls do, but nothing much. This was before he'd started seeing his girlfriend at the time, or at least I assume it was beforehand. I had known nothing of her and the fact that she and Sonny Bill were an item until it was plastered all over the newspapers later. I didn't really know that much about Sonny Bill, except that he was a footballer with the Canterbury Bulldogs and that we shared some friends.

The incident happened on Easter Saturday, 2007, not long after my twenty-second birthday. That day, Llara and I went to the Lawn Party at Randwick Racecourse, something that had become a little bit of a tradition for us. It was usually held after the Ironwoman season had finished, and I used it as a bit of a post-season celebration.

We'd dress up and go as a pair, and then undoubtedly see a cavalcade of people from around our way as we went from marquee to marquee. With our tickets this year, we were given six drink vouchers, and while I didn't get through my allocation, after three or four glasses of champagne I was feeling pretty lightheaded.

When the races ended at around five o'clock, the bulk of our friends were heading to the Clovelly Hotel, close to the path my head-clearing runs took me along. Llara and I wanted to follow, but not before going back home to have a meal that Mum would always prepare for us on days like this.

It was good to eat something, to chat to Mum and to get changed, but I was also quite excited about the prospect of going back out with Llara. It felt really good to want to socialise. Often I just wanted to disappear and tell people I had training in the morning, but I wasn't training the next day and I was in an unusually sociable mood.

Mum gave Llara and me a lift from our place to the Clovelly Hotel and as we entered the pub we could feel that people's nights weren't only just starting. It can't have been much later than about 7pm when we got there, and the sun was barely down, but the pub was in full swing, packed with race-goers, day drinkers, beach-goers and God knows who else.

There's a certain noise in a pub that's just a little out of control and that was what I heard when we walked in. Normally that noise would send me home, but not that night. I enjoyed the energy, even though I was a little confronted by it. Llara and I had a couple of drinks and attached ourselves to a group of people who were friends and friends of friends. An NRL player I knew and had grown up with at Maroubra Surf Club, Reni Maitua, was there, and with him was Sonny Bill.

It was one of those situations, not uncommon when you're in your early twenties, in which you and another person simply gravitate towards each other. We did that, Sonny Bill and I. I'd had some drinks and I suspected he'd had many more, and we were chatting and flirting. The body language, the things that were said, the faint touches all suggested that we were going to kiss. There were eyes on us, though, in this open area. It was uncomfortable.

Outside of the surf club and swimming communities, I wasn't anybody, but back then, Sonny Bill was already a star of his sport. He was still only twenty-one years of age, but had been playing first-grade footy for three years. He was one of the most highly respected players in the game and, at six foot five and over a hundred kilograms, he was also one of the most visible. That night, however, he was just a guy in a pub who I wanted to kiss, and I wanted to do it without a pub full of prying eyes staring at us.

He suggested that we find somewhere less visible. He got up and I followed. First he led me upstairs, but there was no privacy there either, and he then led me through a door and then another door, and we kissed in privacy.

It took me a little while to fully realise we were in the men's bathroom. I also hadn't noticed that some people had followed us into the bathroom until I turned from Sonny Bill and saw a hand reaching under the bathroom partition with a phone. I pushed that hand and that phone aside. I may have said something to the creeping pervert, but I can't recall whether I did.

I think sometimes about how different my life may have been if I'd just grabbed that phone and deleted the photograph. So much pain and humiliation might have been avoided. The thought never occurred to me, however. Cameras had only just become a feature on mobile phones and I didn't think much of the intrusion.

But as I discovered, it was a brand-new way to impinge on someone's right to privacy.

After I pushed the phone away, I could hear people outside and had a sense that a crowd had gathered. I could hear the bouncer, clearing people out of the bathroom, and then asking for Sonny Bill and me to come out. Some of Sonny Bill's mates were there, and they suggested that he should probably go home, or at least leave the pub.

Llara and I left the pub also, but we didn't go home. I was having fun. I was having a night out and I certainly didn't foresee the drama that lay ahead of me. I went from the Clovelly Hotel to the Sapphire Lounge in Kings Cross and there I stayed until a little after 1am, when I started to worry that cab changeover time was looming, so I grabbed a slice of pizza and ate it in the taxi, alone on my way home.

That night I slept without a care in the world, which is something I can't say for so many of the nights that came afterwards.

*

Between my breakdown and that night at the Clovelly, I had managed to find some equilibrium in my life. I'd stopped swimming as much as I had previously been doing, and had stowed any Olympic aspirations. I ran every day, but I also went back to surf lifesaving, just for the love of it. I trained on the board and on the ski, but mostly I was just part of the North Bondi Surf Life Saving Club, where I could just be part of a community.

I hadn't spent the spring busting a gut trying to get back to the Ironwoman series, I'd just trained when I wanted to. I'd actually had a fun summer of competition. Instead of competing only for myself, I had competed for the club in a relay event called the Taplin.

In competitive surf lifesaving the Taplin is an event in which a swimmer, a board paddler and a ski paddler compete legs of a relay, and is often the most prestigious event of any carnival that doesn't include a professional Ironman or Ironwoman event. It's certainly the most prestigious team event, and usually only the very best clubs perform well.

For instance, clubs like Maroubra in New South Wales, where they might have a few standout athletes but not much depth to the talent pool, struggle in events like the Taplin, and traditionally it's been the strong Queensland clubs that end up on the podium.

In North Bondi we had a really good team with me doing the board paddling, a girl called Josie Riakos on ski and Kristy Lee Ogilvie swimming. We became close and really supported one another. We were successful, too – we were the state champions and even won silver at the Australian Championships, beating a number of really prestigious clubs.

I'd actually even started to enjoy my ski paddling that summer. Before, I'd only used the ski for Ironwoman racing, but as I became stronger and more confident, I really got a lot of joy from it. The ski can cut through and ride the surf like a dolphin. With the right operator the ski can be sleek and very fast, and of all the disciplines of surf lifesaving, ski racing is the one that can most elicit moments of cresting joy.

I had become more comfortable socially too. As I'd learned from my counselling sessions, I knew I couldn't force myself to be someone I wasn't, and if I was going to enjoy being out with friends, it was going to be because I wanted to be there, not because I'd just forced myself to leave the house. And I'd finally been able to do that in Bondi, with my club mates, and also elsewhere with Llara. I'd really missed her since leaving Brigidine, and now that I had more time, we were connecting again, having fun again. It was so wonderful to have her back in my life.

I'd been excited to go to the races with her that Easter Saturday, and so happy about how comfortable I was there and at the Clovelly. Perhaps kissing a boy in the bathroom was a bit out of character for me, but I'd been having fun, and I wasn't hurting anyone. This is something I'd have to remind myself in the days, weeks and months after the incident, when people wanted to characterise what happened in a wholly different light.

But it took me a while to remember all of that. While it was happening I was too young, too hurt and too inexperienced, and I was too shocked that the story took off, and then just went on and on, with truth being the first casualty.

*

The first I knew that something was happening was on Sunday; the day after the incident. Max Markson called to tell me two things. The first was that an upskirt photograph of me kissing Sonny Bill was being circulated around the country via text message and email, and the second was that a daily newspaper was going to publish a story about Sonny Bill and me the next day.

I didn't think there was anything to this story, but I didn't get to decide. I was going to be in the paper whether I liked it or not. I was horrified, and a thousand questions started to flood my mind. The two that loomed largest were why any newspaper would want to publish a story about Sonny Bill and me kissing, and how they and other people could legally share a photo of me in a bathroom. Soon those questions gave way to another: how the hell were my family going to handle the story?

Dad was a sober man, and he didn't preach in his house about what constituted good or bad behaviour, but I knew he was going to be disappointed by the story. I didn't tell my parents what was coming. I didn't tell anyone. I hoped it was going to be a tiny little thing, secreted away deep in the folds of the newspapers, only to be seen by the most eagle-eyed readers.

That Sunday night I started what was to become a stomach-churning and increasingly depressing routine. Having found a newsagency that was open all night in Kings Cross, I got in my car after midnight, drove up a near-empty Anzac Parade, parked, pulled a hat down over my face and bought a freshly printed newspaper.

In the car I pored over the pages in the hope that the story only alluded to what had happened, or that it was just a small story in the gossip pages, or that an editor had binned the story altogether, telling the journalist to come back when they had something that was actual news and didn't intrude on anyone's privacy.

None of that hope was realised. Not only was the story prominently displayed alongside actual news, the photograph had been published, which had been shot up and under my skirt inside the bathroom. The story also suggested that Sonny Bill and I were having sex in the bathroom, even though those words weren't used. That would be a plain reading of the story, and was the conclusion that most readers came to.

'Toilet tryst' the newspaper said. That would be a euphemism that I would become disgustingly familiar with. The story just got worse and worse as I read. I read that Sonny Bill had a girlfriend, someone he'd been living with, and there was also a quote from Max Markson in the story, which was a shock to me, which said that I'd been auditioning for the *Kenny* sequel, alluding to the popular Aussie film about a man who works for a company managing portaloos.

I felt sick to my stomach. I couldn't keep it all in my head at any one time it was too big. I could only think about parts of it, like how it would affect my parents and brothers, or how it would affect me in surf competitions, or how it may affect me as I walked down the street. If ever I managed to reconcile one of the aspects of this thing, another would emerge from the murkiness and sit there, ugly and dark in my consciousness.

There was no respite. I felt attacked and defenseless at all times. Surely anyone taking or even sharing such an image, let alone publishing it in a newspaper, were potentially exposing themselves to civil liability and also possibly to criminal liability? Certainly Max never suggested I seek legal advice, and despite my embarrassment and outrage at the article, I was still young and naive so I allowed him to continue to manage the situation.

I drove home with my newspaper and I felt sick. I kept telling myself that I just had to keep going, push through. The story had come, and it would go, like all news stories. Today's news, tomorrow's fish and chip paper, as they used to say.

After all, how interesting was this story, really? Surf lifesaver pashes footy player in local pub?

*

The next day, Monday, was a lurching nightmare. I woke up and the story had grown legs. Every radio station was talking about Sonny Bill and me, and it was on the telly too. It seemed everyone had been invited to give their thoughts. Across radio and television they were also careful not to say that we were having sex, but again the implication was strongly there.

Toilet. Tryst. Photograph. Toilet. Tryst. Photograph. Toilet. Tryst. Photograph. Toilet. Tryst. Photograph.

Those words were everywhere. And so was my name. Sonny Bill was being mentioned too, but he wasn't copping it like I was. Listening to and watching and reading the coverage and the comments, there seemed to be strong feeling that Sonny Bill had just done what blokes do, even when they have girlfriends, but that I was a slut. Only some people used that word, but it was always hanging in the air. I didn't have sex in a toilet. I kissed a boy I liked. That was all.

There was no shortage of media requests that day, but I didn't want to add any fuel to the fire. I said no to them all. I hoped that if Sonny Bill and I both refused to give comment, the story might just go away.

At midnight of that Monday I drove again to the Kings Cross newsagency to buy the next day's papers, with my collar up and a cap shoved over my face, and when I got back to the car I tore open the paper. I felt nauseous when I saw there were more stories about me: some comment, some news, and some just large images of me and of Sonny Bill with little more than an extended caption to justify the inclusion.

There was no 'news' per se, but I could tell that wasn't going to stop this train.

That was my week's routine. I'd be up at night, pacing and anxiously waiting until midnight, then I'd drive to the newsagency and open the paper, hoping against hope that the story was over. Each day there were new stories. There was no new information, but there were endless reactions, responses and comment.

It was a media feeding frenzy. I found out later that for Australia's top news site, the story was the second most clicked-on news event in Australia that year – a year in which a new Australian prime minister was elected, a cyclone killed thousands of people, the wars in Iraq and Afghanistan lurched on, and Andrew Johns retired from footy.

I tried to contact Sonny Bill, as I thought he might be the only one who could give me some clarity about the events of that night and could help me understand more about what had happened. After contacting his manager, I heard nothing back from Sonny Bill. I've never heard anything from him.

When I opened the paper that second night at Kings Cross, the anxiety and horror was overwhelming. The story wasn't going away. It felt like a never-ending nightmare. And again one of the things that was making me feel so ill was what I thought my parents and brothers were thinking.

Dad drinks rarely, and that was part of the reason that I barely drank: not because I thought there was anything inherently bad about drinking, but because the example that had been set for me was that sobriety was a normal and preferable path. Now, here I was at the centre of a drunken kiss, a *tryst* in newspaper parlance, late at night, which everyone in the world, it felt, was condemning.

I never opened up to my parents. After the stories were published I just told them briefly what had happened and then went into my room. I stayed in my room for most of that week, not wanting to face them and not wanting to face the world.

I felt so alone. I also felt mortified, as though there was some shame I owned that was just outside of my field of view.

My agent's advice was that I say something; Max wanted me to talk. I didn't want to do that.

On the Friday of that week, Danny Weidler, a friend who worked at Channel Nine and at the *Sun-Herald*, contacted me and told me that Sonny Bill had agreed to do a cover story and a two-page spread with his girlfriend for the *Sunday Telegraph*. He asked me whether I wanted to respond.

Now that I knew about the *Sunday Telegraph* piece, it scared me; even if I wasn't going to be vilified, I didn't think I was going to be humanised in the story. I was beginning to understand how this whole media cycle worked. That piece would be about Sonny Bill's judgement and redemption, and his girlfriend's disappointment and forgiveness. I'd just be the girl in the toilet: a temptation, a seduction, a mistake.

I trusted and felt comfortable with Danny, and I started to think that perhaps I should do a story with him. He said he could get me on the news that Saturday night and then he'd write a piece for the *Sun-Herald*. I agreed, hoping it would put an end to the story, and put an end to any more speculation about what had happened.

My agent advised me that the best thing I could do was to apologise publicly, for what exactly I could never quite understand, but people seemed to be angry, and repentance seemed to be my role in the whole narrative. I wanted it to stop. I agreed to the story and we put together some talking points and arranged for the journalist and a camera crew to meet me in Cooper Park in Bellevue Hill at about 2pm. There I prostrated myself. I apologised to my family, to the public, to everyone for my part in it, and then went home and waited for the Nine News at 6pm.

An hour or so before the news, a story was published online on a rival news website with all of the details revealed in the interview and also quotes from me. I had no idea how this had happened and felt completely out of my depth, and now Danny's piece would be old news, which added more embarrassment to humiliation. It was a mess.

Over the following two days, nothing changed. The story rolled on, and the characterisation of me didn't change – not in the papers, not on TV or the radio, and not on the streets either. Everywhere I went, I felt all eyes were on me. For every person I passed, I felt there was a conversation about me, either with the person they were with, or one in their head. There's *that* girl.

Toilet. Tryst. Photograph. Toilet. Tryst. Photograph.

There was no respite. Nothing was working. To me, continuing to manage the media response with Max seemed hopeless, and I decided to work with one of his colleagues at the agency instead.

Finally I left the country, but I could only afford to get away so far, and for so long. A friend had offered me some accommodation in Fiji, so on the Tuesday I called Llara and asked her if she wanted to come with me. The very next day we were there.

It was air in my lungs, that trip. It was only a week but it was so very needed. We just talked and swam and walked. It was Llara's birthday, so we had a fancy dinner, which was lovely. I knew at some point I had to go back home, though.

I returned, hoping that perhaps people had forgotten and that I could disappear into the noise of Sydney, but it wasn't to be. The story had kicked on and there was now an entrenched misunderstanding of who I was. It followed me everywhere.

A few weeks after returning from Fiji, Sonny Bill was back in the news after smashing a camera from a photographer's hands as he was coming out of a nightclub in Kings Cross. There was also speculation as to whether he was going to stay committed to his club, the Bulldogs. I would have thought that these stories had nothing to do with me, and yet I was brought up every time.

Sonny Bill was going off the rails, some people were saying, and these people were also suggesting that I was the reason. I'd kissed Sonny Bill and chatted to him for perhaps a couple of hours. I had no idea how anyone could suggest I was an influence at all.

Meanwhile, I was running and running and running. I was really beating myself up then, and had started to take on the things that were said about me. I'd started to believe that I deserved all the scorn that was piled on me. But every day I'd pull a hat down over my face as far as I could, put on sunglasses and try to outrun it all.

Even while I was running, the story was still there; it was in the faces of the people I ran past. It was on the blasting radios of construction sites I paced alongside of, and it was also in my head. It was much quieter when I was running, though. The voice of self-criticism and the scope of the scandal lessened, enough to give me just enough space to find myself again, the intangible me, the inside me, the real me, not the person everyone was talking about. With the ocean at my side, the sun above my head, music in my ears, my heart pounding in my chest and sweat pouring out of me, the story just didn't seem as important, and I didn't seem such a justified object of contempt.

I was just a girl running, with the waves lapping and the birds soaring and the breeze blowing, regardless of whether

I'd kissed a guy in a pub or not. I don't know where I would have ended up then if I wasn't running.

Eventually I decided that I was going to do a paid interview.

The things that had concerned me the most throughout the whole gruelling affair wasn't that the incident wasn't being fairly characterised, it was that *I* wasn't being fairly characterised. I wasn't a party girl. I wasn't a drinker. I wasn't some kind of Australian Paris Hilton. I was just me, Candice Falzon. I wished people knew that. I had a new agent now, a young woman who had just opened her own management agency called Sarah Wagner, had fielded some offers with cash attached, and when one from the TV show *A Current Affair* came with a $20,000 payment, I decided to do it.

I have to say the money was a consideration – not the only consideration, but it was one. It was a lot of money to me. It was money that would certainly make a difference in my life. I also felt that there were so many people benefiting from a false version of me, that perhaps I should be able to benefit from the real version of me.

The interview with *A Current Affair* was with a young female journalist and she went on the offensive quickly. Every question was built around the premise that I was a man-eating party animal. Perhaps the interview wasn't what I expected or wanted it to be, but it hadn't hurt, and I was happy with the way I conducted myself. But, naively, I thought that perhaps this interview would put an end to the story.

Of course it didn't.

*

I've often thought about why the story became so huge. Sonny Bill was a big star in footy, and yes, he had allegedly cheated on his girlfriend which, I suppose, had some kind of strange news value to it, but nothing deserving of what the story became.

Was it the titillation factor? I suppose that must have been a part of it. Was it the fascination with new technologies? I think that was certainly a part of it. In the situation that Sonny Bill and I had been in, a photograph to accompany the story would have been rare before 2007. Previously, a classic paparazzi image might have been of someone pushing their hand in front of a camera lens as they came out of a restaurant, but this was something altogether more nefarious and futuristic.

In 2007, 'user-generated content' was a term that was barely used. Twitter didn't exist, nor Instagram, and we were more than a decade away from TikTok. People had started using camera phones, but they couldn't yet be easily and instantly uploaded to a platform, as phone apps and the iPhone were still just a technological possibility, not a fully deployed consumer product.

This story was right in the zeitgeist, but it was also very unusual because there weren't many other mobile-phone-generated stories around at the time. Soon enough, newspapers would be full of imagery snapped on mobiles, and stories generated and shared through social networks, but around Easter 2007, the story about Sonny Bill and me was unique.

The other technology that drove the story was the brand-new click-economy that the media was starting to embrace. In 2007, newspapers were making the move to publishing online, but were struggling to understand how their business would make money on the internet. The now-antiquated clicks-for-dollars banner-advertising revenue model was the one that newspapers were relying on for online revenue, and in this story they'd found the ultimate clickbait.

The story was like following the white rabbit; it led the reader down a path they were enticed to believe would end in salacious detail, and perhaps even something pornographic. Of course, there were no such details and no such pornography, and only the most gullible readers of news websites would believe what they were being sold, but in 2007 we were all neophytes in the business of online news.

Everyone clicked, and everyone talked, and the story became one of Australia's first huge online news sensations. It was the story that gave and gave: to newspaper editors, who ran stories daily; to talkback hosts, who invited discourse; to advertisers, to those who liked to read about and discuss scorn and faux outrage. Everyone had a take.

There was a by-product of this story: pain and humiliation, but it only really affected me and my family. It wasn't felt in the workplaces of the people who peddled the story endlessly so they could make a couple of extra bucks, but in our home.

The story must have hurt Sonny Bill too, but it didn't follow him around for years like it did for me and my family. It wasn't the first thing people said to him, and about him. He wasn't bullied with songs about him and me, and no one was wearing masks of my face to get to him or his partner.

When Sonny Bill published his memoir in 2021, he had the privilege of not having to dedicate too much time to the incident, because for him it was something that simply came and went. It probably wasn't even the most consequential thing that happened to him that month back in 2007.

It took a long time for me to realise what had happened that night and beyond, and why it blew up the way it did, and it had a lot to do with my gender, my age and my background. I wasn't anything much like the daughters and mothers of the people who made decisions to print and publish. I wasn't the type of woman that these people thought deserved respect. I was treated as a certain kind of disposable person with motivations and hopes and dreams that didn't matter.

I was still expected to apologise, for what I still don't exactly understand.

I know now there was a class and wealth element to this story too. I know now that when newspapers' stories are being assessed by inhouse lawyers, one of their first considerations is whether the potentially defamed person would consider taking legal action, and then if they did, whether they could afford to do so.

Some weeks after the incident, it did occur to me that I could sue, and I put together a scrapbook of all the stories and comments and clips, with a view to taking it to a lawyer in the hope that it might arrest the story. But every lawyer I spoke to told me the same thing: it was a marginal case. Yes, in the headlines and language the media were using in their stories, they were alluding to the falsity that Sonny Bill and I had been having sex, but they never said it outright. Perhaps I could mount a case and perhaps I could even win, but that wasn't assured, and to do so would cost millions.

Obviously it wasn't something my family and I could do.

The illegality of the publishing and dissemination of the photograph was something different altogether, though. I could potentially take that matter to the police and the person who took the photo, the people who shared the photo, and the media outlet that shared the photograph could all be investigated and potentially charged with an offence that had a maximum sentence of three years in jail. It could certainly act as a deterrent for anyone else considering doing it, but it would all come with a significant emotional cost to me, and more importantly to my family, and the last thing I wanted to do was cause them any more pain, and it would probably only make my life worse. I'd be Candice the Toilet Tryst Girl as well as Candice the Dobber. The media had decided that I could just be a punchline. I just had to wear it and suffer it.

I cried my eyes out. After all, when enough people say bad things about you enough times, you start to believe them yourself.

Eventually it got to the point where I thought I wanted to escape. I didn't want to be seen or heard and I wanted the pain my family had been feeling to go away.

I'd tell Mum and Dad that I was going to training and I'd just drive, for a long, long time. There was no destination; it just seemed to me that I didn't want to be where I was, wherever I was. I'd sometimes find myself parked, just bawling my eyes out on my own. I felt so alone, and I wanted to *be* alone; I felt like my actions had affected everyone, and it would have been selfish to inflict further pain on them with my misery.

One day I drove myself to Watson's Bay in Sydney's east and found myself parked at The Gap, which is a place in Sydney that's synonymous with self-harm.

I remember just thinking: 'This is it. I can't take it any more.'

My heart was broken. I just wanted the pain to go away, and I didn't know what else I could do. People wouldn't stop talking about me, and it didn't feel like they ever would. I was hiding from everyone – hiding my feelings, and my face. I didn't see how things would ever get better.

Thankfully in all the darkness of that moment, I recognised that I just needed help. I called my brother Pat and told him I needed him. I told him I couldn't do it anymore. I told him I wanted to die. He came to me immediately. He embraced me, and while it didn't make it all better and it didn't stop the pain, it took me off the ledge and that's something I'll love Patty for until the very end of time.

Pat would check in on me every day after that, and even just that was a golden tether in the dark days.

8

Restoration

For most of that year, I was kind of a recluse. I didn't want to be seen in public, and when I had to leave the house I often hid myself under a hat and sunglasses.

Mum was worried about me and Dad was too, and when people realised that they were my brothers, Tim and Patty used to get jokes thrown at them at the pub. They didn't just cop it and sometimes they got into fist fights over what had been said.

The whole incident was a joke for everyone else, but for me and my family it was serious. I wondered when people were ever going to stop characterising me as that 'toilet tryst' girl. The answer was never, but eventually I did manage not to care quite so much about what people thought, especially the ones who didn't know me. They didn't care who I really was, so I had little interest in their opinion of me.

One thing that amazed me about that period was that while everyone had something to say behind my back, almost nobody approached me about that night, and not one person asked me what had actually happened.

I think it's because people didn't really want to know. They had their own titillating version of events and inserting a real person and some less than titillating facts into their narrative would spoil all the fun.

*

Mum, Dad and I had always planned to go to Europe in June in 2007. We were going there to visit but now, after what was happening in Sydney, I thought I would have to stay there. It felt as if there was no future for me in Australia.

Flying out of Sydney I was profoundly depressed and not a lot of fun to be around. We spent time in London, where I thought I might live, and there my depression deepened. It was summer there, but I still found it an unfriendly and grey place, which I was loath to have as the background of my life. But if not London, where?

After London, we went to Paris, and the pall that had fallen over me persisted. It's one of the world's great cities and yet I couldn't enjoy any of it. I felt trapped and was hating myself for not enjoying such a beautiful place. I was still stuck in my own head and thoughts of the past and the future were destroying any happiness in the present. I know Mum, especially, was very concerned about me.

Dad had been worried since the whole incident of course, but I knew that Mum could actually see the depths of my dejection. She couldn't pull me out, though. That's all any mum wants to do – to fix things, to solve things, to pour so much love into a situation that smiles and happiness return.

She tried so hard in London and Paris to get through to me, and I tried to meet her halfway, but I just couldn't. Until we got to the south of France, on the Bay of Biscay.

It was the ocean. Just being in and beside the glittering water, I started to feel calm. I could swim and walk along the beach, with no one staring or talking behind my back. And I ran, breathing in and breathing out, inhaling the sights and sounds around me as started to find a way back to myself. The voices of condemnation in my head started to disappear. I spent a lot of time just staring at the endless blue. It seemed to give context and scope to everything.

I was starting to accept that I'd been treated unfairly, but also that I didn't have to respond to that unfairness with self-pity. Accepting that I'd been treated unfairly simply meant that I could enjoy the ocean again, and run, and be happy again. Accepting that I'd been treated unfairly meant I could reclaim my thoughts.

Mum recognised a change in my mood when we were oceanside and told Dad that we were slightly rejigging our itinerary so that we'd only be visiting coastal places. This wasn't hugely inconveniencing them anyway, as the main destination of the trip was Malta, an island – a country that was all coast.

After a few more happy beachside stops we arrived in Malta, and that was where my restoration was completed. It was in Malta that I realised my sole focus had been on myself in the here and now, and only myself, and with such a narrow focus I wasn't taking in all of the scope of life.

Malta is an incredible place, and a rich history abounds in the buildings and people. Dad's family history was tied up in that little island, and when we were there I met so many family members who I didn't even know existed. They knew about us though, and they certainly knew Dad.

My grandfather had left my dad when he was just a little boy, and the shame of that event was still felt strongly in the family. There was an apologetic shroud over so many of the interactions we had with Dad's family, but there was also a sense of triumph. They loved and respected Dad, not because he'd done good and become a millionaire, or was a famous sports star, but simply because he'd grown up to be a good man, honest and trustworthy, and with a family who loved him.

It warmed my heart to see it, and reminded me of where I came from and how far Dad had come in his own life. The trip helped me understand him a little better, and perhaps, if that was even possible, made me love him even more.

In Malta I really started to feel like myself again. I realised some things about myself, and also my plans for the future. The way I felt – the malaise and depression – had started with the media deluge and as the stories came and went, I carried it with me, like dogshit on a shoe. No matter where I went, ill-feeling was going to be with me because it was within me.

I wasn't going to live in Europe; I was going to return to Sydney. But once I was back, I knew I needed to do something worthwhile, to engage deeply in my life again.

I still wanted to compete, but simply for the enjoyment of competition, not for winning. I wanted to train to push myself, to get better, but without the overbearing weight of personal or public expectation. With all this in mind, I thought perhaps I could compete in the Coolangatta Gold.

The Coolangatta Gold is legendary in many Australians' minds, but that legend is born of confection, not history. In the early eighties, an Australian screenwriter was looking to build a film around Grant Kenny competing in a legendary Ironman race, and with no such race existing, he decided to create one. For narrative and location purposes, this fictional race was going to be an endurance event like nothing that had existed in Australia before, with competitors racing from Surfers Paradise to Coolangatta, on the border between Queensland and New South Wales.

When it came time to shoot the film, the decision was made to run the fictional event as an actual race. Many of the top competitive surf lifesavers raced, but the event was won by a then unknown teenager, Guy Leech. In the eighties and nineties, the event was held just four times but, as an endurance event, which asked around four gruelling hours of its competitors, it was at odds with regular Ironman racing, which was usually more of a middle-distance or sprint event.

The race returned in 2005, however, with women also being invited to compete. To me, the Coolangatta Gold was an Australian version of the Hawaiian IRONMAN Triathlon, which was a competitive and professional event not solely defined by winning.

Each year hundreds of people competed in the notoriously gruelling Hawaiian IRONMAN race. Often they had a time in mind, and maybe even a place in mind, but from amputees to older athletes, to recovering addicts and people who just needed to break out of a malaise, there were always so many people who knew they weren't going to challenge those in the front of the race, but were going to win by enduring and persisting and crossing the line.

I wasn't an endurance athlete, I was a sprinter with my legs and arms full of fast-twitch muscle fibres. I could give you a competitive twenty or thirty and maybe even forty minutes, but I couldn't sustain peak performance past that (I don't feel bad about it; Usain Bolt will only give you twenty seconds).

Four hours is beyond the limits of what I'm built for, but that's why I wanted to compete in the Coolangatta Gold. It's not the Hawaiian IRONMAN, but it was much longer and more challenging than any of the other surf lifesaving events. I would have to train very seriously, despite having no chance of winning. That's what I wanted too. I'd compete only to compete, race only to race, tested only by myself.

I came back to Australia with a new lease of life, a plan and a goal, and for the first time in a long time, I felt as though everything was going to be okay.

*

I came back home to the rudest of awakenings. Arriving in Sydney, there was a massive package at home addressed to me, which contained hundreds and hundreds of printed pages. Each was a news story or a page of comments from an online article or a message board about me and the Clovelly incident.

There was a handwritten note atop all the printed pages that said: 'Printed these. Didn't want you to miss any of it.'

Someone had taken time out of their day, every day, to print all that had been written about me while my family and

I had been away. This was what someone had chosen to do with their time? Of all the things that can be done with this life, someone chose this?

I pitied the person who'd done this. They were pathetic, whoever they were. I still pity them in the way that I pity the people who comment on articles about Dave and me, or who feel the need to make comments about us on social media. It just isn't a great use of this one life we get.

It didn't get to me. The entire box was thrown away immediately. It wasn't so long ago that something like this would set me spiralling, but I came back from Europe feeling like a different person, with a goal and a future ahead.

I almost felt sorry for all the effort this person had made, all for no effect.

*

Of course, I was expecting some kind of commentary about me and my past when I entered the Coolangatta Gold, but I wasn't expecting it to come from someone I'd always looked up to – former Ironman Phil Clayton, who was now coaching Queenslander Hayley Bateup, winner of the previous two women's Coolangatta Gold races.

In the days before the race, Phil was quoted by the media saying that mistakes I'd made in my personal life were effectively bringing the sport into disrepute. It was disappointing to see, especially as Phil was someone I'd always admired for his ability in the surf, and it was even more disappointing as I'd resolutely kept my head down, training hard, and hadn't made myself available for media or interviews in preparation for the Gold.

When other competitors did media, they were often asked what they thought about me and the fact that I was on the start sheet for the race. Most batted the questions away, but Hayley Bateup, the reigning Coolangatta Gold champion, seemed very clear in her opinion – she was quoted as saying that if I thought I was going to win, I was kidding myself, and that I'd be lucky to finish.

It hurt, especially since it would be my first race since the incident at the Clovelly Hotel and the prospect of not finishing was something I feared. I wasn't there to win; in fact I knew I wouldn't, and I'd never suggested anything to the contrary. That said, I did want to finish it, and the comments I'd seen actually gave me extra motivation to get across the line.

I trained incredibly hard in the lead-up to the event, which would be held in October. There weren't many other people from the North Bondi club who were going to compete, but one of the guys there, Matt Colquhoun, coached me and essentially helped me with all of the training I needed. An exceptionally strong ski racer, Matt taught me so much about the tactics required for such a long event and trained me in drafting behind other competitors and following in their wake; not fighting the surf, but working with it. He was so generous with his time; I was so grateful. In fact, the whole club gave me incredible support, and even mounted a few miniature Coolangatta Gold-style training events, with people dropping in and out of relay legs in the race against me.

Not competing with a team per se, I had to personally generate the support group that was required for an event like this — ideally I'd need four people to help me, moving my equipment during the race, providing gels and fluids at crucial times, and giving me moral support for the long, final run leg. Llara had started going out with my swim coach Chad, who didn't see me as often now my Olympic ambitions had gone but who still trained me, so that was two people supporting me, and of course Mum and Dad had graciously agreed to help, giving me the four I would need. I couldn't have found a better support team.

I went up to Queensland feeling great. I'd done the work and I was with people I loved. However, as I joined the athletes' briefings the day before the race, I started to feel quite apprehensive. I had no idea what kind of reception I was going to receive.

Hayley and Phil were there, and a large group of competitors from Queensland clubs, including Hayley's, the super-club BMD Northcliffe from Surfers Paradise, which was one of the first Australian clubs to pay its high-performing athletes to train and compete using revenue generated in the club, including revenue from poker machines. There was definitely a chill in the air from that quarter, but there were other athletes there who were welcoming and supportive. More than a few, some of whom I didn't know, came over to say hello and wish me well, and also, touchingly, to congratulate me for picking myself up from the year I'd had. Their kindness meant a hell of a lot to me that day.

The race started with a surf ski sprint from the shore, out to the back of the break to the first turning buoy, where the

127

pace would settle into an eighteen-kilometre paddle, before a run to a three-and-a-half-kilometre swim, and another run following to the five-kilometre board paddle and the final seven-kilometre soft-sand run.

I was placed next to Hayley on the start line and my strategy was to stay with her and her group as long as I could, not because I wanted to try to get in her head, but because I knew there would be a large group in front of the race and then an atomised tail, and I needed to stay in that main group at the beginning or it was going to be a very long and difficult day.

The gun went off and the race started at a blistering pace. I think the top girls knew that the rest of us were going to try to stay with them in the ski, so the pack tried to blast off as many of us as possible.

A few kilometres in, the muscles in my forearms started to blow out. The pain was excruciating, and I wasn't even an hour into the race. But one stroke at a time, I managed to work through the pain. I did get shaken off the main pack eventually, but at that point I'd settled into a good rhythm and soon I was through the first run and was into the swim. The swim was hard but fun, but the board was where I really hit my stride. Even though I'd been going for three hours by then, I found out later that my time on the board was the fastest split of the whole event.

I gave everything to the final soft-sand run leg, and had Mum, Dad, Llara and Chad there spurring me on when I was close to the point of exhaustion. As I approached the finish, not in the first group, but not in the last group either, I was full of emotion, and as I crossed the line, my eyes welled up and soon I was a mess of tears.

This race had meant so much to me, because it wasn't just me who'd competed. Llara and Chad had been there for me, and Mum and Dad. Not only had they barracked for me during every moment of my training, and every moment of the race, they'd been there for me during what had been the hardest year of my life. Any achievement of mine in that race was for them, every second of it.

I went back home to Sydney with an immense sense of satisfaction, but also a renewed love for my sport, and also for training. Six weeks after finishing the Coolangatta Gold I went back to Queensland for the Ironwoman series trials – with all of the work I'd been putting into my ski racing that year, I thought I may have a chance at success. And by a stroke of luck, the qualifying event was longer than most and the endurance training I'd been doing paid off. I qualified for the 2007/2008 series easily.

Qualification was a strange moment. I'd been out of the Ironwoman series for years by then, and there had been a time when getting back in was all that I'd possibly wanted. Now it had just sort of happened, without too much fuss, and I didn't really have strong feelings about it.

Perhaps too much had happened since. Perhaps something in me had broken.

Or perhaps I felt that way because I knew I was going to have an interrupted season, with intermittent training anyway – between finishing the Coolangatta Gold and being accepted into the Ironwoman season, I'd been approached to compete in another kind of competition altogether.

*

In 2006 and 2007, Channel Seven aired a television series called *It Takes Two* in which notable Australians who didn't have a singing background were trained by some professional singers and paired in weekly live singing duets. The competitors of the first and second seasons included cricketer Michael Bevan, actor Kate Ritchie, presenter Ernie Dingo and actor Lochie Daddo. They'd been paired with really impressive singers, like Troy Cassar-Daley, Kate Ceberano, David Campbell, and Glenn Shorrock from the Little River Band.

I'd been asked to be part of season three and a love of music was one of the reasons I agreed to do it. I wasn't a great singer, but I wasn't awful, and I thought, with the training that the show offered, perhaps I may even be able to be better than 'not-awful'. Another reason was that I hoped I'd be represented in a way that would transcend the figure I'd been reduced to in the gossip columns, with another being that they were going to pay me, and well.

I knew it would impact my training for the 2007/2008 season as the recording of the show was going to coincide with the Ironwoman season, but my expectations for this season were relatively low anyway as I'd spent most of 2007 training for the Coolangatta Gold. I'd stopped working in real estate, had very few sponsors still on board and I was running out of money, and when I saw what they were going to pay me each week, I couldn't refuse.

I really enjoyed the season and working with my partner, Anthony Callea, who had been one of the breakout successes of the television show *Australian Idol*. Anthony has an incredible voice, and he was an excellent teacher as well, but one of the best parts of my experience on *It Takes Two* was the friendship that I developed with fellow contestant comedian Julia Morris.

As a twenty-three-year-old with very little television experience, and someone who was still quite wary about the media, I was a bit overwhelmed when we started filming, but Julia really took me under her wing and cared for me through the recording of the show, which soon became very enjoyable.

As the show progressed, I also got an opportunity to promote my beloved sport. Each week the remaining contestants had their song performances preceded with a short segment about what they'd been doing during the week, and a few times the camera crews came along to film me training or competing. While competitive surf lifesaving was still as strong as ever as a participation sport, coverage was drying up and professional Ironmen and Ironwomen were no longer household names. None of the events were being televised live and only a few were shown in packaged shows, meaning they weren't broadcast live, and were heavily edited.

The sport was becoming like volleyball, netball or hockey, with great grassroots support but little interest to the general public. I was glad that I could put a little bit of a spotlight on the sport, in a primetime television slot, and as I raced professionally that season, some of my fellow competitors thanked me for helping to raise the profile of the sport. Of course, though, for every action there's an equal and opposite reaction, and I copped criticism from others, primarily from members of some of the Queensland clubs, who felt I was somehow hogging the limelight without performing at the high level they were. But I'd learned how to shrug off worse calls than those in the last year or so, and just focused on enjoying myself.

That Ironwoman season was middling for me, with no standout finishes, but also with no events where I finished near the back. I had a really fun and successful team season, though, as the board competitor in a number of relay events representing New South Wales. Meanwhile, Anthony Callea and I were really clicking on *It Takes Two*, and we were also getting a lot of love from the public and judges, until one production meeting when Anthony reminded the producers he was only available for one more week – he was booked to go on tour with Celine Dion. The next week, in Week 7 of the series, we sang a song by the Veronicas, 'Hook Me Up', which, wouldn't you know it, the judges didn't care for, and we were eliminated. Julia Morris went on to win the series, and I couldn't have been happier for her.

And with a little bit of money in my pocket, I made a drastic life decision.

9

A New Beginning

Each year I competed in the New South Wales State Surf Life Saving Championships, at which all of the clubs in the state meet up and take part in individual and team competitions. At this meet after *It Takes Two*, I competed strongly, taking out the state open board title.

That win gave me the opportunity to travel to Western Australia for the national titles, which that year, 2008, and for the next three years, were to be held at Scarborough Beach in Perth. Although I didn't win any national titles that year, I fell in love with the place, and made the decision to move there.

There were a few things that helped me in my decision. One was that there seemed to be excellent training possibilities in Perth. Despite the reported posturing of Phil Clayton and Hayley Bateup in the lead-up to the Coolangatta Gold in my season, Hayley was beaten to first place by the Western Australian competitor, Alicia Marriott, who trained with the City of Perth Surf Life Saving Club, situated at beautiful City Beach. Alicia was becoming not only the best long-distance competitor in the country, but the best competitor overall, also dominating the Ironwoman series.

In a sport that was usually dominated by Queenslanders, Alicia was the new star of the sport. She wasn't the only one, either. There were other high performers coming from Western Australia, and especially from the City of Perth club. I'd also developed a burgeoning relationship with a Perth man: Brent Staker, a professional footballer who played for the West Coast Eagles. He and I had met in the most 2008 way possible. Brent and I had a mutual friend on Myspace and we ended up chatting via that early social media site. After hitting it off, we saw each other in Sydney when the Eagles came to play the Swans, and I also went to Perth to visit him.

In Perth, I saw a place of immense beauty – glorious sunsets over golden sands, salt in the air and fit and beautiful people. Best of all, the city was familiar but it also felt like it was a world away, and it was, in reality, a whole continent away.

All of these added to my determination to move to Perth, but the main factor was my belief that I needed change in my life.

I kept thinking that my instinct to move away to Europe was a good one, but driven by the wrong motivation. Back then, I'd wanted to leave Sydney because I was running away – from the media, from the gossip, from the seemingly never-ending talk about me and what people thought of me, all after one unguarded night in Clovelly. I'd realised though, that running away wasn't the answer – but moving to Perth wasn't about running away from something. It was about running *towards* something.

I knew I was still quite sheltered. Even though I was now twenty-three, a grown adult, I still lived at home, rarely cooked for myself or washed my own clothes, and considered myself to be still quite emotionally immature, which was a state of being that was pretty common in many high-performing athletes.

When I came back from Europe I'd started to reframe my role around the hurt that was caused after the incident in 2007. Thankfully I'd stopped beating myself up and blindly believing the things that the media had said about me, and I knew I'd done nothing wrong that night. If I had my time again, perhaps I'd have fewer drinks, and perhaps I'd behave in a more 'ladylike' manner – or simply choose a far more private place to kiss a boy. But there was something else I knew, and that was that a lot of the hurt in me following the incident was because of a lack of maturity and emotional development. I realised that I could have been more resilient; I could have been more independent.

I'd relied too much on other people to speak for me or to act on my behalf, and I'd brought hurt on others, including my family, by responding to rumour and gossip when it would have been better left alone to let it wither on the vine. The incident was always going to be what it was, and the media was always going to report what they wanted. It wasn't anything much to do with me, but I hadn't been mature enough to see it.

Now I could see Perth as a wonderful opportunity in my growth as an adult, so I decided just to up sticks and go. I spoke to Mum and Dad and I was quite surprised, but heartened, when they said they also thought it might be a good idea. So it was in a heartbeat, it seemed, that in June 2008 I was packed and booked to fly over.

Leaving home was pretty devastating, though. Everybody loves their parents, but Mum and Dad had been intimately intertwined with every aspect of my life for twenty-three years, including some of the toughest things I'd been through. We ate most of our meals together, watched telly together; we were best friends. They cried and I cried when I left for the airport, and I kept crying for pretty much the whole five-hour flight west.

But moving to Perth turned out to be one of the best decisions I'd ever made.

I joined the City of Perth club and was instantly accommodated, accepted and welcomed. They were such a lovely bunch of people, and also excellent athletes and competitors, who I think really appreciated that I'd moved across the country in order to train with them. In our sport, people usually decamped to Queensland to train, as traditionally that was where all of the best athletes in the sport were from. It's where all the best coaches and the most events were, too. 'Train with the best athletes, train in local conditions' – that was what we were encouraged to do, and there were well-travelled paths from surf clubs all across Australia to Queensland, and especially to the Gold Coast, but from what I'd experienced of the Queensland surf lifesaving culture, it didn't look like something I wanted to be a part of.

It was a punt, going to Perth. I didn't know anyone who'd moved there to train, but with beautiful beaches and athletes like Alicia, I just felt like it may work for me and decided to go, basically on instinct. In this instance, my instinct was right.

I can't overstate how incredible it was to move to a new city and to drop straight into a community of like-minded people. Under my new coach, Rick Turner, the club really motivated me to get my arse into gear again, and I was training as hard as I ever had, managing to get in up to twenty sessions a week under that glorious Perth sun.

I trained early in the morning and in the afternoon and sometimes at night too, applying myself to a club program that was one of the best I'd seen. Unlike other clubs, which had individual coaches for each of the disciplines, Rick was in charge of them all with his own super program, and it made such a big difference to the way we trained and competed. Rick also cared genuinely about every competitor, and he invested and believed in me personally and could see what I was made of. That care only made me want to repay it in kind in my own effort and work, and soon I was getting faster and stronger and fitter. I met people outside of the club too. I met new people through Brent, and also through a job I took in real estate, working as an administrator.

One night, when I'd been out with some new girlfriends, our group mingled with another that included a fascinating fellow who ran a local business. His name was Paul Tonich, someone who, I found out later, had been a rising young detective with the Western Australian Police Force when he was jailed for a short time over the interrogation of a suspect. Getting back into the community, he became a public speaker, talking about his journey and experiences, about taking courage from the past, and developed a very successful real estate agency.

After telling him about my work background on that night out, he gave me his card and told me that if I needed a job I should call him. As it turned out I did need a job, and Paul was true to his word and took me on board, and I worked directly for him. Paul was an inspiration: he was dedicated to his business but made it fit around his family, his marathon running and training and other aspects of his life. He allowed me to work in that way, too, which meant my training tempo never dipped.

With that dedication to training, I started to see results. I flew to Queensland to compete again in the 2009 Coolangatta Gold in October, and this time I performed far better. I'd been training for the Ironwoman distances primarily, but felt that I could push myself and compete in a long-distance race again. As it had been the case a year earlier, I knew it wasn't realistic to expect a win, but I performed really well and finished in the top ten.

Next up were the Ironwoman trials, which I was excited about. I felt ready to compete at a high level again.

*

Looking back now, Perth was where my emotional strength was built, tested and, I believe, strengthened.

Brent and I moved in together, but the honeymoon period was brief. We weren't compatible. There were many nights when I left the house and checked into a hotel, alone and lonely. On those long, forlorn nights, the instinct to go back home to Sydney and to Mum and Dad was strong. They'd fix it all, like they had before; I knew that. I could just move back, with my room ready for me, and I could pull the covers up over my head and disappear from the world.

Things came to a head with Brent on the eve of the 2009 Ironwoman trials at Wanda when everything fell apart. I was absolutely devastated and that affected my performance; my head just wasn't in it. We were too busy burning the last of the fuel in our relationship.

Fleeing back to Sydney would have been the easiest thing to do, but then I would have just been back at square one, with any maturity and emotional growth gone. And there was still so much I loved about Perth. It was the only aspect of my life that wasn't great – I was performing well, training well, and I had good friends. By then, I'd been in Perth for around eighteen months and I didn't want the negativity of my relationship to define my time there, where I really did feel like I was growing.

I tried to maintain my routine and keep training, but after one ski training session in which we were all paddling north from Trigg Island beach, I hit a reef, and my ski broke in half a few kilometres from the shore. I was stranded and feeling a bit desperate before my ski trainer rescued me and towed me in to the beach. I was a good six kilometres from my car, and I walked back barefoot in my cossie, sobbing and shuddering with self-pity all the way. But deep down, I knew how to get through this. I knew what to do. Just breathe, just run. And that's what I did along those beautiful Perth beaches, clearing my head and my heart, finding my feet again.

After talking to my boss at work, Paul, I knew I had to find my own place to live immediately, but where? Fortunately, another of my Perth friends, a businessman named Tony Sage, the owner of the Perth Glory A-League soccer team and a sponsor of mine at the time, offered me an apartment of his, which he maintained for international players coming to Perth. As soon as Brent had gone interstate for his next game, I moved everything of mine to Tony's apartment, and a couple of weeks later, I'd rented my own place in Subiaco, not far from the City of Perth surf club, which Mum came over to help me move in to. It was as if she appeared magically as an emotional backstop, reminding me that she was always there, no matter what, and perhaps was even subtly telling me that I could always come home.

But I'd already fought my instinct to retreat. I was determined to stay in Perth for a bit longer and keep living my life. I'd missed my chance for the Ironwoman series that season, but I still had the state and national championships ahead of me so I just kept working and training.

The state championships in early 2010 ended up being a great success. Our club dominated and I performed really well, winning eight medals including gold in the Ironwoman event. Afterwards, I was awarded the Bernie Kelly Medal for most outstanding athlete in the state.

But the national championships in March that year ended in a moment of sadness and tragedy, and I didn't end up competing. In huge surf, a nineteen-year-old competitor named Saxon Bird drowned after his head was struck by a loose ski in treacherous surf. It was a sobering time, especially for someone like me who had always struggled to push themselves to get out and compete when the surf was violent.

Later, a coronial inquest cast blame saying that, 'To a cohort of notorious risk takers ill equipped to realistically balance their best interests, [the organisers] offered powerful inducements to participate even if the conditions made doing so unduly dangerous.' What happened was a tragedy, but I didn't blame the organisers, nor did what happen diminish my desire to compete. In fact, it was as strong as ever.

*

In April 2010 Perth, a friend of mine and competitive surf lifesaver, Andrew Mosel, was invited to the Splash Festival, a surf-based multisport event in South Africa, in a city that was then called Port Elizabeth, but is now known as Gqeberha, after the Xhosa name for the river that flows through it.

The festival would be an international carnival, with teams of four athletes coming from a number of competing countries, and racing in events in Nelson Mandela Bay which included beach sprints, long- and medium-distance swims, ocean ski paddles, and a final blue-ribbon event in which athletes would sprint along the beach, swim around buoys a short distance from the shore, body surf back in, and finally race on foot to the finish line. The winners of this event were to be crowned the King or Queen of Nelson Mandela Bay.

Andrew suggested that I should be part of the Australian contingent, and when the organisers requested I join I was thrilled. It sounded like fun. On that first trip to South Africa,

I was staggered by the beauty of the place, both the city and the countryside, which I saw while on a short safari. Everywhere I went I was greeted with friendliness, but now I can't help but acknowledge how ironic it is that this beautiful country would eventually become the site of much anxiety and misery in my life, and in the life of my future husband.

Thinking back to that first trip, I remember well the warmth of the South Africans I met – as well as the bitter cold of the southern ocean, being fearful of sharks, and primarily concentrating my efforts on the final blue-ribbon race – the Queen of Nelson Mandela Bay. It sounded like a very cool thing to be crowned, I thought, and my skills matched the race perfectly.

I knew who my primary competition would be. Melissa Gorman in the Australian team was one of the world's best middle-distance swimmers and was a world champion ocean swimmer, having recently won the five-kilometre open-water event at the FINA World Swimming Championships. She was heavily favoured to win the Queen of Nelson Mandela Bay, but I had a Spidey sense that if I could manage the conditions and use the waves in a way that Melissa couldn't, then I might have a chance of beating her in and out of the surf.

That's exactly what happened. I went out fast into the surf, and Melissa started gaining on me and then passed me, then I reeled her back in as we came back in to the beach and beat her in the sprint across the line.

It was a dream race, and as I competed, I felt something new, something exceptional – and something I'd foster and feel more of in a few years' time. It wasn't just confidence, it wasn't just calmness – it was a deep sense of personal self-knowledge and power. It was such a great trip, and the cherry on top was being crowned as the Queen of Nelson Mandela Bay.

I travelled back to Perth beaming.

*

I did move back to Sydney, but I did so on my own terms. I realised I'd done what I needed to do; I'd become who I wanted to become. I felt completely different to the person who'd moved to the other side of Australia two years earlier.

In May 2010, Mum, Dad and Tim flew over to Perth to help me pack up my things, and while Mum and I flew back to Sydney, Tim and Dad had an adventure of their own, driving my car across the Nullarbor and all the way back to the east coast.

I loved Perth, but Maroubra was my home, and still is my home. It's where my heart has always been, and where it will always be.

10

Hitting the Peak

The journey to success is a strange one. It's been a strange one for me, anyway, taking a route that I couldn't have possibly predicted.

When I first qualified for the Ironwoman series as a fourteen-year-old, I had certain expectations of what the road to success would look like. I expected steady progression, like points on a map towards a destination. I expected success without change. Struggle, of course, and hard work – I always knew that that was part of the equation – but I'd never expected the change that would happen, the change that would be required of my thinking and to my mind.

It's strange, the way it worked out. It's strange, it's wonderful, it's exhausting, it's exhilarating, it's bizarre. And then it was over, unexpectedly, but at the right time and for the right reasons, and to give way to a new life.

After what felt like a very slow journey to me, success seemed to just happen, and happen very quickly.

When I moved back to Sydney, my coach Matt Colquhoun had moved a couple of hundred metres south down Bondi

Beach, from the North Bondi Surf Life Saving Club to the Bondi Surf Bathers' Life Saving Club. Rivals for decades, both clubs had a strong and storied history, but recently the Bondi Surf Bathers' hadn't been as competitive as the North Bondi club had. However, I wanted to train with Matt, so I joined him at the Bondi club and started training.

It was a strange, disjointed and pretty unfulfilling competition season. I really enjoyed training with Matt, as I always had, but there simply wasn't the quorum of competitors to push the results. Matt was always there when it was time to train, but often there weren't any other athletes out on the water.

While training wasn't exactly what I wanted it to be, I'd at least found a job that I loved when I came home from Perth. As much as I'd enjoyed working in real estate, I wanted something different. I found a job working at a company called Sydney Harbour Kayaks, on The Spit in Middle Harbour on the way to Manly. There I generally provided guided kayaking sessions for people who lived nearby: mostly people who had a bit of money and who, in most instances, brought their own kayaks. They needed someone to get them out on the water, working their arms and legs, and who could perhaps teach them a little bit of technique along the way.

I loved that job. I had a great boss, great customers, great work and it was in a stunning location. The only aspect I didn't love was the drive north across the harbour, which from Maroubra was a bit punishing, but soon I moved my early morning swimming training to the Warringah Aquatic Centre in Frenchs Forest, further north of The Spit, where I had a great swim team and coaches, and there was never much traffic on the road at 4.30 in the morning.

I'd been spending so much time in Middle Harbour anyway that I thought I should perhaps go the extra couple of kilometres and start training at Manly Beach, which I knew had a large competitive surf lifesaving community. I contacted Trent Herring, who I knew as a coach at Manly Surf Life Saving Club, and he was really excited about the prospect of me joining the club. He drove down to Sydney Harbour Kayaks during my lunchtime to tell me about their training program. I thought it sounded quite professional, but it wasn't until I actually joined one of the sessions that I recognised that this club was going to be a home for me.

In the first training session I joined, there would have been forty people in the water, and before and after training they were just so welcoming and friendly, and quick with a joke and a smile. But during training they were all fire, brimstone and effort. I knew immediately that these were my people and that I wanted to be with them.

The 2010/2011 season was a magical season, on and off the beach. I loved training with the Manly crew and I learned so much from Trent, especially on the ski. He and his family had been ski racing for decades and from him I learned that there was so much more in ski racing, board racing and ocean swimming than just technique and athleticism. I'd been in the sport for more than a decade now, but there were little things about waves and rips and conditions that I was still learning, and Trent really sped up my education.

On the ski I was becoming fast. Really fast. In training, I was becoming a standout, but unlike other situations I'd been in, the girls I was training with at Manly were only ever supportive. Manly athletes competed for Manly, not just for themselves. Naomi Flood, a world-class ski paddler and two-time Olympian, and I were both competing in the Ironwoman series and we were training for that, but just as much we were training for the club events and the Australian Championships in April in 2011, which would be the club's hundredth year since incorporation. Once again it was Kurrawa Beach that hosted the Australian Championships and, once again, the surf was dangerously large.

In every major competition, the last event of the meet is the Taplin Relay, the blue-ribbon team event in which the club's best swimmers, board paddlers and ski paddlers compete in a relay. This is the event that Queenslanders, especially athletes from the BMD Northcliffe Surf Club, usually excel at, and with the championships taking place at a beach just a couple of kilometres south of Northcliffe, the expectation was that they'd take out most of the events.

I was to be racing last in the ocean on the board, after Naomi Flood competing in the ski leg and a girl named Devon Halligan, daughter of league legend Daryl, competing in the swim leg. Both had done an amazing job and I was happy to get into the water second behind a Northcliffe competitor named Elizabeth Pluimers, who wasn't only the reigning Ironwoman champion but the Australian individual board champion. She hadn't been beaten on the board for years.

Trent had identified that there was a rip to the left of the course and I figured that after smashing past a few waves, I'd be able to let the rip take me out and miss much of the surf. I'd have to fight a little to get around the buoys before coming back, but that squeeze seemed worth the juice.

Elizabeth battled to keep her line, fighting against the waves after being hit a few times. I got dragged down the beach but managed to get into the rip relatively easily, turning around the buoys first. Coming back into the beach, there was a break in between the sets of waves. Now all I needed was the right one to bring me back in. Too large a wave and I knew I could be spat out, losing my board and possibly the race. Too small a wave and I might be overtaken by Elizabeth on a stronger, longer wave.

But nothing came. There were no sets, no waves. Now I was fighting to get back to the beach – but so was Elizabeth. I willed the ocean to send me a wave to catch, but would be ready for her if we happened to be on the same wave. I was the faster runner and I was hungry for a win. There was no way I'd allow second place for my team if Elizabeth and I hit the beach together. I would be all legs, all elbows, literally ready to fight for position.

It didn't come to that. A wave came: the perfect wave. I rode it all the way to the beach and, with hundreds of people watching and my teammates on the wet sand already celebrating, I crossed the line first.

It was a moment of victorious ecstasy. We all hugged and fell on the sand together. We, a New South Wales club, had been victorious over Queensland *in* Queensland, and in Manly's hundredth year, to boot. It was a watershed moment, for the club, my teammates and myself. It was the start of a period of personal success as well, and a period of growth.

The next national championships were again on the Gold Coast a year later and again we won the Taplin Relay, but also the ski relay, a race I won after getting past Elizabeth Pluimers who had been in front of me when I went in. I worked so damn hard to help us win that race, and just as hard in the double-ski event with Naomi, which we also won.

The Australian championships came after my first season back in the Ironwoman series since I'd moved to Perth, which was a middling season for me. I had a strange feeling of dissonance at each race, feeling as if I was absolutely the equal of, if not better than, every competitor in each race, and yet also totally an outsider.

Approaching each race I had nerves. In fact, it was more than nerves: it was anxiety. As I got closer and closer to the line there was an increasing cacophony of negativity in my ears. It was the other athletes saying: 'Here we go again with Candice, the attention-seeker.' It was myself saying: 'It's not going to happen.' It was the newspaper journalists asking: 'How is she going to embarrass herself this time?' Every time I lined up in a professional Ironwoman race I felt like a pretender and a pretend Ironwoman, yet as soon as I raced, I'd realise I was perfectly acceptable.

I'd trained hard and worked hard, and I was consistently in the top ten of every race that year. I never led though, not once. I never considered that I'd reach the podium or, heaven forbid, win. I was just there, racing. I was never at the back, never at the front; I was always just in the race.

After the second Australian championships I competed in as part of the Manly team, I started to consider why I wasn't breaking through. While competing for the Manly team I had fire and vigour and endless positivity, but individually in the series, I had nothing of the sort. I had doubt. So much doubt.

I didn't know what to do about it, and then it occurred to me to speak to Trevor Hendy about it. Throughout my career, Trevor had always been very supportive and that had meant a lot to me. He was one of the icons of professional surf lifesaving, and had been a dominant force at the peak of Ironman racing. Since retiring, he had remade himself as a successful life coach and motivator, and I thought he could be the perfect person to identify and hopefully address the negativity that I felt was plaguing my Ironwoman races.

Trevor suggested that if we were to speak in a professional capacity, I should come and sit down with him at his place in Queensland and talk. And talk we did.

Even though I desperately wanted to be done with it, that one night at the pub in April in 2007 was still lingering in my mind. Despite all the progress I'd made personally so far, growing and maturing, and processing and rationalising the events and the actions of others, I still carried a lot of shame about it, and still felt, deep down, that the media were right to pile on me. Deep down, I believed that what was said about me was probably right. I'd never talked to anyone about the shame and the weight I'd been bearing – not family, not boyfriends, nor friends, and whether it was out of love, compassion, loyalty or politeness, no one asked me about how I was feeling about it.

Despite the acres of newspaper columns and hours of radio and television interviews that had been dedicated to it, no one had ever asked me what had happened that night, how I felt afterwards and how it had affected me. I certainly wasn't going to bring it up. I didn't blame anyone, because I think people like my parents and Llara thought they were doing what was best for me, and what I wanted, and I now know those two things were mutually exclusive concepts. It was a wound that had simply festered, until the moment Trevor asked me about it.

It started when I told Trevor that I knew I was there athletically when I was racing but that it felt as if there was a barrier in front of me, stopping progress. I told him I wanted to be confident on that start line. I didn't know how to make myself confident. He asked what, in lieu of being confident, I was feeling when I lined up. I told him I felt sad. Why particularly then? Because that was where emotions ran high. Because that's when I was alone and about to be tested. Because those moments were the path out of heavy thoughts. Because those were the moments in which I thought there was the possibility to once again make my parents proud of me after all the embarrassment I felt I'd put them through.

Tears welled in my eyes. Trevor told me to cry when I tried to stop. He told me to get it out and to cry and cry and cry. I did just that. And I didn't just cry, I bawled. He asked me about Clovelly and I told him. I told him what happened and how I felt, and I cried some more.

I wanted to win so badly, but the reason I wanted to win was because I believed it was a path to redemption, not only for me, but for my family. I wanted people to see my dad at the surf club gym and for them to come up to him and say: 'Candice is doing well in the series.' I wanted Mum to be able to celebrate me as an athlete, rather than supporting me as a subject of public scorn.

These were the intrusive thoughts that came when I lined up in the series. It would all come rushing back as I lined up, linking Sundays at Maroubra Surf Club with Mum and Dad and my childhood dream of success in the series with a moment of shame and embarrassment and public humiliation.

I had no idea how much psychic weight I was still carrying until I unloaded it with Trevor. I was feeling so much, and none of it had been expressed – in fact, most of the time it wasn't even sitting in my conscious mind. It was there, though, just waiting for me to line up in an individual Ironwoman race. In team events and at practice I performed exceptionally, but on race day I was driven by negativity. And ultimately, when I approached a race with so much negativity, I felt as if I didn't deserve to be there. The term 'Ironwoman' was always attached to my name and yet so often I didn't feel I'd earned it.

Trevor helped me purge myself of these intrusive thoughts and helped me learn so much about myself. Astonishingly, his help was what kicked off what would be my most successful season and the peak of my athletic career.

After that first session and some follow-ups on the phone with Trevor I wanted to keep going with the work that he and I had started. He'd got me back on my feet and now I was keen for more of the same kind of rehabilitation and therapy – in my case, psychological rather than physical.

When I'd been training for competitive swimming, I'd done a couple of group sessions with a sports mindset coach called John Novak. I knew Novak as someone who'd worked with Olympic swimmers and was greatly respected by, and always worked with, NRL coach Des Hasler. In the lead-up to the 2011/2012 season, I worked a lot with John on getting my mind where it needed to be for the upcoming Ironwoman series. Through exercises – some visualisation, and some closer to meditation – I prepared my mind in the way that I'd always prepared my body: with absolute commitment.

I applied myself to the tenets of what John calls the boomerang effect, which stipulates that whatever you put out into the world, comes back to you in some way.

Words, thoughts and actions: always positive, no exceptions. That was now my mantra and the golden rule in the lead-up to the season, and I lived and breathed it, twenty-four seven. By the time I was lining up for my first race of that season, I'd done an incredible amount of physical and mental work.

*

I decided that if I was to be more competitive in the ski leg, I was going to need more explosive power. Trent and I decided I would benefit from another five kilograms of lean body weight, and so I did everything I could to achieve just that.

I still ate clean, avoiding sugar and fats and eating mostly a lot of lean protein and vegetables, but had larger meals and more of them, and when I was in the gym I did lower repetitions and more weight. Eventually the muscle came: one, two, three and eventually the five kilograms that we thought I needed.

It made a difference. I think it ended up becoming hugely beneficial, but it's a strange thing, changing your body – literally the biomass that is you – for the benefit of your sport. Ever since I'd started training at fourteen, I'd kept myself to a certain frame because that was what was considered best for my sport, and I'd never once thought about changing it, until now.

Five kilograms doesn't seem much, especially when that weight is mostly muscle, but I noticed the change and I had mixed feelings about it. Sometimes I'd see myself in the mirror or in photographs and be a little taken aback. There was one particular instance when I did a shoot in the off season for Finz Swimwear in their costumes, and I felt like I looked a bit puffy, something I'd never thought of myself before. I found it hard looking at myself in those images – I didn't feel like I was in my own body. It was strange. My body was what I wanted it to be, and what I'd worked hard for it to be, and yet there was this nagging need to be thinner and leaner, as I had been before.

I guess I heard other people's voices – the voices of people looking at those images and saying I was fat or masculine looking. Did those people even exist outside of my head? I don't know, but I heard them nonetheless. I now really appreciated and understood what other female athletes meant when they talked about the feeling of losing control of their own bodies while training because of judgement from people, people who had no place commenting on a woman's body.

Like most women, I wanted to look beautiful, and like most women I didn't really know what that meant in any given moment. I often judged myself against other people's expectations, and people's expectations about feminine beauty often did not involve large amounts of muscle.

However, I was still also proud that I'd managed to achieve that useful extra weight, and when I was on the ski I did feel the difference, especially when I needed an extra push to get on a wave.

*

As well as training twice a day in Manly – swimming in the morning, and then board or ski training in the afternoon – I was running both for myself and for fitness, and also finding time to visualise that first race, over and over again.

For every local race I competed in, I used the processes I was planning on using for the races in the Ironwoman series. If my race was at 9am on a Saturday, at 9am on the Friday I'd be there in my mind, telling myself that today was my day. Today I belong.

I'd visualise my warm-up and then I'd pace through the race from start to finish, in fast forward. Then I'd do it all again, this time in slow motion. I'd slow myself down for the day, even walking more slowly so I'd find myself with a relative spring in my step the next day. I'd assign trigger words to individual races and write them on my hand to remind myself, and all of this was logged in a diary of affirmations, inspiring aphorisms and guidance.

The first race of the 2011/2012 professional Ironwoman season was at Scarborough Beach in Perth, which I practically considered home turf. The format suited me to a tee; the competition had three individual discipline races, concentrating on either ski, board or swim, but starting with a fifty-metre soft-sand run. Points would be awarded for each race and then there would be a full Ironwoman race with triple points awarded. Between each race there would be ten minutes of rest.

I wrote the word 'explode' on my hand. I was going to get in the water first, exploding off the line and then try to hold my position. For the most part, it worked. I had an excellent day. I *believed* I was going to win this final race and the whole event. In fact, I *knew* I was going to win the race. It was a strange feeling and like nothing I'd felt before. It wasn't confidence; it was something much more powerful than that.

And then ... I didn't win.

Going into the last leg of the event, the ski leg, I was in second place and felt pretty good. I was looking forward to, potentially, a sprint finish that I felt I could explode through and win, but after coming through the beach and into the surf, I was shocked to find I couldn't steer my craft left or right.

Under each surf ski is a rudder which is controlled by foot pedals on the top of the ski. It's essential for manoeuvring. But no matter how much pressure I put on my left or right pedals, it wasn't responding, and there was more drag than expected too. I knew instantly what was happening. The rudder was probably stuck in position after being jammed by a rock, twig or some seaweed from the shore. I hoped it would dislodge before I had to turn around the buoys that marked the midpoint of the leg, but it didn't. As all of the other competitors were nimbly paddling around the marker, I had to cut a huge crescent berth, which cost me place after place after place.

I came into the beach, exhausted and defeated, crossing the line at second-last. My emotions vacillated then – was I momentarily unlucky, or was I permanently cursed? I finished the day in fourth overall.

I did think that perhaps getting a podium finish for the Ironwoman just wasn't to be. Perhaps my childhood dream was never going to come true – after all, there are as many dreams as there are people, but there are only so many Oscars in the film world, only so many top spots in the music charts, only so many champions in each sport.

I turned those thoughts over in my mind as though inspecting fruit at the market. I found them soft and rotten. I was going to finish this season at least, and if I was going to keep going, what good did such thoughts do? Who did they help? Perhaps they helped my competitors, but they did nothing for me at all.

Positivity cost me nothing, so positivity I would keep with me throughout the season. Going into the next race, which was to be in Newcastle, north of Sydney, I maintained my routine of visualisation and relentless positivity, planning a successful race in my mind many, many times before I lined up on the sand.

This time I decided it wouldn't be a verb like 'explode' or 'fly' that I'd write on my hand, or even a noun like 'determination' or 'strength'. It would be a proper noun. While the sport I loved was centred around the beaches in Queensland, I didn't spend time training there, nor was I close to the athletes from there. I loved New South Wales: the beaches, the people, the clubs. I had a sense of pride competing for my home state and for this, an event in my home state, I decided to write 'NSW' on my hand.

That day was one of the hottest I'd ever competed on, and when we lined up for our first race it was already well into the thirties, soon to be forty and then ultimately a searing forty-three degrees.

The format of the Newcastle event was to be an eliminator, meaning we'd all race a number of times, and each time four athletes would be eliminated until there were just eight girls left in the final race. This type of race was one that I was least suited to. I was not genetically gifted as an endurance athlete although, having competed twice in the Coolangatta Gold, I knew I had reserves to draw on. I was undoubtedly fit, and trained as hard as anyone, but I knew I faded somewhat in events like this, especially when it was debilitatingly hot.

I performed well through the heats though, and made my way to the finals by competing and then getting straight into an ice vest, often without even a warm-down jog and a slow stretch. I was exhausted and depleted going into the final, but still feeling happy and positive. The mindset change had been profound but it was going to be a long, tough final race.

Until the last leg, I managed to maintain a decent level of energy and I used that energy to stay in the top group of girls. But then fatigue finally set in. I was just throwing my arms into the water, one by one.

I told myself: just keep going, just keep moving. Two girls got out of the water before me and ran across the line – one of them was Naomi, who came second. I dragged myself out of the water with Courtney Hancock, an athlete originally from New South Wales who had moved to the Gold Coast for an incredible Ironwoman career.

She and I were shoulder to shoulder, fighting for the last spot on the podium. We were running up a sand hill to cross the line, and underfoot I could feel a spring, just a little one. I felt a boost and a lightness, and before I knew it, I was across the line and lying down on the sand, being hugged by Naomi.

I had beaten Courtney and come third! For the first time in my career, I was on the podium of a professional Ironwoman race, the same beach where I'd competed in my first professional race as a fourteen-year-old. That third felt like a first to me. With my family there at the race, I felt a rush of pride and happiness and joy and, above all, acceptance. I was an Ironwoman; I felt it now.

I had no idea the best was yet to come.

The next event was in February 2012 in Coolum, on Queensland's Sunshine Coast, and I arrived there with a lightness I'd never experienced when arriving at a competition beach. I had no nerves at all. I was just walking on air; open, ready and calm.

I lined up with only the race in my mind. I'd done my

visualisations: I'd run to my ski, and then race around the buoy before coming in to the beach thirty metres or so to the left of the main course, on a second break. I'd run again and then power through the swim before another run, and catch whomever I could in the board leg, my strongest.

I felt nothing when the race started – I felt nothing and I thought nothing. I just flew. It's a transcendent feeling, and something I've heard other athletes describe as 'flow state' – when everything just happens. The athlete is conscious and unconscious, working and not working. It's a synthesis of past, present and future, with past being all the work, all the effort, all the preparation; the present being the athlete in the race; and the future being the outcome that is, to a certain extent, ordained, whether it's success or failure.

I came into the beach on my ski in fifth place, and was bolstered by that. The ski was still my weakest discipline and I knew I would move past at least some other competitors as the race progressed to the other legs. And that's what happened.

I powered through the run to the swim, and then powered through the swim. I wasn't the fastest in the swim leg, and knew I wasn't, with Rebecca Creedy ahead of me – one of the fastest pool and ocean swimmers in the world – but I was very fast. As we came into the beach, Rebecca was in front with another girl, and I was behind with another girl. The pair of us caught a wave that the two in front didn't, and Rebecca and I were neck and neck as we bodysurfed into the beach.

As I sprinted to my board, I was in first place. I'd never led a professional Ironwoman event before! I could imagine even a year earlier, it would have been an overwhelming and depleting experience. Not now. I'd flowed to the front and there I stayed.

This was like running: the running I'd done for me – the running I'd done to find myself, be myself. I raced that race as I'd run before, with me and for me, for the sky, for the ocean, for the rhythm of life. My heart beating, my body moving. Air coming into my body and out, feeding my soul.

I turned the buoys in the lead and led as I paddled to the beach. Only the conditions could stop me now. I only needed a wave to win.

No wave came. Nothing. Nothing. And then finally, there it was. I flowed into the beach and across the line. That's when I came out of flow, and my emotions and feelings rushed in.

These emotions were singular though, clear and uncrowded and welcome. It was joy I felt – and relief. Mum and Patty were there on the beach as I won, and I shared that singular feeling with them. It was joy and relief, and accomplishment. It was progress. It was finality, too.

I'd won! That was something to talk about, something to think about. It was an event to attach to my name at last, an event that I owned. There was great coverage of the race. It led *Sports Tonight* and was on the back page of a few papers, and there were no snide comments in the text, no backhanders or smutty allusions.

It was just me: winning. This was something people could talk to Dad about, on the street or in the gym. 'Saw your girl in the paper, Mickey. She's done good.' Or Mum, being able to take calls from her friends about her daughter the athlete, and not about anything else.

That was all I'd ever wanted. It was the moment I'd dreamed of. Emotions are welling up in me as I write this now. I had everything I'd ever wanted. I'd reached the top of the mountain.

And, just like that, I was done. I came second last in the next Ironwoman event, not because I had crowding, intrusive thoughts as I'd had my entire career, but because I didn't have the drive that had pushed me through the last three races.

I kept training because that's who I was, and I raced more, but I'd taken what I needed from the sport, and hopefully I'd also given back. I was still young — still years away from thirty — and I was certainly still improving, but I was essentially done.

That season did see the achievement of three world championship wins at the Rescue 2012 Life Saving Championships at Adelaide's Christies Beach, which were all shared with team members from Manly, including Naomi Flood and Devon Halligan. The Rescue championships are administered by the International Life Saving Federation and in 2012 they were held in Australia, attracting competitors from all over the world and we took out first place in the Taplin Relay and the Tube Rescue. In 2013, I also went on to win the NSW Ironwoman and a number of other medals in the state and national championships, and while it was thrilling to win these titles, somehow I just didn't need competition anymore: it was as simple as that. For years I'd felt I had unfinished business — ever since I was that fourteen-year-old qualifying for the series — but after Coolum, I felt like I'd done what I wanted to do, and learned what I wanted to learn.

The final nail in the coffin of my Ironwoman career was that the trials for the 2013/2014 season trials were scheduled on the same day that my brother Tim was getting married. Although I'd had two podium finishes, including a race win the season before, and now some world titles, I'd also had some miserable results.

I was training hard and thought, if the spirit returned, I could win some races. I planned to qualify for the season and then make a decision about my future, but with Tim's wedding obviously taking preference over the qualifiers, I requested one of the wildcard spots, which was afforded athletes who couldn't, for one reason or another, qualify through normal channels but who the organisers thought should be competing nonetheless.

I was confident I'd be given one of the wildcard spots, and when I got a phone call telling me I hadn't been, I was disappointed, but far from gutted. There would have been a time when this news would have created some kind of disconnect, negativity and even anger perhaps, driven by some kind of perceived failure. In any other year, when I was another Candice, I would have also questioned my identity, my purpose, my ability.

Not now, not this time. I was ready to move on – and something momentous was about to happen. David Warner entered my life.

I don't know what would have happened if Dave and I had met while I still had all that unfinished business on my mind. Perhaps it wouldn't have been what it was when we did finally connect: glorious and fast and with both of us recognising that we'd never be the same again, and we'd never be apart.

11

An Inauspicious Meeting

The first time I met David was at the Beach Road Hotel at Bondi, having just run the 2010 City2Surf, truly one of Sydney's great events. I thought he was possibly the rudest man I'd ever met.

I lined up with 60,000 other people, many raising money for charity (mine was the Cancer Council), in Sydney's CBD to run, jog or walk the fourteen kilometres to Bondi Beach. Along the way there would be bands and well-wishers and all the glory of the views of Sydney's sparkling eastern suburbs. Lining up alongside me was my brother Patty, who wasn't as fit as me, but was a decent runner and who I'd promised to stay with until the end of the race.

We stopped a couple of times along the way, so he could go to the bathroom or to catch his breath, but we had a great time, working our way down the course, shoulder to shoulder. But then, with the finish line in sight, Patty put the hammer down and sprinted away from me. It took a couple of seconds for me to realise what he was doing and I sprinted after him, but I didn't catch him before the finish line.

Patty's chest was heaving but his face was beaming.

'Wondered when you were going to turn up,' he said. Classic Patty. To this day, he likes to remind me about the time he beat me in the City2Surf. After the race he and I went home, but a few of my girlfriends were meeting at the Beach Road Hotel, the unofficial site of the warm-down for the City2Surf, so I decided to join them.

It's a great vibe in that pub after the race, once you get over the smell of stale sweat and percolating sneaker. Everyone there has done something big with their day, and often for the weeks and months preceding too, if you count their training. People go there to enjoy themselves, to blow off a little steam and bathe in the endorphins that the run has just stirred.

I met my friends upstairs and we were joined by cricketer Brett Lee, someone I knew through friends of friends. While I knew the names of some of the more well-known cricketers, I knew nothing of the game. I was talking to Brett about my neighbourhood, and he said I should meet a mate of his who grew up nearby in Matraville, a stone's throw from where I grew up.

Like Maroubra, Matraville is a fiercely, singular working-class suburb, whose residents are very proud and who overperform in many sports.

Dave was leaning on the bar when Brett introduced me to him. I said 'Hello' or 'Nice to meet you', and I can't remember whether he just grunted or whether he even acknowledged me at all.

I certainly didn't see him as the future love of my life, the father of my three beautiful girls and the rock around which my entire life is now built.

*

Sometime in 2013, three years after that City2Surf, I watched a piece of branded content sponsored by ASICS, the sportswear company, about cricketer David Warner playing in the Indian Premier League T20. T20 is a shorter, faster form of cricket, which was introduced in 2003 to find new, younger audiences. With innings limited to only 20 overs a side, hence the name, it's focused on big hits and high scores. It was very quickly picked up by cricketing nations around the world and is especially popular in India. The piece I watched had colour and fun and excitement, and at the centre of it all was one athlete, someone who I didn't recognise at all as the recalcitrant bloke I had met at the Beach Road Hotel.

He had a funny smile, and a lovely way about him. He was reticent in the television show, but also charismatic in a way, and while it was hidden under steeliness, I could see an intelligence and strong emotional centre. I could see a little bit of the Dave that I know and love today.

Watching that show, I got a sense that Dave and I were similar spirits. Growing up so close to one another and being roughly the same age, it made sense that we'd be similar people. While I hadn't felt that way the first time we'd met at the Beach Road Hotel, I felt it now. In that little piece of branded content I saw, for the first time, the man I see every day now.

I jumped on Twitter, planning to write about how entertained I was by the show, and wanted to tag ASICS and Dave. When I went to do so, I found that he and I were already following each other, so I sent him a direct note instead, simply saying how much I had enjoyed watching the piece. He wrote back and I replied, and a few months later we were chatting online regularly. It all felt so easy with Dave. I'd never been so open with someone – there was no miscommunication, no artifice, no façade, just honest, real chat mixed naturally with warmth and whatever we found hilarious.

When we started messaging each other, David was at the beginning of a long tour of Great Britain. First he was to be part of Australia's ICC Champions Trophy team competing in the one-day cricket tournament, and then he was expecting to be part of the Australian Test team contesting the Ashes, directly after the conclusion of the one-day cricket competition.

There was a road bump, however. After losing to the English side in the tournament opener, Dave had gone to the Walkabout pub in Birmingham for perhaps one too many drinks, where English batsman Joe Root and an English fast bowler had also invited themselves. Dave had been particularly galled by Root, who was mucking around with a green and gold wig he'd found and was wearing it like a beard, which Dave thought was intended to mock a Muslim cricketer.

Joe Root found a fist on the end of that wig – Dave's fist. And Dave found himself on the end of some swift Cricket Australia punishment, being relegated from the top tier of Australian cricket to the second-tier Australia A side who were playing in Zimbabwe.

Dave accepted he'd done the wrong thing punching a bloke, drunk at 2am, so it was what it was. He wanted to talk to me about it. He opened up to me, and I to him. It just seemed the most natural thing to do, so that's what we did. It was really the start of our relationship.

Day and night we'd message, developing a bit of a routine. I was still training every morning, getting up before 5am, and when I did wake there'd be messages from Dave greeting me as I met the morning. We'd chat as I prepared for training and he for dinner with the team, and I'd leave messages for him to start the day with. It was just lovely. There wasn't anything yet that was romantic or sexual, just two people who were instantly connected. We had mutual friends from the neighbourhood and a mutual interest in the NRL, so we talked about that. We had both recently ended relationships and we talked about those break-ups. We were both at the same stage of life, so we talked about that. We talked about his sport and mine.

Soon we started chatting over video on Skype and an even stronger connection developed. I saw something in his eyes – a sort of deeply embedded kindness, and an honesty. I saw the place where he grew up in them too, which was just down the road from where I had grown up. It was a special feeling, being close to someone like that, even though I'd only met him in person once – a meeting that hadn't been successful.

Soon some little gifts arrived at the house: chocolates and little teddy bears and champagne, and all the while as we were messaging, I was watching the cricket on the telly with Mum and Dad. I hadn't told anyone what was going on, but my parents knew something was up. I was very happy, and attached to my phone at certain parts of the day. They were just happy that I was happy, after such a difficult few years.

Dave and I talked about marriage and having kids before we'd even met properly. These weren't serious conversations obviously, just general chats about what we both wanted in our lives. But it meant something to us both that we were so comfortable talking about it. It all meant something. Something big and serious was happening in my life, and in his. It was unsaid, but it was clear.

It didn't take long for me to realise I was falling in love.

One day Dave told me that he was sick of waiting for us to be together. He was back in the Australian Test side after a brief stint in the Australia A side in Zimbabwe and would be in England for at least a couple more months. He didn't want to wait to see me and to be with me. He and the team would soon be in Manchester, contesting the third Ashes Test, and he reckoned I should fly over for that.

To me that seemed a bit – I don't know – forward, or extreme. Of course, I wanted to join him, but it seemed like a slightly mad thing to do. Dave wouldn't relent, however. Now I know that's just Dave. When he has an idea, he makes it happen. His life is one that he's fashioned through sheer tenacity and will, coming as he had from a housing commission background. Now he wanted us to be together, and the only way to do that was for me to go to England.

I talked to Mum about it. She could already tell something was going on and when I told her that something was David Warner, the guy from the cricket who had grown up in our area, and who I was thinking of going to England to see, she was wary but supportive. She could tell that I, now in my late-twenties was falling head over heels, but she was wary for the same reasons I was.

Dave was in the middle of a news story. He was still painted as the bad boy after the Joe Root incident, and with a large media contingent likely to be swarming around the team, the last thing Mum or I wanted was for another media mess to emerge around me.

I spoke to Dave about that and he said we'd manage it. He'd talk to Michael Clarke, the team's captain, to make sure it would all work out. While we were discussing it, one of Dave's close friends, Usman Khawaja, who had already popped up on a few of our video chats, jumped in to say hello again, and he was so welcoming and lovely. I hoped the rest of the team were just as friendly.

Ultimately, the reason I decided to go was because I really wanted to, and damn the consequences! I'd go and be with Dave, and keep my head down. If it turned out that I was in a delusional bubble of infatuation, I'd be in Manchester, and from there I could escape to London, or anywhere else I liked. What did I have to lose? The price of an airline ticket. What did I have to gain? The realisation of the feelings that had started to take hold, and perhaps even the idea of a whole shared future.

Just before leaving, I was driving back from training in Manly with Patty, who was curious about my mysterious trip.

'So, what's in England?'

I told him about Dave and our online romance.

'You're an idiot!' he yelled at me. He kept saying that I was setting myself up for disaster, saying many times over that

Dave was going to romance me in England and then 'upgrade' me as soon as he came home.

I yelled back that he didn't know me, nor did he know Dave, and that he certainly didn't understand what was going on between us. I told Patty I was going and that he could shut his mouth about it, and that was that. Little did Patty realise that it wouldn't be that long till he'd be one of Dave's groomsmen at our wedding.

With my flight arriving in Manchester at the start of day five of the Test, Dave had arranged for me to be met by a friend of his, Griffo, at the team hotel – Patty also knew Griffo, which was comforting, and he was welcoming and warm. A key was waiting for me at the front desk, and I went up to Dave's room, a bit tired, but also very excited that we were finally going to see each other face to face. Part of the exhilaration was the joy of travel, but most of it was this mad run towards love.

There was a part of me that knew I could leave if I had to. Although I'd come across the world to see this man, I knew enough about myself and the world that if I got a sense that I should leave, I would. I never felt I needed to, though. Not once.

When I went into Dave's room, I found that housekeeping had already come, but there was a very faint lingering masculine scent. This was his space, his personal space, and I was here at last. I already felt so connected to him, it felt like home. I couldn't wait to meet up with him.

After a quick shower and change to refresh myself after the long flight, Griffo took me to the Old Trafford Cricket Ground, where there was a rain delay. We found the seats that Dave had arranged for us and then Griffo asked if I wanted to walk around and see Dave on the other side of the ground, where the Australian team was. At that moment a shyness came over me, especially knowing that the rest of the team would be there, but Griffo convinced me – he said Dave had been waiting for me to arrive, and that he was really excited. We ended up waving from around thirty or forty metres as my heart pounded.

Griffo and I chatted in our seats under a grey sky with intermittent rain until, late in the afternoon, the Test was abandoned, so we went back to the hotel. As was the routine at the end of each Test, Dave would be spending time with the team to debrief and decompress and he sent me some messages telling me that he didn't know when he'd be free, but hopefully it would be soon.

I waited with anticipation and then Dave messaged me with good and bad news. The good news was that he was on his way back to the hotel, but the bad news was that he was only going to be able to stay for ten minutes before having to go out for a team dinner. I was getting a sense even then that the Australian cricket team kept its players on quite a tight leash.

It was an awkward but wonderful ten minutes. Dave walked through the door, we kissed for the first time, which was barely more than a peck, then we said our hellos. He rushed to get changed and then he was gone again. It was really quick, but so lovely. I was so happy. I could tell I'd made the right decision.

My heart wouldn't stop pounding.

Griffo and I went out to dinner together and he told me that he'd actually advised Dave against inviting me over to

England. In fact, a few of Dave's mates had done the same, but Dave was adamant. Happy and adamant.

Throughout dinner, Dave and I were messaging each other, inching our way closer to being together, and then Griffo, Dave and I decided we would meet up at a bar nearby. By now it was the early hours of a Tuesday morning, and there weren't too many places open, but we found a sparsely populated bar where we found some members of the English team Dave had just been competing against. There was some fun music and cold drinks, and Dave and I danced our tails off. Again, all I felt was ease and that everything felt so, so right. In his arms, I felt like a key in a lock, one that was to open a whole new life.

Normally the team travel together from place to place in England on a team bus, but Dave was given permission to rent a car and drive to the location of the next Test, which was in Durham. In the break between Tests we spent some really wonderful time together in nearby Newcastle upon Tyne.

We ate at restaurants and wandered the streets of that small city, which was new and old, industrial, and grand and charming. We saw the raucous local nightlife, which was like stepping into an episode of *Geordie Shore*. We went to exclusive bars where Dave indulged in one of his passions: French champagne. (I tried to share the passion with him but my tastebuds were dulled by the shock of someone spending so much money on a bottle of wine.)

I thought perhaps Dave was going to be stressed in the day between Tests, but he wasn't at all. He was light-hearted and fun and able to compartmentalise. It's a great skill, and one

Dave has in spades. It was a wonderful time for me, and he said it was for him too, telling me that normally when on tour he mostly stayed in his room, watching the telly.

The day before the fourth Test at the Riverside Ground in Durham was to start, Dave asked me if I wanted to sit with the other wives and girlfriends in the stand. I absolutely did not. I'd only met one of them so far, Shane Watson's wife, Lee Furlong, and while I really liked her, I didn't see myself in the company of the other wives and girlfriends, and felt embarrassed meeting them.

They wore designer outfits and had seemingly perfect hair. I was a surfie chick from Maroubra, with the clothes and hair to match. I didn't know what I'd wear, I didn't know what I'd say, and I was also worried that the cameras might drift over to me and the media might make something of the fact that I was sitting with the other partners.

I had no idea what the media may make of Dave and I being together, but I knew they wouldn't be complimentary.

Dave and I considered ourselves pretty lucky in that no stories had been run about the fact that we were together in England. Of course, we had no problem that people knew we were together, but both of us were twice shy having been once bitten by tabloid media, and although we couldn't see a negative angle to us being together, I reckoned the tabloids would be able to find one.

I told Dave that I'd rather sit in the public stand, not only because I wanted to avoid potential embarrassment, but because that's how I like to enjoy sport, with other fans. Dave thought that was fine and found me a seat with one of Usman Khawaja's brothers, Arsalan.

Usman and Dave had grown up together and played junior cricket together, and Usman and his brother knew a lot about Dave and the way he played. As I watched him out on the pitch in his baggy green, Arsalan told me that Dave was a special cricketer, and I agreed. But Arsalan said it was even more than that – that Dave was a phenomenon.

The truth was, although I'd been watching this Test series with Mum and Dad at home, I didn't know much about cricket. As was much explained and lauded by Mark, one of Dave's friends and manager of a London nightclub who I was sitting with in the stands as well, Dave opened the batting and was out early in the first innings, but managed a hard-fought 71 on a fourth-day wicket. At the time, it wasn't something I understood at all – not like I do now.

A larger-than-life character, Mark enjoyed his cricket with Pimm's and he asked me to join him in some of his rounds. I found Pimm's very refreshing under the rare British sun, but when I stood up again to leave, my head was swimming a little and, in front of the entire stand, I stumbled head-first into a wall.

Some of the punters erupted in cheers and I was so very glad that they had no idea who I was. I hoped that whole incident would just disappear like almost every other interaction in the stands does, and I was very relieved to find that it did.

I waited for Dave in the hotel and we went downstairs where the team was having some end-of-Test drinks. I felt incredible trepidation, but it dissipated completely when Dave walked me straight up to then-captain Michael Clarke and introduced me.

'We're really happy you're here,' Michael said. 'You make Bull so happy.' Bull was the nickname the team used for Dave back then, describing his obstinance, his refusal to ever take a backward step and his willingness to charge the opposition if provoked.

After dinner and a quick punt and drink at the casino, Dave and I went back to the hotel and I really started to feel the fact that we only had a few more days together. We lay in bed together and it just came out: words rushing from my mouth that couldn't be put back in.

'I love you.'

As soon as I said it, I threw the covers over my head. In many ways both of us are very shy, and I stayed under the covers waiting for Dave to say something. He didn't say anything. Under the doona I sweated, not quite regretting what I'd said, but feeling very much off kilter and totally unsure what Dave's reaction would be.

When I finally pulled the covers from my head – I mean, I had to at some point – there was Dave, laughing at me. He'd wanted to make me sweat. He knew how uncomfortable it was for me to say it. That's the joker in him!

'I love you too,' he said, with a gorgeous grin.

He's also an absolute sweetheart.

The last Test was in London, and my flight home was at the start of it. Before I flew home, Dave and I had a few whirlwind days of dreamlike handholding in the magical city of modern skyscrapers and old pubs. We spent our last night together at Mark's bar and, again, he proved a wicked influence on me, the lightweight. Mark was plying us with absinthe and, at 6.30pm, with the sun still high in the northern sky, I had to be taken home. I have no memory of what happened but Dave told me the cab had to pull over so I could slick the London streets with my dinner.

I woke up at 4.30 the next morning and I was furious with myself. It had been our last night together and I'd ruined it by embarrassing myself. I lay in bed not able to sleep and not able to calm myself. Eventually I jumped out of bed and started putting on my running gear. The only way I knew I could sort myself out was with a very early morning run.

Dave woke, bleary-eyed, and asked me what I was doing. I told him, and it took a while for that information to process.

'Why?' he asked.

I just had to. My head was spinning and I was so angry with myself.

I was in a bit of a state, but Dave thought it was hilarious. I was mortified. I told him that this drunken woman – the woman of the night before – wasn't me. I was an athlete. It was all wrong, I told him. This was all wrong.

He just hugged me, stroked my hair, and told me to stay in bed with him, which I did. In his arms my head stopped spinning, my thoughts quieted, and soon I went back to sleep.

He'd seen me at my worst, and it only amused Dave, and it endeared me to him. I loved him for that, and I always will.

12

Meant to Be

'You're going to move in with me, right?' Dave had said, out of the blue, while we were in England. I assumed I would. After only a few days of being together, I assumed that we'd be getting married, having kids and spending the rest of our lives together – and Dave, as he told me later, had also assumed the same. Neither of us had ever felt like this before, but it was clear to both of us that we simply belonged together.

When I came home I gave Mum and Dad the news that I was moving out, but the good news was that Dave's place was only ten minutes away, in Little Bay, the next beach suburb south of Maroubra. They were happy for me. I'd been speaking to Mum and Dad pretty much every day while I was in England, and they could tell how ecstatic we were and how much in love we were.

I moved some stuff over to Dave's house while he was away, but mostly stayed at home until he returned to Sydney, which he did via Dubai because, as I found out later, he'd been at the gold market in Dubai looking at wedding rings.

When Dave returned to Sydney, I took him to Mum and Dad's place for Monday dinner, which had become an institution at our place. Since the Falzon kids had started to stray from the nest, with Tim and Patty moving out of home, Mum had insisted that everyone, when in Sydney, had to meet up around the family table for dinner, once a week, on Mondays.

It was quite lovely seeing how nervous Dave was, meeting Mum and Dad for the first time. They hit it off immediately and I think the reason my parents got on so well with him was because they saw how happy and contented we made each other. After that, Dave was family too, and obliged to be in attendance for Monday dinners, and it was at those dinners that Patty and Dave became the closest of mates.

Then Dave arranged for the two of us to go up to Hayman Island, part of the Whitsundays in Queensland, and there the magic returned and perhaps even intensified. I didn't think I could be even more in love, but in Hayman, I fell in love with Dave even more. We snorkelled and ate and drank and talked about the life that lay ahead of us. It had only been a few months since we'd met in person, but neither of us had any doubt that we'd spend the rest of our lives together. Dave mused about the prospect of us having a child, and although it wasn't something I'd even considered before, I said I would be happy to have that adventure with him. But when?

He said perhaps such an idea was best left to chance; after all, we might not even be able to fall pregnant, with neither of us ever having tried before. That very day we agreed that I'd go off the pill and let the cards fall where they would.

Above: Growing up at Maroubra, I lived my life on the beach.

Below left: Mickey and Kerry Falzon — Mum and Dad — and (*left to right*) Patty, me and Tim.

Below right: As a young Nipper at age six.

AUSTRALIAN SURFING WALK OF FAME

CANDICE
WARNER (NÉE FALZON)

2017

NSW Ironwoman Champion 1999 & 2013
Professional Series Coolum 2012
Outstanding contribution to Surf Life Saving

Randwick City
Council
a sense of community

Opposite top left: New South Wales Ironwoman champion at age fourteen, and winner of the 1999 Maurice Singleton Trophy. © *Stephen Chu*

Opposite top right: Professional Ironwoman series champion at Coolum in 2012.

Opposite below: My childhood dream came true when I was inducted into the Australian Surfing Walk of Fame at Maroubra Beach in 2017.

Top right: In action during the women's qualifying final for the 2003 Ironwoman series. © *Getty Images/Chris McGrath*

Below left: Screaming in on the board at Kurrawa at the 2012 National Championships. © *Harvie Allison*

Below right: Celebrating with Naomi Flood (*centre*) and Devon Halligan (*right*) after winning the Taplin relay for Manly at the 2012 Australian championships at Kurrawa. © *Harvie Allison*

Opposite: Completely in sync with Naomi Flood (*left*) to win the double ski event for Manly in the final at the 2013 national championships on the Gold Coast.
Top © Getty Images/Matt Roberts; Bottom © Harvie Allison

Above: On my way to winning the 2012 Ironwoman series at Coolum.

Right: Feeling it with Naomi Flood after competing in scorching conditions at the 2012 Ironwoman series in Newcastle. I wrote 'NSW' on my hand to remind me I was competing for my home state.

Opposite top: Early days with Dave, celebrating Australia's Ashes win in 2013.

Opposite bottom left: With Llara at her wedding in Greece in 2014, both expecting our first babies.

Opposite bottom right: With baby Ivy Mae and Dave, thrilled for the Australian team's win in the World Cup in 2015.

Below: Marrying the love of my life in April 2015. *Photograph by GM Photographics*

Above: With my two gorgeous baby girls, Ivy Mae and Indi Rae. *Photograph by GM Photographics*

Below left: Our family is complete with the birth of Isla Rose at St Mary's Hospital in London, 2019.

Below right: At home in the heartland, Maroubra Beach, January 2022.

It's only in retrospect that I recognise now that things were moving very quickly, but then, things were moving exactly how they should have been for both Dave and me.

When Dave and I moved in together, I was preparing to again compete with Manly Surf Life Saving Club in local competitions, so I kept up the same routine I'd maintained when I was in the Ironwoman series – out the door well before dawn, and the last training of the day taking place when the sun was setting.

I think Dave started to feel a little bit embarrassed that he was the professional athlete and I was the one doing all the training, so his regimen started to change. Dave began getting up when I did and used those extra hours to work out with a mate of his who was a personal trainer: boxing, lifting weights and running.

He started to become very fit indeed, and with it developed even more of a killer mindset. Dave had weighed almost ninety kilograms playing for his country in England, and when I met him he was already in good shape, but became something else altogether that spring. As I watched his body and stamina change I started to think about how dangerous he'd be next time he stepped out for Australia.

When Dave returned from England, there was a little bit of a break before starting another Ashes Test series in Australia over that summer of 2013/2014, with the two series landing back to back because of rescheduling required due to the 2012 London Olympics the year before, which had postponed that year's Ashes. In the meantime, Dave was home and playing for the New South Wales Blues. At one game, Dave and I were photographed together in the stands with an accompanying story published in the papers suggesting that Dave's focus may be wavering due to my influence. This made me very wary and nervous that there might be a bit of a press reaction to our relationship to come, as media interest, even to this day, makes fires burn that were lit at the Clovelly Hotel.

The first Test was at the Gabba in Brisbane in November and now that Dave and I were living together, I was going to be in the box with the other wives and girlfriends. I was still pretty nervous, though, so I called Michael Clarke's then-wife Kyly and asked her what I should wear. Kyly became my cricket-whisperer then, telling me what to wear, what to do and who all the people were that I was about to meet.

It was a full-on adrenaline ride, that Test. I was starting to understand cricket a little better, and I really understood Dave's desire to help win back the Ashes after having a broken series in England that had been marred with the Joe Root controversy and also on and off form.

It was incredibly gratifying, watching Dave smash out a century in his second innings and becoming the highest run scorer of the match. It was amazing watching him so happy, fit and strong; as he batted, I felt that we were connected. With Australia's Mitchell Johnson throwing down thunderbolts and the English team scattered and, at times, seemingly scared, Australia won easily.

I became completely invested, as though I was out there playing too.

The series went to Adelaide, and Australia also controlled that match. Australia declared in both innings, with Dave smashing most of the 132 second innings' runs. Mitchell Johnson dominated again with the ball, and England fell more than 200 runs shy of victory.

In Perth, Australia then won the series by 150 runs, with Dave scoring another hundred and also a half century. It was a hell of a thing, being part of it all, as the trophy had resided in England since the 2006/2007 series. They wouldn't be presented with the urn until the end of the series in Sydney, but that night we partied with the rest of the team and their partners at a luxury villa that Shane Warne had rented at Crown Casino. The atmosphere was incredible, with the very dear now-departed Warnie making sure every glass was full of champagne, and every hand was holding an expensive cigar. Dave and I were having one hell of a summer.

I was obviously having a great time, but I did feel just a little bit like it was someone else's good time. As Dave was competing, I sometimes felt a few pangs that I wasn't still competing. I was so very happy for him and genuinely believed that I was helping contribute to his success, but we were living solely on his schedule and I knew that would continue.

I also knew our relationship was going to gain more interest in the media. Throughout that summer of cricket, Dave and I were pretty much stalked by paparazzi everywhere we went and it was unsettling being back in the public eye again. However, this time I think I was better suited to reconcile with it, and also perhaps to manage it, too, because this time, I knew we had absolutely nothing to hide, and that we were doing absolutely nothing wrong.

A few days before the Boxing Day Test in Melbourne, Michael Clarke warned us about all of the exposure. The team and their partners were all meeting for drinks at the Quay West Hotel on the Yarra, and Clarke sat Dave and me down to say that we should try to minimise the coverage of our relationship in the media as, from his experience, it wasn't always a positive thing.

But of course, we hadn't done any media at all; it was simply a case of photographers snapping us when we were out in public, and people talking about us, journalists or otherwise. We couldn't control that, which is what we told Michael. From our own experiences, we knew the media would do exactly what they wanted, including reporting on the new relationship of two well-known people, as well as Dave's blockbuster form.

On Christmas Day, which I'd always spent with Mum and Dad and my brothers, I did feel some angst knowing that I was moving from one life to another. I certainly didn't feel bad, as I was with the person I most wanted to be with at all times, but you always lament the former stages of life when you're moving on to the next.

Boxing Day was a strange day though. I was catching a taxi from the hotel to the grounds in Melbourne with one of the team's partners and, apropos of nothing, I was told that a lot of the girls used to make really nasty comments about me.

It had only been a few months since I'd been with Dave, and I thought it was a very weird thing to hear. I suppose all it meant was that some of the partners had a certain perception of me and my relationship with Dave, and that that perception had changed once they'd got to know me. I didn't press further for any more details as everyone had been so lovely, and shrugged it off. All that mattered was that Dave and I respected and loved each other, and outside of that, whatever happened, happened. Besides, I was too physically uncomfortable then to think too much about it – lately I'd started to feel bloated, with an urgent need to pee seemingly every half hour or so.

It was crazy. As soon as the Test was underway, I couldn't go anywhere that wasn't a short jog to a bathroom. I didn't know what was going on. I mentioned it to Dave and he said he'd talk to the team doctor. When he did, the doctor had said there could be a few things going on, but the first thing I should do was to get a pregnancy test.

I did just that and it strongly indicated that I was pregnant. Later that day I spoke to Llara, telling her what was going on. She said she'd had the same symptoms lately too, and joked that perhaps she was pregnant too, to her partner.

As soon as the Test was over and we were back in Sydney, my doctor confirmed that I was a few weeks pregnant. I was so happy with the news. This was all just written in the stars, with no qualms or reservations felt by either Dave or I, only love. Afterwards I got a call from Llara, who told me I wasn't the only one who was having a baby. My joys were having joys piled on them. It was early days, but should all the cards fall where I hoped, I was going to be a mum and Dave a father.

Before I'd met Dave, parenthood wasn't something I'd ever really envisioned for myself, and not something I'd ever planned or discussed with a partner. It was something other people did, something other people wanted. My goals and dreams had always been individual and athletic, and yet life had grabbed me by its forceful hand and dragged me in a different direction – towards a different type of life – and I found I was happy to be there. Dave couldn't have been happier either.

I'd never been in a relationship anything like the one Dave and I had developed. I'm not sure I really even understood ever what a partnership was prior to meeting Dave. I was quickly discovering that the people in a true partnership are still who they are with their own strengths and identity, but that partnerships have wants and needs and their own unique characters, too. A good one, I was learning, was more than the sum of two parts, and ours was becoming very good indeed. And with all fingers and toes crossed, we'd soon be a trio with new characteristics of its own.

This pregnancy was very much an expression of love and with it came gratitude and blessings, but also responsibilities. I felt that. That's what I had imagined motherhood would be because that was what I had seen growing up. Mum had worked hard when we were kids, especially when she was working for Nutrimetics, but never once had I seen her shirk her responsibilities as a mother, as to her, those were sacrosanct.

When we returned to Sydney, Dave and I did the rounds to my parents and his. At the house in Maroubra where I grew up and in the Matraville apartment where Dave grew up, we were greeted with unmitigated excitement, and also with tears. It had all happened so very quickly, but our parents had seen that this was a significant once-in-a-lifetime whirlwind. That the storm was taking us to territory that neither of our parents would have thought we'd end up in so quickly was only cause for celebration.

It was early days in the pregnancy but we were both in our twenties and strong; there was no reason to think that things wouldn't proceed as expected. Dave and I started making plans through the fifth Test, which Australia won after also winning the Melbourne Test: where we would live, which hospital we'd go to, whether Dave would be at home or whether he'd skip a tour. It was such a great summer – a 5–0 sweep of the English, we were in love and we were pregnant.

My feelings of that period are perfectly encapsulated in a photograph taken just after the end of the fifth Test where Dave, still in his uniform, is carrying me in his arms and inside of me is our baby. In the image we are grinning like maniacs. I can still feel the joy of that moment. It felt like we were floating.

Two weeks after the end of that Test, Dave was to fly to South Africa for a Test series, and while we were still some time away from telling people other than family that we were going to have a baby, Dave felt that he had to tell the coach Darren Lehmann and his captain, Michael Clarke. Of course they were ecstatic for both of us, but shortly after there was an incident reminding us that in our public and private lives, there were always media sharks circling and someone ready to throw chum to them.

Still only eight weeks pregnant, a gossip columnist from the *Australian Financial Review* called me and told me I was pregnant. He didn't ask me, he told me. I was shocked, as we'd only told our families, and so few other people. It was still too early to tell anyone else our news, let alone the media, so I denied I was pregnant, and he essentially threatened me with disclosure, telling me that if I didn't give him quotes and details about the pregnancy, he'd run the story without them, which he did, with my denial as a quote.

I was in tears when I got off the phone and called Dave straight away, who was by then in South Africa. It was a stark reminder to us both that even our most private of private news was fodder for the media. We were both well used to the machine's need for clicks, but this was about a tiny defenceless new life in the making, and it made us even more determined to keep the drawbridge up on our personal lives, and to start building a moat of safety around us as we started out on life's biggest adventure together.

13

A Nest of Love

All sins are forgotten when you're winning, and the South African tour was a winning one, with Dave again being an integral part of that success. I joined Dave in Johannesburg, in the north of the country, where the first Test of the three-Test series was contested at Centurion Park. Dave scored a century, Mitchell Johnson was brutal with the ball and Australia won easily.

The Test circus then moved on to Gqeberha, a place that I was very comfortable in, having competed there before, and where I was named Queen of Nelson Mandela Bay.

Dave scored half-centuries in both innings of the Test. Afterwards, on the way out of Gqeberha, he ducked away and said he had to make a phone call. I found out later the call was to my dad, scheduled because Dad is absolutely hopeless with his mobile phone and never uses it. (Dave knew that if you want to catch him on it, you have to arrange a date and time beforehand, which Dad will write down on a paper calendar to make sure he's sitting next to the phone when you call.)

At the Gqeberha airport on our way to the next Test, Dave asked my dad if he could propose. When Dave told me the story later, it sounded to me as if Dad had genuinely tried to warn Dave to be wary and think about what he was doing.

'Are you sure?' Dad had asked, and Dave said he was sure.

'Well, good luck then,' Dad then said, giving Dave his blessing and making his own little fatalistic joke.

The next Test was in Cape Town, a beautiful city on a peninsula jutting into the Atlantic ocean under the shade of the stunning Table Mountain.

While in the city, and unbeknownst to me, Dave was making preparations. He'd contacted Janine and Brigitte from Infacet Jewellers, two friends who source ethically mined diamonds, and bought a cushion cut diamond, which he had mounted to a ring that he knew I'd like.

Previously he'd shown me some engagement rings, trying to gauge my preference, and I told him I couldn't choose. They were all too flashy, too expensive. I just didn't know where to start. Dave asked me to at least tell him which ones I didn't like.

On the day he was to pick up the ring, I had arranged to have my twelve-week scan at an imaging facility in Cape Town. He couldn't come along because he had a mandatory recovery session, and I was disappointed for him, but that's the nature of being in the Australian national cricket team – some things are movable and some immovable.

One of the partners who I'd become closest to on the tour, Anna Weatherlake, then Peter Siddle's partner, said she'd come with me. There I saw and heard the little heartbeat of the tiny person who was going to be our child. And then the sonographer told me the gender of the child: it was a girl. Dave and I were to have a daughter. When I told him, Dave was ecstatic with the news.

Dave had made plans for us in the clutch of days that we had to ourselves before the Test. Warnie had recommended we stay at a place called Element House on Camps Bay, south of the city. It was such a dreamlike place, with a gorgeous open living and sleeping area, all opening out to a large pool deck with sunset views over Bakoven Beach.

Dave told me he'd planned a full day for us the next day – we were going to hike Lion's Head, one of the smaller but more picturesque peaks nearby, then he'd arranged a picnic on the beach for us. It all sounded wonderful to me.

But when we woke, we were told it was too windy to trek Lion's Head. Dave seemed a bit off, but I thought it was just because his plans had been thwarted. Instead we went to the beach for our picnic, which was lovely if not a little strange, because most of what had been set out – champagne, soft cheeses, prawns and cold meats – couldn't be consumed by someone who was pregnant. I think Dave had been so stressed about what was coming, he hadn't noticed that I wouldn't be able to eat much of it.

I essentially sat on a beautiful beach watching Dave eat his way through the picnic and drink the champagne, which I now know he was using as Dutch courage. When we came back to Element House, a path of beautiful rose petals had been laid artfully on the floor, leading to the spa, which was steaming hot and waiting for us with another bottle of champagne in an iced silver cooler and two glasses.

Dave's plan had been to return from the beach engaged and into a little nest of love, but he hadn't had the courage yet to propose. Instead he did a pretty admirable job of suggesting that the hotel must have confused us for honeymooners.

I honestly still didn't know what was going on. Dave jumped in the spa and poured more champagne, but I could only sit on the edge as again, neither hot baths nor champagne are on the pregnancy menu. I sat there chatting to Dave as I took what I now think are hilarious photographs of him.

Another romantic gesture Dave had planned was a private dinner on the deck, which was constantly interrupted by him getting up to go to the bathroom after drinking so much champagne. After the fifth or six time I was starting to get annoyed.

Little did I know that each time he was going to the bathroom, he was practising a speech he'd constructed about me and him and our life together, and our future together – a speech that would end in a proposal.

After one of the last trips to the bathroom, he came back onto the deck trembling, and before I could ask him what was wrong, he'd produced the ring he'd worked so hard to design for me and asked: 'Ah, Candice, will you marry me?'

Now it was my turn to tremble. Even though we were pregnant, and we'd spoken about rings, and we'd both decided very early on that we wanted to share our lives forever, Dave's proposal was still a surprise when it came, even though it made sense now, all of those attempts at romantic gestures.

I couldn't even look at the ring, and barely even at Dave. 'Are you sure?' I asked, feeling honour-bound to give him an out.

Was he sure? I didn't want it to all blow away, like sand in a storm, all of this happiness. I felt elated, shaky, strange, unstable, in love. I needed him to be sure.

He said he was definitely sure.

It was all I needed to hear. I told him of course, absolutely, undoubtedly, yes, yes, yes.

Dave and I were on a high after that, and in the deciding Test Dave smashed the bowling to all parts of the ground, in both innings. At nearly a run a ball, he scored back-to-back tons, sealed the match and the series, and was awarded player of the match and then also the player of the series.

I could tell our engagement and my pregnancy were a bit of a shock to the Australian cricket establishment, including some of the partners of Dave's teammates. In the space of only a few months, after having been dropped from the Test side, Dave had gone on a scoring tear as he and I became an item, and were now planning for our future and our baby's. We certainly felt there was a degree of shock about how quickly things were happening between us, and I'm sure there was some speculation about how long it would last.

The most important thing was that we knew it was going to last, though.

Cape Town is so much like a beautiful mini-Sydney. It had become a special place for both of us as we'd experienced so much joy there. We thought that it would be a place we'd come back to over and over again, recreating one of the happiest times of our lives.

Now I don't ever want to go back, especially not with the Australian cricket team. How quickly things can change.

14

Perfection

After the Test in South Africa, Dave and most of the players were going to Bangladesh for the T20 World Cup, which was the premier competition in cricket's shortest and very popular but less respected form of the game. I went back to Sydney and after a couple of weeks I was really missing Dave. He was missing me, too.

He called one day and said he was really suffering. He'd previously been used to the solitary life of a touring professional sportsman, but he didn't want to do that anymore. In fact, he couldn't bear to do that anymore. We were really becoming a team, he and I, and he was more comfortable when I was with him, and he also played better when I was around. I was dedicated then only to my pregnancy and my new relationship, so I decided to join him in Dhaka, which set a precedent for us, being together as much as we could. We were going to tour together, and so some allowances were going to have to be made, both on our part and on the part of team management so that could happen.

In the years to come with our growing family, our kids would have to travel more in their first years of life than most people would in decades, and that was something we made work or accommodated, but on the other hand, if team management and coaches wanted Dave's best performances, there needed to be some new thinking around how partners and children travelled with the team. Cricket Australia had some strict rules around when partners and families could stay with players, including a partner ban period in which wives and girlfriends were strictly forbidden from seeing the players. For most players it worked well; it gave them dedicated time to bond with their team-mates with no distractions and the result was a team which worked seamlessly on the pitch. But as a one-size-fits-all rule, I didn't agree with it – not all players played across all the cricket formats like Dave did, meaning he was working most of the year, and not all players had young families. The ban didn't recognise that some players were better off mentally and simply played better when their families were around, like Dave.

That year we'd started looking for what we both called a forever home. Dave and I had been living with mates in a house in Little Bay, but it didn't feel like *our* place, nor was it necessarily the kind of place where we wanted to raise a family. I liked the house, but I'd always found it a bit creepy, especially after Dave told me that there was a ghost that had probably been spending a bit of time there. Even if he'd told me half in jest, I was spooked.

Both of us ideally wanted to stay in Maroubra, too, as our two greatest wants were that we were close to the beach and close to both of our families. There was one particular street that we loved too, but there was nothing on the market, so we started looking nearby, from Vaucluse to Bronte to Rose Bay, and while we certainly saw some beautiful places, we both knew it would feel too strange to be away from family and close friends, even if they were only half an hour away.

Dave was going to be away a lot playing cricket. I really didn't know how much he was going to be away, even when he told me that it could be up to a couple of hundred days of the year. I knew the number, and I knew it rationally, but I didn't know what that was going to mean emotionally. Dave told me it was going to be a lot to take. He knew what the reality of that was. He'd seen it, with teammates who had families, and had lived it also when he was single. When he was at home, he wanted to really be home, and another thing he wanted was for my brother Patty to live with us.

Almost as soon as Dave and I got together, he and Patty became the best of mates. Dave absolutely loves and trusts Patty, and only very occasionally reminds Patty that he'd once insisted Dave would 'upgrade' me after my mad dash to Manchester.

Both Dave and I wanted him living with us for so many reasons, an important one being that there'd always be someone else living with me and our baby whom we totally and wholly trusted when Dave was away. With Patty living with us, my life would be easier; our baby would have at least one uncle with her all the time, and Dave's mind could be a little calmer and clearer when he was touring, knowing we had immediate support.

Ever since Patty came and saved me when I was at The Gap feeling no hope, and even before, he's always been a special person in my life, and I knew he'd be a strong figure for the child to come.

Eventually we found a beautiful house that was just a few hundred metres away from the street we'd dreamed of living in, which ran from the south end of Coogee Beach to a pedestrian-only pathway that led to the South Coogee stairs. It was such a beautiful place, with all the room we needed, a pool next to a lovely patch of grass, and views over the ocean to Wedding Cake Island. It was perfect – the realisation of a dream.

I must have run those South Coogee stairs a thousand times, when training or on one of my head-clearing runs, and I had always noticed the houses at the top of those stairs. In my mind's eye they were places of such happiness and achievement. They were like castles to me, as if from a fairy tale, and now I was living my own fairy tale.

When I was around four months pregnant, Mum and I travelled to Greece for Llara's wedding, who was making a family too. It was magical to be there for her big day, and to know that we were no longer just friends, but connected families, with both of us due to give birth at roughly the same time. When Dave came back from Bangladesh, we were already partially moved into our wonderful new home, which seemed perfect, except for the intermittent intrusion of British tourists ringing the doorbell, as apparently the cast of the sixth season of *Geordie Shore* had lived there.

*

I was so happy, but there was a small, gnawing concern that just wouldn't leave me alone.

I'd never been maternal. I'd never loved a child before, or even a dog or a cat. We'd had a dog when I was much younger, but it was Dad's dog. I was twenty-nine and I was also pregnant and engaged at a time when I'd never even thought about getting married. I hadn't moved in circles where people were settling down and having kids, and there was no precedent set for me – no trail laid down.

What if, when the baby came, I wasn't going to feel the love that I wanted to give the baby, the love that the baby truly deserved? I was in love with Dave and so excited about our new life, but I'd been a very independent person for a lot of it. Was I ready to be a mother?

When I was in Greece for Llara's wedding, and then back in Australia, I quieted the doubting voice in my mind with the only thing I knew would help. Everywhere I went I took running gear and shoes with me, and when the gnawing questions in my mind started to become a bit much – or to stop it from becoming a bit too much in the first place – I'd run. Preferably somewhere in sight of the ocean and the beach and waves and cliffs and seabirds.

Obviously I wasn't running as hard or as far as I had been, but even so the time I spent pounding the path was so restorative for me.

It was all working well until, after one of the scans, the doctors said they were concerned that the baby was, perhaps, a little undersized. It wasn't anything to be concerned about yet, but using an abundance of caution, they advised that I stop exercising except for gentle exercise, like walking.

Soon I started to swell, and then bloat and then balloon. The pregnancy was an easy one, with few complications except the lower-end baby weight issue and almost no morning sickness, except that I put on weight, and then more and then more. Eventually I put on around twenty-five kilograms and I really started to hate the body I was living in.

When I saw myself in the mirror or in photographs or when I tried to move around, I felt a physical revulsion. It wasn't vanity, as I didn't really care how other people saw me, and I was getting truly incredible support from Dave, who loved me inside and out, but I just didn't feel like I was living in my own body. I'd always been in control of my body, strict with what I put into it and regulated with what I did with it and how I trained, but now I was no longer in control. As the pregnancy matured and I grew larger, I struggled, and those struggles were exacerbated by the fact that I couldn't hit the pavement and paths.

Many women love being pregnant, but for me, it was a test of patience and will. I didn't enjoy it, and I was counting down the months, weeks, days until it would be over. The only thing holding me back from wanting it to be completely done was the fear that I was going to be handed my baby and that perhaps I wouldn't have the feelings for her that I wanted to have. That fear only grew stronger as the pregnancy progressed.

I had long conversations with Mum about it, and she said that it really wasn't something that I had to worry about. Time and again she reassured me that it would all just click into place as soon as the baby arrived. This was from Mum though, who I had only ever known as a mother, and a fantastic one at that, and I wasn't that person yet. I just couldn't see it in my mind.

My worries continued to grow and when my doctor told me they wanted to induce me ten days prior to my due date, I was elated, but also filled with trepidation.

Our plan was for me to be admitted at the Royal Hospital for Women at Randwick the night before I was to be induced. After Dave and I had a lovely dinner with Patty, Dave drove us all to the hospital, where I broke down. All of a sudden, I felt alone and isolated with my thoughts. I was with my fiancé and with one of my beloved brothers, and I was starting a family, something that I was really excited to do, but was suffering intrusive thoughts that I couldn't completely articulate.

Dave held me, and told me things were going to be okay. When someone you love says that enough, you really do start to believe it, and soon I started to feel better and even started to feel a bit excited about what lay ahead.

I didn't get much sleep that night and at 7.30am I was taken into the birthing suite and given the hormones that would induce birth. They worked a little too well. I was told that most likely I was going to dilate one centimetre an hour and that I'd probably need to start pushing sometime late in the afternoon. After an hour I was in a lot of pain, with contractions wreaking havoc with my body. We had a plan for the birth, but that was all thrown out the window very quickly.

I told the midwives that I was getting to the threshold of what I could handle and they told me that we had a long day ahead of us. I think they thought that I simply wasn't handling the adversity very well, but when they checked, they found that I'd already dilated to seven centimetres, which was very quick.

Once a racer, always a racer.

They asked me if I was ready to push, but the last couple of hours had been so hard wearing I needed an epidural. They told me to rest and to sleep if I could before starting to push at around midday.

We did rest, both Dave and me. We were both shattered. Somewhere deep in my mind, I had the idea that childbirth was going to be a kind of spiritual journey, with us as the soon-to-be parents holding hands and staring soulfully into each other's eyes as new life came into the world, but it turned out to be a far more primal experience than that for both of us.

Finally it was midday and I was fully dilated, and it was time to push. And when I did, Ivy Mae Warner came into the world.

I was shocked when she came out. I had never, ever seen a person, baby or otherwise, have such a conical-looking head. She really did look like an alien, which did nothing for my worries about loving my baby, but the nurses assured me that the shape of her head was still settling.

Then the moment I'd been so wary of and nervous about arrived, inevitable like a sunrise. Ivy was placed on my chest and instantly all of my fears and worries and trepidation disappeared.

She was beautiful – tiny, healthy and perfect – and, as her skin touched mine for the first time, there was a rush of emotion. All I felt was wonder and a fierce, powerful love that I knew would last forever. I felt a calmness, too, and I think that came from being in the moment and nowhere else. It would be okay. Whatever was to come, it would be okay.

I'd been so concerned that I wasn't going to feel that love, partially because I couldn't envision what those feelings may be. But now I knew exactly what they were.

There was nothing I wouldn't do for this child, who had once been an idea or a concept, and was now a pink and purple bundle, breathing and crying and blinking on top of me. When Ivy was placed on Dave for the first time, I knew he felt exactly the same.

This perfect baby was instantly loved. Mum and Dad were outside, soon to come in and meet their first grandchild, and Dave and I would soon be planning our wedding. All my doubts were gone. Life was perfection.

15

Making it Official

There were only a few days between us leaving the hospital after Ivy's birth and when Dave was scheduled to fly to the United Arab Emirates for the 2014 Test series against Pakistan. In those very early days, I was floundering a bit as a new mum, but Dave was an absolute rock. In hospital, people and flowers kept coming, and while that was all very nice, I was trying to breastfeed and get the baby to latch and found it all very difficult and overwhelming.

It's a real shock to the system, that first child, and I wasn't really confident in anything that I was doing. I'll never forget that first car ride home. Ivy was so tiny and fragile, she just seemed to disappear into the baby capsule strapped into the back seat of the car. But Dave was calm and solid and reasonable and exactly what I needed. Dave has two nephews, Kaden and Logan, whom he adores and had spent a lot of time with, which meant that he was a lot more comfortable with babies than I was and also understood how stressful those first few months would be.

He knew I wouldn't be alone when he left, with my family and his around, but he also knew that having some professional help, especially through the difficult nights, would make things easier for me. We arranged for a nurse from a service called Mothercraft for Babies to spend some nights at the house, and she proved to be an absolute godsend.

It didn't take long for Ivy and me to get into a routine, and spending so much time together – just the two of us – in those first few weeks was lovely. I didn't have to worry about cooking or what I was wearing, I just got to learn how to be a mum and also reconcile myself with the reality of having a partner in the Australian cricket team who was going to be away from parenting duties out of necessity. Dave being away was just a fact of life. It wasn't a choice, it wasn't a lament, it just *was*, and we all had to move our lives around that fact.

Gee, I missed him though, and I couldn't wait to see him.

We arranged that Ivy, Mum and I would join Dave in Dubai once Ivy had her six-week vaccinations. I was incredibly nervous about the flight and breaking the baby's routine, but we all felt it was very important for us to be together. It turned out I needn't have worried, as Ivy was a champion little traveller, staying on routine and filling her daddy's heart up as soon as she arrived in the Middle East.

In the UAE, we went to the games only a few times as it was very hot, but being together in the evenings in the hotel benefited all three of us, I think. Dave had scored a hundred in the first innings of the Test before our arrival, his third on the trot, and was establishing the start of a routine that would see him scoring a ton soon after I gave birth.

*

There's a little window in Australia when the weather's still sunny and warm, the summer of cricket in Australia is over and international cricket is yet to begin. That window generally occurs around Easter, and it's in this window of time when almost all elite cricketers get married.

It was around November 2014 when Dave and I started planning our wedding, just a couple of months after Ivy's birth. We knew it had to be on the Easter weekend in 2015, between the end of the T20 World Cup and the start of the Indian Premier League (IPL) competition, where Dave was going to be playing for Hyderabad. Dave was keen to do something splashy, having always seen himself getting married in a night of some spectacle.

Before I met Dave, I'd never seen myself getting married, and always baulked at any affair where I was going to be the centre of attention. Even now, if we have a birthday dinner or celebration for Dave, I have the time of my life, but if we do the same for me, I wriggle and fret. Still, I wanted to do whatever Dave wanted to do and I wanted to celebrate our love with as many people as possible, because I really believed it was something worth celebrating. One point that tripped me up though was the cost of everything.

We were concerned that media interest in the wedding might become a bit too much, so we decided we'd have it somewhere relatively close to but not in Sydney. Every venue we contacted, with all of the extras that Dave wanted, was going to cost a fortune. As the daughter of a council worker, though, I knew I just wouldn't enjoy myself at a wedding that would cost many times my dad's annual salary. It just seemed wrong.

We decided to offset the cost by doing a deal with the magazine *Woman's Day*, releasing photographs and information that we were happy sharing with the public. This also served as a way of managing the media somewhat, and keeping the feeling that this was a wedding owned by us.

Eventually we handed the planning over to a professional, who told us that a historic country house, Terrara House, near Berry on the New South Wales South Coast, could host the entire proceedings, with extra accommodation for guests just twenty minutes away. The place looked beautiful, set in the lush green surrounds of the Shoalhaven region, between the coast and the hills, and another benefit of that location was that there were aviation restrictions over the house, which would make it difficult for any media organisation to intrude aerially without prior approval.

Some women obsess over every detail of their wedding, but I had more immediate things to deal with, like looking after our baby and setting ourselves up at what was now a family home in Coogee.

Everything was organised pretty easily, from the beautiful Pallas Couture dress that was made for me, to the crèche at the wedding that was to be managed by Lorraine, the nurse from Mothercraft, who Ivy already knew and loved.

Even though we were only inviting family and close friends, David has a huge family and the guest list swelled and swelled, and we ended up booking out pretty much all of the accommodation in Berry. On the night before our wedding, Dave was staying at a house in Berry, and I was staying at a motel with my mum and my close girlfriends. That night, Mum held a little get-together with many of the people who'd come for the wedding, while Dave and his parents, Howard and Lorraine, his brother Steven, Patty, Tim, Dad and a few of Dave's other mates had some drinks.

The only person left out that night was me. I was with Ivy, who had gone down to sleep at around 7pm, and I felt a bit peevish that everyone else was out having fun without me. I was also a little perturbed that rain was predicted the next day, even though we had a pretty comprehensive wet-weather plan.

Sitting there, on my own, heavy thoughts about isolation and self-worth started to gather. I loved Dave, and my new life, but I wondered whether I deserved it. I knew these thoughts to be perfectly normal on the wedding evening, but I feared I'd still be feeling them on the big day. I decided to combat those thoughts in the way I'd learned to do over the last decade. I messaged a bunch of people, including Trent and Naomi from my Manly club, asking them whether they'd go for a run with me in the morning before the ceremony. We managed to get a little group of six runners together and did a lovely ten kilometres or so around beautiful Berry, through woods and past locals in refreshing, misting rain. As soon as we finished, I knew I was now in the right mindset to have the best day of my life.

My bridal party was Llara as maid of honour, Naomi Flood and another old friend and surf lifesaving team-mate, Kelly

Jury, and we had arranged to have our hair and make-up done professionally. Fortunately the wedding venue had its own salon and beauty room, and the feminine ritual of it was quite lovely – one of the aspects of the wedding I really enjoyed. All we had to do then was walk to the gardens speckled with bright flowers of red, white and yellow, where the ceremony would take place, and there I would wait.

Who were we waiting for? David Bond, 00-Groom.

Dave had told me he really wanted to arrive at his wedding in a helicopter, looking sharp in a tuxedo. This is one of the ways in which we were – and still are – very different: I couldn't bear the idea of such an entrance, but I loved that this is what he wanted. I loved that he'd had dreams of a flashy wedding ever since he was a boy – very specific dreams, including a helicopter – and that those dreams were being realised. I also loved that I was the realisation of that dream, too.

He looked so damn handsome, arriving in his tux. My heart was bursting with love, but I also felt the nerves and reticence I always felt when I was the centre of attention. As I walked down the aisle towards Dave, I could tell that he was welling up with emotion, brought on as Kaden, Dave's nine-year-old nephew, wearing his little tuxedo, carried Ivy, in her own tiny little gown and wearing a garland of flowers in her hair, down the aisle ahead of me.

It was a moment of generational change, and the realisation of hard work, sacrifice and will. Dave and his brother, Steven, hadn't been born into a world of plenty. They were kids from a housing commission flat in Matraville, born of loving and caring parents, but not people with means. The Warner boys' future had been something they had to carve out for themselves.

Traditionally, there's a lot of privilege in cricket with many players coming from generationally wealthy families and from expensive private schools, with all of the coaching and equipment any boy could want. That was not Dave's experience. He had to fight with single-minded determination to get to the life he's enjoying.

He had earned a helicopter to fly into his wedding. He had earned those tears he shed. He has earned everything he now has. God, I was so happy to be able to say yes to Dave's proposal and 'I do' at our wedding.

There was one thing I put my foot down about, though. Dave wanted to dance, and not only that, he wanted for the first dance of our wedding reception to be a choreographed ballroom dance, and then the entire Johnny and Baby dance from the end of *Dirty Dancing*, including the lift that was made famous in that movie and *Crazy, Stupid, Love*, which had come out a few years before our wedding.

I just couldn't. It's not in my DNA. We had '(I've Had) The Time of My Life' as the song for our first dance, but we invited everyone to join in pretty quickly, and then the real party broke out. Everyone danced, around and with us: family, friends, cricket people, people from surf lifesaving, everyone. It was a dream come true.

At about 11.30pm Dave and I left the reception under a guard of honour, and at that point I was exhausted in the way I reckon only new mums can be. Everyone was heading to the pub and Dave wanted for us to join them. Lorraine, the mothercraft nurse, was with Ivy, but I just couldn't do it. I went to bed, but that wasn't the end of the celebrations just yet.

The next day we drove back to Sydney, and hosted some friends of mine from Perth at the Coogee Pavilion, a pub that was walking distance from our place. We were all having so much fun that we ended up rolling to a club near Oxford Street in the city for more dancing.

Married life was definitely all right by me.

*

A few days after our wedding, Dave packed his bags and was off to India for the Indian Premier League season where he was to be captain of the Hyderabad team, the SunRisers.

I'd first travelled to India with Dave when I was pregnant with Ivy, and my eyes were like saucers pretty much the whole time. It's a place with so much life and energy and excitement, even seen from the windows of cars, buses and hotel rooms, and it was the place where I first understood cricket as truly a phenomenon.

For the Indian fans, cricket is something else. The cliché is that in India cricket is a religion, but that's not what I've seen. Religion bears the weight of life, the seriousness and solemnity, but in India I see the people enjoy cricket as a thing of pure excitement and positivity.

There are plenty of places where I've seen people cry into their beers while watching sport, almost hoping that their team loses so they have something to be upset about, but this has no bearing on what cricket is all about in India. They are so exuberant, so positive, so *excited* about the game, and I saw this the first time I ever went to India: at the grounds, and also whenever they saw Dave.

Every stadium I have watched Dave compete in is absolutely packed, and the events seem to be more of a celebration than a competition. Obviously people cheer for their team to win, but it doesn't seem to be the only thing they are cheering for. They are cheering for life and for cricket and for each other, and when superstar Indian players are batting or bowling, the entire stadium of fans cheer, regardless of what colour the player is wearing.

When I saw Dave play there for the first time, it really did make me realise how relatively tiny, by way of participation and also sponsorship and fan interest, my own sport was by comparison.

Dave had previously tended to stay in his room generally when touring, and especially when in India as, when there, he had to be assigned bodyguards any time he went out. I thought the juice of seeing a bit of the country was worth the organisational squeeze, even in India. From early on in our relationship, I tried to press Dave to go out a bit more, and now it's something we do to this day. We've had a few hairy moments, with one instance in a café in a shopping mall getting so packed our bodyguards had to call in the police to create a cordon in the crowd so we could escape, but in every instance when things have got slightly out of control, it's because of the crowd's absolute enthusiasm, and nothing dark or nefarious.

Not long after our wedding, I took Ivy to meet Dave in Bangalore and then Visakhapatnam, and he began an incredible run of IPL form.

That season Dave was awarded the Orange Cap, an IPL award recognising the batsman who scored the most number of runs in the season. That season Dave averaged almost 50 runs, which in T20 cricket, where there are only so many balls to be faced, is a hell of an achievement.

It was a purple patch of form that would continue pretty much as we were having babies, with Dave being awarded the Orange Cap twice more over the next four years.

We'll always keep travelling back to India, even when Dave is no longer playing cricket there. The colour and excitement and energy is so addictive, and it's a place that our kids now absolutely love. In fact, in many ways I'm looking forward to returning after Dave has retired, so we can set our own itinerary and visit the places that have been outside of Dave's itinerary when playing with the Australian team or his IPL team.

We yearn to see the other Indias. I hope one day to take the family and tour India by the sea, and especially Goa, a place where Dave has been and loved, but the girls and I haven't been able to travel to. We hope to travel around India's north, and Dharamshala, in the shadow of the Himalayas where there's an India that's cold and lush and, I'm told, very beautiful. I also hope, one day, to see the Taj Mahal. I know it's a very touristy hope, especially for someone who has been to India so many times, but I dream about visiting that temple, which was built as a dedication to love, with the whole family.

We'll always have a connection with India, which we'll always remember as a place that welcomed us and our family with open arms, after the very worst of times that we would experience in the not-too-distant future in another country.

16

A New Challenge

I t was only a few months after Ivy's birth that Dave and
I started planning to have another baby. We'd always
wanted more kids – well, 'always' being relative as we'd
only been together for a little more than a year by then. In
fact, as soon as I'd had Ivy, I started to think about another
child. Then perhaps another. And perhaps even one more. All
of the worry I'd had about having a baby had dissipated in the
sheer love and joy of our new family unit and it's safe to say I
got a little baby crazy. Dave and I fell so naturally into being
parents that we couldn't wait to have more, we wanted them
to be as close in age as possible because that seemed to be the
most fun way of doing it.

We wanted them to be a unit, playing and loving and
supporting and pushing one another along as they experience
similar phases of life together, and so we planned our next
pregnancy. Six months after Ivy was born we started trying
for another baby, and fell pregnant very soon afterwards.

Both Dave and I were ecstatic. We were already a family,
but two kids creates a household, a little community. I was far

more confident in this pregnancy. I can't say I enjoyed it much more as I, once again, became heavy and bloated, but I could always see the light at the end of the tunnel this time, because the light at the end of the last tunnel was crawling around me, being an unmitigated joy.

I discovered we were having another girl, and both Dave and I absolutely adored the idea of having two little sisters in the house. She was small again, this developing child, but healthy, and her development was monitored closely, without showing any significant issues.

We planned an inducement just shy of full term, not really for any pressing medical reason this time but because Dave was scheduled to fly to New Zealand for a series in January 2016 and we wanted to make sure he could be there for the birth of his second daughter.

I went into hospital for our second baby feeling quite confident, especially in comparison to my last birthing experience, but the night before I was to be induced, I had quite a freak-out. This time it wasn't because of any stress over the birth, or because I felt like I wasn't going to connect with my baby.

It was more that I knew I *was* going to connect with my baby and felt that when I did, when that love rushed in for her, it would have to come from somewhere, and I was scared that the new love was going to have to come from the place where so much of my love was already residing. In other words, I was worried that when my new baby arrived, I was going to love my first daughter less. I called Mum in tears and again, she reassured me that I didn't have to worry. She said that wasn't the way love works, especially not maternal love. It multiplies, but never divides. She loved Tim, and then when Patty came along, she loved him too without losing an iota of the love she had for Tim, and it was the same again when I came along.

I still had trouble shedding the feeling that I was betraying Ivy though, throughout the night before the birth and the next morning. I was induced early in the morning and again the drugs hit me like a Mack truck. It took even less time the second time round for me to become fully dilated.

But when our second little girl was placed on my chest, I had yet another moment of realisation and revelation. Mum was right, as she always was. I loved this baby absolutely and with all of my heart, and yet I didn't love Ivy any less, nor Dave nor anyone else. My capacity for love had increased, just like that, and it has never wavered.

Indi Rae had arrived into the world.

*

In 2017 Dave was at the forefront of high-profile renegotiations between Cricket Australia and all of the players who were paid by Cricket Australia, and being so visible, he copped some heat.

Two decades earlier, it was agreed that players' earnings were to be tied to the total revenue generated by their play, be it gate earnings, TV deals and/or sponsorship. This was a model embraced by some US sports leagues, with the NBA and NFL players associations negotiating a nearly 50–50 revenue split with their team owners. It was agreed that a quarter of the total revenue should go to the players, and this had been the basis of the contracts that Australian cricketers had negotiated since the nineties.

In 2017, however, the agreed framework between the players and Cricket Australia was to lapse, and Cricket Australia wanted to move away from the revenue-sharing model, and offer players whatever they could negotiate individually.

Cricket Australia had two seemingly contradictory positions, one being that a large rise in revenue meant that players were being overpaid, and the second was that some of the money meted out to players as part of the revenue-sharing model was needed for grassroots cricket development.

Negotiations were so fraught in 2017 that a tour of South Africa was scrapped, and the Ashes series that was meant to happen in the summer over 2017/2018 was in jeopardy.

Dave's position in the negotiations was that the men in the national side should continue to be remunerated based on a profit-share model, but that players competing in the domestic league and the elite female players should also benefit from revenue sharing. The current agreement only offered a little more than $7 million to all of the paid female cricket professionals in Australia.

I wasn't surprised to see Dave push himself front and centre as negotiations were ongoing, providing comments to the press, not only as the vice-captain of the men's Test side, a position he had held since 2015, but as a man of unyielding principle. Dave is one of the kindest and most generous people I've ever met, but if he thinks he, or anyone he cares about, is being treated unfairly, it brings out the fighter in him.

I was proud of him. He would have benefited, financially and reputationally, just to keep his head down and give no public statements as he was one of the most valuable players on and off the pitch to Cricket Australia and, in private negotiations, could have pressed for one of the bigger personal contracts. That just wasn't Dave, though. He knew he was right, and eventually he and the other players won.

An agreement was hammered out in August, with the revenue-sharing model still intact and a massive increase going to the professional female cricketers, with that $7 million pot becoming more than $55 million. Dave negotiated hard on behalf of himself, the other players in the men's team and those playing domestic or women's cricket, and he didn't make a lot of friends at Cricket Australia doing so.

They didn't see him as part of their brand, but they loved to win so they were in a bit of a bind. He had a great relationship with coach Darren Lehmann and the other players, and he was getting runs, so they just had to accept him, and me, whose manner and attitude wasn't always in the 'quiet wife in the box' mould.

I did wonder what the situation would have looked like if Dave's game hadn't been sailing in such favourable winds.

*

In 2017, I took my running to a whole new level. I'd always run when I could, always making the time, and I'd never done it to push myself, just to treat myself. I ran ten kilometres, twelve, fourteen. Whatever was required to get the effects

I wanted, which was a clear head, a healthy body and a modicum of equanimity. Then, with two little girls to look after, I was looking for a challenge that would be my own. I decided that it was time to run a marathon.

I loved looking after my kids and supporting my husband, and I dedicated myself to the task in the way I'd watched my mum run our house, with love but also regimented totality. Growing up, Mum and Dad were both very hands-on parents and, like them, I wanted to be there for every minute of my children's lives. I didn't want to miss any of it – I still don't. Sometimes it's to my own detriment, but I know it will all be gone in a flash, and I love seeing them learn and achieve; I love seeing their smiles when I'm there to pick them up at the school gate. But now I needed something else in my life, too. I had been a professional athlete on top of my game only a few years before, and there was something inside of me that needed feeding. I wanted to carve out a little mental, physical and emotional space to do something for myself. I wanted a challenge, and a marathon would be that.

I called Paul Tonich, who I'd worked with in Perth, and who had completed literally dozens of marathons, asking where I should start. He told me I should train and then start with the Gold Coast Marathon, which was held in July during temperate weather. With quite a flat course, he said it'd be an excellent 'starter' marathon, and not only that – Paul said he would fly over and run it with me.

There were sixteen weeks between that conversation and the race and, with a solid fitness base already established, Paul thought that was enough time to train to complete the marathon. An app from ASICS that was recommended to me had a sixteen-week marathon training plan and, if I stayed completely dedicated to the schedule and stayed injury-free, I should be okay. The only problem was that many of those sixteen weeks would be spent overseas, supporting Dave at work, competing in India and then in the UK.

I didn't really know how that would work until I sat down with Dave and found him fully supportive of the idea. I wasn't going to be able to pound the streets in some of the Indian cities we'd be staying in, but everywhere we went there'd be a gym with a treadmill where I could get the kilometres in. It would be monotonous, but also possible and perhaps even restorative, as I envisioned getting dual use from that time, dedicating that time to training, but also to listening to music or a podcast or a meditation app, things I simply wouldn't have been able to do otherwise.

That's what I ended up doing, just getting kilometre after kilometre under my belt under fluorescent lights, with business people coming and going around me as they tried to shake off jetlag. I was slavish to the app, getting long running sessions done, often before dawn. I knew I'd have to get my training done before the day started, so I'd mostly get up at 3.30 or 4am and slip down to the gym to get in my day's training, before the sun and the family rose.

It might sound obsessive, training like this, but I was absolutely dedicated to supporting Dave as he worked and being a hands-on mum for my girls, so it was the only way I was going to find the space and time to do it. The idea of getting up so early didn't daunt me at all as I'd done it for so long in my teens and twenties, and nothing motivated me more than knowing I was going to drag my body over forty-two kilometres of bitumen in the not-too-distant future. I don't think I missed even one session of the app's program.

By the time we got to England I was getting to some of the longer runs the app was instructing me to do, close to the distance I'd be running on race day. Some of those had to be done on the treadmill, with rain hampering not only my training but the ICC Champions Trophy tournament that Dave was there to compete in (only one of Australia's matches ended in a result, and even that was decided by the Duckworth–Lewis system, which uses an algorithm that decides the winner of a cricket match without all of the overs being bowled). I did get to do a lot of kilometres in London's Hyde Park and in the very early morning, pounding through the dark, I became part of a silent, sweaty community of runners that populated the greens every morning.

Some of those London runs were glorious, and there were mornings when I felt like I could just keep going forever. This is the nature of athletics sometimes, it can create a state which is part physical, but mostly mental, and creates resilience and perseverance beyond what you think is possible. I've found it can also be used a reserve for the rest of your life too. When I came back to Sydney, I felt truly ready.

The whole family came to the Gold Coast to cheer me on – Dave and the girls, and also Mum and Dad. Paul and I ran in different groups, and the way the race worked was that we all ran with a standard bearer, meaning a runner with a flag who was going to keep pace for the time that we planned to get at the end of the race. My marker was for three hours and thirty minutes, and at the beginning of the race, adrenaline pushed me along with the standard bearer, but at a tiny little incline and with ten kilometres to go, I crashed.

I'd had my energy gels, I'd had my sweets, so I was on my own to get through the last quarter of the race. It was such a tough slog, but I got there in the end, with a tiny bit of help – I'm not ashamed to say it – from some lollies that another runner had dropped! But the main thing that pushed me through was knowing that Dave and the girls and Mum and Dad would be waiting and cheering at the finish line.

I slowed down a lot near the end and was a little bit disheartened when some of the novelty runners passed me. It's hard to see yourself as an athlete when you see someone dressed as Kermit the Frog striding faster than you are. But I made it across the line, and with a time of three hours and forty-six minutes, only sixteen minutes off my goal.

Afterwards I was on a high, with a huge sense of achievement and accomplishment that lasted for months afterwards. I actually think Dave might have been a little jealous, and for my part, I was looking forward to a time when we could do something like this together. Dave has some running aspirations after the end of his cricket career, and those are even broader in scope than a marathon. He has spoken a few times about wanting to run the Marathon des Sables, a multi-day 251-kilometre race across the Sahara Desert in Morocco, which is considered by many to be the toughest foot race in the world.

I'd probably need a bit of convincing to do that one with Dave, but I can tell you one thing: Dave and I are going to be that sixty-year-old couple crossing the line of some endurance event together, holding hands, exhausted and happy.

Not long after the Gold Coast Marathon, I also saw the completion of my long-held childhood dreams as a young Nipper at Maroubra Surf Club: seeing my name among the legends of surf lifesaving. It might not have been a photograph of me up on the wall of the club, but in my eyes it was far better, a plaque set in stone in the Australian Walk of Fame on the Maroubra Beach promenade for everyone to see, celebrating my 1999 and 2013 NSW Ironwoman of the Year wins, and my 2012 professional Ironwoman series win at Coolum.

I was inducted into the Walk of Fame during the 2017 Beach Breaks Carnival, which celebrates the surfing history and culture of Maroubra, alongside the Olympian and national surf lifesaving champion Graham Johnson, the pro-surfing pioneer Tony White, and surfer Kevin Davidson. I love that Mum and Dad and my girls can walk along the beach and see my name there and the words inscribed on the plaque for my 'Outstanding contribution to Surf Life Saving' – it's as much Mum and Dad's plaque as it is mine, enshrining their love and support of me through my surf lifesaving career and one of the toughest times of my life.

It seemed life couldn't get any better.

*

The 2017/2018 Ashes series eventually went ahead in Australia after the pay dispute ended. It opened in Brisbane, with Dave and captain Steve Smith guiding Australia to an excellent win. Australia managed a small first innings lead, but with England scoring fewer than 200 runs in the second innings, Australia needed not much more than 170 runs in the final innings to win.

That innings was opened by Dave and a young Western Australian named Cameron Bancroft, and the two of them dismantled the British bowling, breaking the record for the highest unbeaten run chase to win a Test. It was a superb performance from Dave, scoring a very quick 87 not out, and from Cameron Bancroft.

But during that innings the beginning of something quite concerning happened.

The Barmy Army, England's official supporters who attend each Ashes Test as a block, had started singing a song about Dave that alluded to the 2007 Clovelly incident involving me. This was a crude attempt to put Dave off his game, which was not only standard behaviour for the Barmy Army, but something that was accepted at sporting grounds across the UK.

The song wasn't graphic or particularly malicious, and I ignored it in the box as it was sung, but it certainly didn't feel good. When people mentioned it, I smiled and laughed about it, trying to make light of it, but I was surprised at how much it hurt me. I'd done so much work on myself since that incident, but it was still a barb that cut deep.

I was thankful, however, that it didn't seem to concern Dave, who smashed the English bowling around the park that innings and that series. A 239-run stand at the WACA in Perth from Steve Smith meant that he was the highest run getter in the series, and also the man of the series, but Dave was the third-highest run scorer of the series and an integral part of Australia winning the series 4–0.

During that series, Dave and I had been trying to fall pregnant with our third child, but it had been strangely difficult. Our first two girls had come easily and quickly, and as we were still young and fit, we assumed that getting pregnant for the third time would be just as easy. After two girls, I did wonder whether Dave wanted a boy and I talked to him about it, knowing that there were some medical measures we could take, not to assure a specific gender but increase the odds of a certain outcome. He said he'd be happy with a boy, but that he would also be just as happy with another girl, so we decided we'd just leave things to fate.

Fate was playing games with us, however, and decided it wasn't time for us to fall pregnant. I was habitually doing pregnancy tests, refusing to accept that it wasn't happening. This difficulty was challenging for me. I was used to my body responding in the way I wanted it to, but in this instance chance was very much at play. I didn't want to accept that lack of control. I was changing test brands and staring at what I hoped may have been faint positive lines but proved not to be, trying to will another baby into existence. But that child just wouldn't come.

We arranged to see a specialist, and, after a raft of tests, they told us that physically there was nothing wrong with either of us. It was just that the cosmic dice throw wasn't giving us the numbers we needed. Stick with it, we were told, and stick with it we did.

Then, finally it happened.

There were so many reasons for us to be happy. Primary of all of those reasons was that we were going to complete our little family as, at two kids, we'd decided that three would be the magic number for us. Another reason I desperately wanted to fall pregnant was that some stress would be taken out of our lives, which was important because I could see that Dave was absolutely exhausted.

In the year before, Dave had been away from his family and away from his bed for about 300 out of 365 days. As well as playing Test cricket, which was the fulfilment of Dave's childhood dreams, he was also playing Indian Premier League T20, which contributed significantly to our family earnings, and he was also playing international one-day. At the time he was the only Australian player to compete in all three forms of the game internationally.

In the small break between the Ashes and the next series in South Africa, Dave was heading to New Zealand where he'd be captaining the Australian T20 side in a short series, then, after that game, he'd be getting on a plane to South Africa, missing the tour and going straight into the first Test match.

There was no end in sight, but this was a tempo of Dave's choosing. Dave was never going to be a guy to say no, or to say that anything was ever too hard. Dave was one of those people whose competitive switch had been turned on and never turned back off. He never wanted the easy route, never wanted the rest, and certainly never wanted to miss an opportunity to play for Australia, with performance in the national side his childhood and then ongoing dream. He wanted to play as much cricket as he could, play as well as he could and win every match he could. He flew straight to South Africa from New Zealand cooked and exhausted – but also excited for the series.

He and I were certainly looking forward to going back to South Africa together. We had experienced so many joyful moments there, from seeing the scan of our first baby (and for me, hearing her heartbeat), to our engagement in beautiful Camps Bay. We had so much personal connection to the place that it sometimes felt like another home. Dave had high hopes for the games ahead. The last time he'd played Test cricket in South Africa he'd scored hundreds in half of his innings, helping Australia win the series, and was named player of the series.

As the vice-captain of the team, now he wanted another series win and also another stellar personal tally, hoping to head home triumphant having scored at least three centuries.

But our South African homecoming wasn't something we could ever have envisioned.

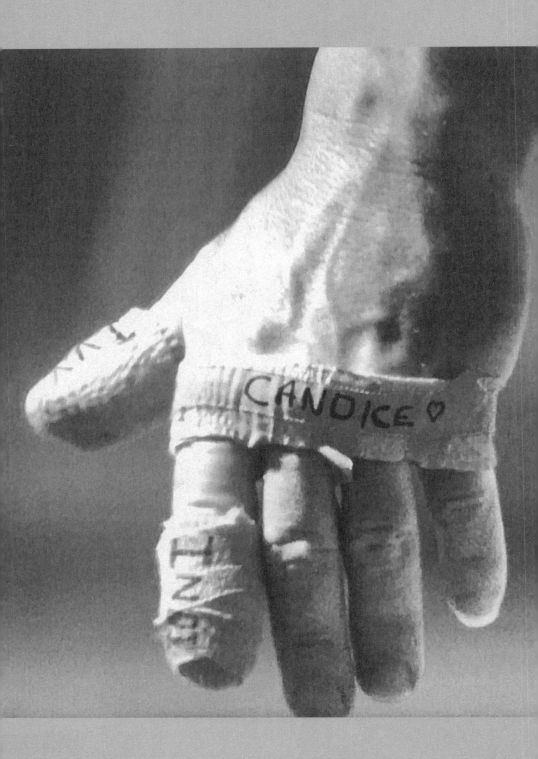

17

Dark Days

We were all excited to go to Durban, the location of the first Test of the 2018 series between Australia and South Africa. Neither I nor Mum, who now often travelled with me and the kids, wanted to miss the trip. It was always so wonderful having Mum with me to help, especially now I was pregnant again. The city didn't disappoint.

Quite often our favourite destinations are those that are very kid-friendly, and the smallish, coastal city on South Africa's east coast, with lots of child-friendly sites, a couple of which were directly across the road from our hotel, instantly became a favourite.

In lovely warm weather, Mum and I took the girls to a water park and to a swimming pool for swimming lessons, and then went to the cricket ground for the first day of the Test, which was a staple of our touring life. With little kids, it doesn't make sense to go to each session of every Test, but we always go for the first day, to give Dave and the team our support. Half the time, we get to watch Dave open the batting and set the team up for the Test ahead.

On the first day of the Durban Test, Australia won the toss and decided to bat, with Dave scoring a half-century until he was caught by his close friend AB de Villiers off Vernon Philander's bowling.

The kids and I watched or listened to days two, three and four either from the stands or on TV or by listening to the radio. Australia put together a solid first innings, scuttling the South African batting for a substantial first innings' lead, and then built on that lead, dashing towards an unobtainable last innings' total. At the end of day four, Australia needed just one wicket to win the Test with most of the South African batsmen giving their wickets up very cheaply, except for an opening batsman who scored a century, and their young batsmen-keeper Quinton de Kock, who was still defiant at the close of play.

I could only see and hear so much on telly, but I could tell that things were getting heated on the pitch. I didn't know how heated they were until Dave came back to the hotel that night.

He was pretty fired up, and it turned out he'd had an off-field confrontation with Quinton de Kock who, Dave told me, had made some very sexually explicit comments about me, making reference to my past at the Clovelly Hotel.

I felt a bit sick. I was also embarrassed, and grateful for my supportive husband and a thousand other emotions. The Clovelly incident seemed to be a poison that I just couldn't completely draw out from my body. I'd done so much since then, in my life and in my efforts to learn how to cope with the fall-out, and yet I couldn't get away from it. Now Dave was having to deal with it, a fact I really hated.

I was proud of the girls' and my ability to support Dave at work. That's why we were here, in South Africa, and now he was having to deal with my past and my mistakes. I was so proud that Dave had stood up for me, but hated that he had to.

It was encroaching; my past was returning. I felt the shame again, fresh as new snow. I was that kid again, that dumb kid who didn't know how to deal with what seemed like the whole country turning against me. I felt culpable and ashamed, even though I couldn't quite place where the wound was. It was like returning to a nightmare that had been absent for so many years.

I apologised, and he told me there was nothing to apologise for. We both hoped the whole incident would go away and that the series would move on to Gqeberha without any more hitches. Unfortunately, that wasn't to be.

That night CCTV footage of a mostly verbal altercation between Dave and de Kock in the stairwell at teatime was leaked by someone from the Durban Cricket Association to the media, and a quick investigation was to be undertaken. In Gqeberha, Dave was to face sanction for 'bringing the game into disrepute'.

Cricket uses a points demerit system and although Dave hadn't accrued any points since the incident with Joe Root years earlier, he had to explain himself, otherwise he was in danger of missing the next Test, which I knew would have devastated him as he would have felt he was letting down his teammates.

He was also furious that he'd been charged and would have to defend himself. Other players, both Australian and South

African, had heard what de Kock had said about me, and Dave didn't think anyone on either side would have accepted someone saying that about their wife. Undoubtedly Cricket Australia and the match referee knew exactly what had been said. As Dave said in some interviews after the incident, he was used to copping sledging on and off the field to put him off his game, and it never got to him, but he drew the line at disgusting comments about me, or about any woman in fact. He'd always defend his family no matter what. I loved that about Dave; his fierce love was like a fiery sun and I was so proud of him, but I had push down the anxiety that was rising in me.

Eventually Dave accepted a lesser charge, meaning he'd take a fine that would be equivalent to most of his match fee and some points that would essentially put him on a good- behaviour probation period for two years, but the series would roll on with him still a part of it. Neither of us were particularly happy with how the whole incident had played out, because Dave felt that he wasn't at fault, nor would he have acted differently if the exact same situation arose again, but we moved on to the next Test, just hoping it was behind us.

Again, it was a naive hope. In fact, the drama had only just begun, and I gleaned that when I was in a car with the girls and Mum, on our way to day one of the Test in Gqeberha. I received a whole series of notifications on Twitter, and when I opened the app, my feed was full of South African cricket fans sharing photographs of themselves as they headed into the grounds, armed with songbooks containing lyrics about my past, as well as with masks bearing the face of a grinning Sonny Bill Williams that they were going to wear at the game.

There were so many posts in which South African fans had tagged me. It wasn't just one group of friends taking the piss; this was big and organised. Some entity was handing out masks and songbooks at the ground.

That sick, anxious feeling rushed back in. I was regressing, I know that now. I was going back in time, becoming that young person I'd been in 2007, eleven years before, driving to the Kings Cross newsagency fearing what may be written about me in the papers that day.

I felt guilt, too, I'm embarrassed now to say. I knew I hadn't done anything wrong, but I still felt the guilt in my bones. It was all because of what I feared Dave was going to have to go through. I couldn't believe he was going to have to cop this because of a meaningless mistake I'd made as a young woman after one too many drinks. I was angry, but I was also devastated.

When I saw those notifications piling up on my phone, all I could do was put my sunglasses on to hide the tears welling in my eyes. I didn't want Mum or the girls to know anything was happening; or that my heart was breaking. These songs were different to the ones that had been sung in Brisbane. They were graphic, and weren't just ribbing Dave, but attacking me as a woman, aggressively and sexually.

I knew I would just have to sit there and wear it. If I turned the car around and went back to the hotel, that would be devastating for Dave and the game. If he saw the masks and heard the songs and then saw that I wasn't where he thought

I'd be, he'd know how affected I'd been, and that would affect him. That wasn't going to be good for anyone.

I just had to be staunch and stoic. I had to be visible, I had to be indomitable, and yet inside I was crumbling.

Once a year on an overseas tour, Cricket Australia has a visiting period for partners and families of the players, and they are invited to join the team, but this Test wasn't falling in that period, so when Mum, the girls and I went to the box where we'd watch the game from, thankfully it was empty of Australian wives or partners. That was a small mercy because, throughout the day, it felt as if everyone was staring and laughing at me as the songs rolled in from the stands, full of punters wearing masks. Mum ignored those boorish fans, as I attempted to as well.

On the way back to the hotel after the day's play, I called the Australian team's media manager, Kate Hutchison. She was someone whom I liked and trusted, and I wanted to check in with her and make sure she knew what was going on, just in case there was some media that she became aware of around what had been happening.

When Dave came back to the hotel, he was furious that the South African fans had been so hateful and disrespectful towards his family, and to me. To coin a phrase, it just wasn't cricket. I was despairing for Dave. He'd had a good day with the bat, but just couldn't relax afterwards and prepare for day two as he should have been able to do. Instead he was on the phone with all kinds of Cricket Australia people, trying to make sure that the masks and songbooks wouldn't be allowed in the grounds for the rest of the Test.

One of the people Dave really liked and respected from Cricket Australia was Frank Dimasi, a former Australian Federal Police investigator and head of security for the team. Dave contacted Frank and asked if there was anything that could be done about the situation. Frank was very sympathetic and said he would get in contact with his Cricket South Africa (CSA) counterpart to see what could be done to stop the harassment.

As much as I appreciated what Dave was doing, making sure this incident died down, I really wished he didn't have to do it. It was a huge distraction for him while he was in the middle of a Test match. He was burning mental and emotional energy that he needed for the game, not only as a batsman but also as the vice-captain of the team. I wished I could tell him not to worry about it, but he knew me and I knew him. This was going to affect him because he knew this would affect me.

Then things got even worse. Images were being circulated of CSA's commercial manager, Clive Eksteen, and CSA's media and communications manager, Altaaf Kazi, in photographs posing with some fans who were wearing the masks. There were also rumours going around that the ground staff had been taking the masks off punters who had been wearing them at the ground, but that CSA had intervened and told the ground staff to allow the masks to be taken in.

I was angry, but Dave was apoplectic. The whole incident had put him off-kilter, and the fact that Cricket South Africa seemed complicit in the whole thing had raised Dave's ire and activated his finely honed sense of right and wrong.

There wasn't a public statement from CSA about the incident, and I was asked by a representative of Cricket Australia not to voice any opinion or statement in public about what was going on. I had no interest in saying anything publicly, but I became increasingly annoyed that Cricket Australia didn't want me to make that decision myself. This was about my family, and my reputation. They didn't ask me how I was coping, and they didn't offer me or my family any support. I felt silenced.

I watched most of day three of the Test from the hotel room, and on the coverage I saw something that both filled my heart and broke it. Having suffered a number of jarring hand injuries, quite often Dave has a lot of strapping on his fingers when he's fielding, and in this Test one of his hands was quite heavily strapped. In one period of play, the broadcast was focusing on one of Dave's hands, and eventually they homed in on the writing on the tape. Across Dave's hand he had written 'Candice', with a love heart, and along two of his fingers, he'd written 'Ivy' and 'Indi'.

I'd tried not to tell Dave how I was feeling, and how much of a nightmare this had become for me. He hadn't been there in 2007, and he didn't know what the aftermath of the Clovelly incident had been like for me. He knew about it all, of course, but hadn't told him about the depths of despair I had plumbed then, and I surely wasn't going to tell him now, because the last thing I wanted was for my feelings to affect his cricket. I was so proud of the way I'd managed to support Dave, and that he played better when we, his family, were in the ground or in the same city as him. If I couldn't do that, it felt like I couldn't do anything.

But seeing the strapping on his hands was so touching – he knew how I felt, and he wanted to show how much he was thinking of me and our kids. I loved him for that, but I felt an immense sense of guilt, too. When we travelled on tour, we were there solely to support him, so that he could play his best cricket, and I felt terrible that the tables were turned, and that he had to show his support for us.

*

The Test rolled on, which was won on day four by South Africa.

Eventually, the Australian coach Darren Lehmann spoke about the sledging and was quite forceful, saying that there were some things that were just beyond the pale and attacking players' families was one of them. Again, I appreciated the public support when it came but I was also hugely embarrassed that the coach of the team was having to spend energy defending me when he should have been dedicating that energy to winning this series.

The whole thing sickened me, and while I never told anyone how much it was bothering me, I started losing sleep, staring at the ceiling and thinking about Dave, thinking about my pregnancy, thinking about humanity, when I should just be dreaming.

The only person from the South African side who spoke to me about what had been happening wasn't really a South African at all, but a West Indian. Ottis Gibson, the South African coach, sought me out when I was at the gym at the back end of the Test in Gqeberha and told me he was sorry about what had been happening. It was a classy gesture from a classy man.

Before the Test moved to Cape Town, Mum, Dave and the girls and I were joined by Patty and Dad who were coming with us on safari. I was thrilled to have my brother and Dad with us after the last few weeks; especially Dad, who was someone we could almost never get to travel with us.

The safari was something that we'd all been looking forward to for months and I really hoped that it would help turn this trip around and help us leave South Africa with a positive feeling. There was a cruel twist of fate, however, when I read in a news report that the New Zealand Super Rugby team, the Blues, was soon to play against the Cape Town-based Stormers, and that the Blues were staying at the same hotel the Australian cricket team would be staying at.

The article gleefully noted that that would mean that David and Candice Warner would be sharing a hotel with Sonny Bill Williams. I couldn't believe it. I didn't want to stay there. I just wanted to be somewhere – anywhere – else but I felt that if we did move to another hotel, or if I went home, then the media attention would be even worse.

I couldn't run away; I wanted to support Dave. I needed to put on a face that suggested that this was all water off a duck's back, even if that was a long way away from the truth.

When I arrived at the hotel, there were banks of cameras parked outside. The Stormers' game against the Blues was to be in three days, and we were leaving in two to go on safari, so when we returned, Sonny Bill Williams and his team would be gone. I spent most of my time in my room, steadfastly refusing to allow that wide-angle shot that the tabloid journalists would have sorely wanted. They managed to take photographs of us each entering or leaving the hotel, but not at the same time.

I knew how much stress this had all put on Dave, and I often also thought about Sonny Bill's wife and their children. She and Sonny Bill are conservative and religious people. I couldn't believe that this was something that we still all had to deal with.

I wondered, not for the first time, whether the South African rugby fans would attack Sonny Bill in the same way – making my face into a mask, and attacking him and his wife in public. Probably not, I told myself. This whole thing had been a gendered and selective attack, then and now. The world of high-profile sport was still primarily a man's realm, and in that world a woman was vulnerable to attack in ways that a man still wasn't.

The reset we'd been looking for since Durban did come, though, when we left that hotel for Sabi Sabi Earth Lodge, in the Sabie Game Reserve, on the Mozambique border in the middle of nowhere.

There the angry and encroaching world of cricket and the media and abusive fans seemed so far away. As we woke in the morning there were giraffes next to us, eating the canopies of trees, and at night we could hear the distant roars of predators. It was an amazing time for all of us, especially the girls, and it was a lovely reminder that this was the world too – a world beyond the drama we'd been facing elsewhere in South Africa.

The African bush was sparse and yet full of life and beauty. There were moments in which it looked very much like the Australian outback and others in which it seemed so foreign, especially at sunrise and sunset when the colours of the sky become otherworldly and the animals become full throated and active.

One of the best aspects of the safari was that we had no phone reception, so even if there was continuing coverage about the Gqeberha incident, we didn't know about it. This was a family trip we'd always remember.

There was a part of me that wished we could just stay out there in the bush, with the animals and the savannah scrub and my family. There was also a part of me that wanted to get back to the cricket and see this thing out.

It had been a tough series. Throughout the tour, Dave had been staring into the distance and thinking, probably overthinking, and he wasn't sleeping well. He wasn't eating much, either, and he wasn't his usual gregarious self; he was very quiet. Dave had goals that he'd set himself for this series and those goals were still within touching distance, with the series in the balance and still two Tests to go. I wanted to see what he was going to do – what he was capable of. I wanted Dave to get out there and smash the ball around and grab this series by the throat. I know that instinct was in Dave too – that instinct for competition and victory is always in him, and it's one of the reasons why he's one of the greats. He was exhausted, and the year and the tour had taken a huge toll on him. He needed a break from cricket and the furore, but I knew that he could always find a way to bounce back and I was looking forward to seeing it.

*

Back in Cape Town for the beginning of the final Test, South Africa opened the batting and were all out for a decent score on the morning of day two. Mum, Dad, Patty and the girls and I had all come to the ground for day one, as we always did, and then also for day two, so we could watch Dave bat.

Dave was hit by a bouncer in the first few balls, but after recovering he belted it around, getting a handful of fours and sixes before being clean bowled after fourteen balls. I could feel just how dirty he was with himself as he walked back to the rooms. Then he was stopped by a South African fan who had waltzed straight over from his seat to where Dave was about to leave the ground and, nose to ear, started screaming abuse at Dave.

Dave told me later what the man was saying, but even from where I was, I could tell what kind of vile stuff it was. Dave doesn't take rubbish from anyone, and he yelled right back at him, telling him what he thought of him.

As Dave went back to the room, I was incensed. Not so much at the fan, but more that there'd been no intervention and no protection from ground staff; they had essentially let this guy get right next to one of the players and let loose. To me, it just wasn't good enough; none of it was. I felt our family hadn't been supported or protected throughout this tour, and this was just another example. Ever since the abuse started from the South African fans, no one had come to see how we were, nor addressed how the abuse was going to stop.

I was angry, and I wasn't the only one.

Patty had come a long way from the days when he thought Dave was going to upgrade his sister. He lived with Dave, me and the kids. He had been one of Dave's groomsmen at our wedding. He and Dave were brothers and best mates. And he couldn't believe that this bloke had been allowed to saunter right up to Dave and scream at him, and then didn't seem to have been admonished at all.

Patty had had enough. He is mostly a calm and lovely guy, but Patty has a breaking point, like all of us in our family, and when that point is reached and breached, he becomes a man of action. Patty left the box, jumped a couple of fences to where the particular fan was, and chased him down. When Patty got to him, he throttled him while giving this bloke a piece of his mind.

When he came back to the box, he and I were sought out by representatives of Cricket Australia. They were upset and said Patty's actions would now only inflame the incident further. I lost my temper then – team management and security had an obligation to protect their players and their families, and it felt as though we'd been hung out to dry, with no help, no support, and with no choice but to look after ourselves.

Eventually the fan was ejected, and the altercation between him and Dave was publicised, but thankfully not the one involving Patty.

That night David Peever, who was then chairman of Cricket Australia, sat Dave and I down at the hotel and told us that we were being supported, but that we just didn't know it. He said that in the wake of the previous Test, they'd decided that if the abuse continued, the team would have walked away from the tour. I was sceptical, to say the least.

After that conversation I decided that we'd watch day three of the game back in the hotel room.

I'd started to get a better understanding of the game and now knew there were some days and some sessions that were of greater importance than others. That day, I was watching one of those days and one of those sessions. With one Test apiece, South Africa managed to eke out a small first-innings lead, and after lunch, South Africa had pushed the lead past 100 runs with only two wickets down. AB de Villiers was at the crease. The match and the series were in peril and things had become spiteful on the field.

As I sat in the hotel room with our daughters asleep, I saw, on the television, a lot of chat, a lot of anger, and then something else.

I'd missed the original incident, as I'd been trying to get the girls to go down for their afternoon sleep, but a scene was being replayed over and over again. It seemed to show Cameron Bancroft taking something from his pants and then rubbing it on the ball. I didn't really understand the significance of what was happening, but the commentators were making a big deal of it, replaying it over and over again and discussing it as a potential breach of the laws of the game, not to mention the ethics of the game.

I texted Dave's friend Macca, who was also in South Africa and is a cricket tragic, asking him what was happening.

I didn't fully understand what I was watching, and I certainly didn't envision the days, weeks and months that were ahead of us, but at that moment I knew I had to get to the ground for Dave. That was my instinct. When the kids woke up, we all went straight to Newlands to show our support.

There weren't many people in the box, just a few of the partners of the support staff, and we didn't have access to the commentary, so we just watched the cricket as it played out for the rest of the day. But when we got back to the hotel, I started to gain a little bit more of an understanding of the magnitude of what was going on.

There were a lot of meetings going on – official meetings and unofficial meetings. I could sense that there were a lot of people scrambling, getting stories together. I didn't see Dave much that night as he was drawn into a lot of those meetings, and when he wasn't involved in those, he was distracted or on his phone.

I was just there to support him, fully and without judgement. Whatever had happened was to do with cricket, and I don't question Dave about that. I love him, I trust him, and I was just there to support him.

That night I asked Dave if the game was on the next day, and he said he thought it would be. We went to bed and, although Dave normally sleeps well during Tests, he didn't that night, nor for many nights afterwards.

The next day was strange. At the hotel there was an area sectioned off for players and staff and their wives and partners, and that's normally one of the loudest and most social parts of the touring day. It's the one time and place that we're all there together, and while we were all there together physically that day, there was a stilted pall over the restaurant. The quietness that morning was stifling. There was little conversation, and the chat that was happening was about the fact that Dave and captain Steve Smith were to be stood down and that Tim Paine would be taking on the captaincy.

Every tour we usually have a wives and partners' WhatsApp group so we can share information and just generally chat to one another, and on that morning I posted a message saying that I thought we should all get down to the game, at least for that first session, to show that we were there for the boys, regardless of what was happening and whatever would happen. I didn't get many responses.

That morning the South Africans extended their lead past 400 and when Dave and Cam Bancroft went out to bat after lunch, the Australian side was a deflated mess. Dave and Cam held on for a session, but after they got out there was a procession of single-digit innings.

The South Africans won the Test easily. The Australian team was barely a team anymore, just a collective of shattered individuals.

Back at the hotel there were more meetings, and one very long meeting. It seemed to me that a lot of fingers were being pointed at Dave because he was someone who often managed the ball on the field, and perhaps because of people's perceptions of Dave as someone who challenges the line, especially in the wake of the Joe Root incident, and with de Kock.

A very rushed investigation started and some people were called to give their side of the story, but certainly not all the players and staff. Players, officials and coaches broke off into groups. There was a lot of sitting around and waiting for people to be called for interviews with Cricket Australia representatives.

I watched it all from the pool, where I was playing with the kids. So often I saw Dave there sitting, waiting on his own for his interview. It broke my heart to see that, and there were so many times that I wanted to run over and hug him. He was working, though, and he just had to go through his interview and accept whatever the outcome would be. Even now it kills me to think of it. He just had to white-knuckle it alone, and he did.

In my own way, I was going through it alone too. I didn't talk to Dave about it as he was going through so much himself, but in some way I felt, deep down, that it was all my fault. I know it makes no sense intellectually, but my gut was telling me that if there hadn't been a confrontation between Dave and Quinton de Kock, then there wouldn't have been the Sonny Bill masks and songs, and if there weren't the songs and masks, whatever had happened out there on the grounds in Newlands wouldn't have happened either.

I felt as if Dave was having to deal with a stupid decision I had made a dozen years earlier. My gut was turning over and over with guilt. My sleeping got worse, and I tried to minimise my stress and push the guilt away as best I could, not to make myself feel better as I didn't really feel as though I deserved to feel any better, but because I owed it to Dave to be in the best place to support him and also bring some kind of normalcy to the kids' lives during this period.

I did worry sometimes about the baby, still so tiny in my belly.

The team and families all flew to Johannesburg, and that particular leg of our travel felt as if we were going to a funeral. No one spoke, no one joked, no one was enjoying one another's company. The players and partners arrived at the hotel in Johannesburg in different buses, and when we pulled in I saw an army of camera people and journalists waiting for us. When the kids and I got out of the bus, they all flocked to us, shouting and filming and photographing. It was horrifying. I kept my head down and tried to get the kids and Mum into the hotel as quickly as possible, but in the back of my mind I was starting to fear what things may be like when we arrived back in Australia.

That night Dave received a message telling him he was to come in for a meeting with Cricket Australia chief executive James Sutherland and Pat Howard, the team's general manager. I could tell his stress levels were sky-high before that meeting. Dave normally responds to stress particularly well, minimising extraneous energy and focusing that stress and using it well. Now he was just bottling it up, saying little and doing little, unable to direct that energy. I worried he was going to blow an emotional gasket.

The meeting was a long one and when Dave came back into the room, he kept it together for only a few seconds before he broke down in tears. He told me he was to accept the blame for devising a ball-tampering plan, which was known about by captain Steve Smith and enacted by Cameron Bancroft. He said he was being sent home, and sent home immediately.

I grabbed him and held him. He just kept apologising, over and over and over. I told him he didn't have to apologise for anything. I just held him and told him things were going to be fine. Eventually he calmed down and I asked him what had happened in the meeting. He told me he feared that he may never play cricket again – this was the tone of the meeting he'd just had.

He was so crushed. Dave's whole life was cricket and his family; they were what all his goals were centred around, and he felt that he'd jeopardised both. We weren't so concerned about his livelihood, in jeopardy as it was, but the fact that Dave felt he may no longer be able to play cricket competitively – the sport he so sorely loved – was heartbreaking.

My role in that moment was to be steadfast, and steadfast I was. I kept it together, for the most part, telling Dave that everything was going to be okay. In my mind, I knew that what I was saying was true, but once again, my gut said otherwise. We stayed up that night, packing and talking. We leaned on each other, hugged each other, and loved each other. Flights were arranged for us and for Steve Smith, who was also being sent home.

Steve Smith was to fly directly back to Sydney from Johannesburg on Qantas, the airline we usually fly on, but we were told that his flight was full and that we were to be flying from Johannesburg to Dubai on a different airline, and then from Dubai to Sydney.

It was a very arduous trip home: incredibly long, but almost not long enough for all that we had to prepare for our arrival, knowing that the press would be waiting for us.

We were going to be returning to a strange circumstance. Before leaving for South Africa we'd found a dream block on the cliffside street between Coogee and Maroubra that Dave and I had always wanted to live on. Right on the cliff, this address was on the street we'd been monitoring since we first met. We'd bought that block, and the old house that sat on it, but we'd had the house torn down with a view to building our own dream house. This was actually going to be our forever home, built just for our purposes. In the meantime we were going to rent a family home, but while we looked for a place, we were going to be living with Mum and Dad.

Dad, who had already gone home with Patty earlier, told us that photographers and journalists were already staking their place out.

We had to find somewhere else to stay, and somewhere the kids would be comfortable and safe, and also somewhere we wouldn't be inundated with media. We also needed a car to take us from the airport. We knew there would be press waiting, and the idea of standing around in the often interminable taxi queue with the kids and a press pack was a non-starter. Dave had other aspects of the incident to consider, too. Steve Smith was going to have a press conference at the airport — something that would have already happened by the time we touched down. Dave had been advised to give his own press conference a few days later, not immediately.

Many of the logistics were handed over to my new manager, Roxy Jacenko, who had been managing me for only a short period then. Roxy is well known in Sydney, if not all of Australia, as a PR expert with her own reputation and profile managed expertly.

We arrived at Sydney Airport at about 10pm, exhausted and very wary of what may come next. We were ushered from the plane through customs and passport control to a private waiting area as the airport made preparations to guide us through the media throng waiting for us.

Mum went first. She had a car waiting to take her home, and I didn't want her to have to run the gauntlet that was awaiting us. Then Dave and I had to front up. The girls were exhausted, so we carried them, one each, and we waded in.

It was unlike anything I'd ever experienced. There was a wall of cameras and flashing lights, journalists and photographers jostling and pushing for access, and a cavalcade of baying questions. It was scary, being in the middle of it, and I could feel all of the attention bearing down heavily on Dave's shoulders. Dave didn't want to just plough through, as it's never his style to run away, so he stopped quickly, saying that he'd have more to say in a few days but that right then he just wanted to get the kids to bed and clear his head.

I tried not to respond to any of it, but those cameras and those questions and all of that agitation felt not only like the angry energy of a story being chased, but the mood of the entire country. Under that shaming spotlight, all of the feelings from 2007 rushed back again and I tried to push them down, and do what I could to protect my kids and support my husband at the centre of the storm. I could see how much Dave was hurting and how much emotional energy it took to front the pack. Cricket was his life, everything he'd worked towards, and now he was looking down the barrel of losing it all. As we were led out through the scrum, all I could do was hold him close with the girls, my heart pounding with adrenaline and shock.

I started to cry, even though I desperately didn't want to. I fought those tears, but they just kept coming. There was something in the bottom of my stomach, dark and heavy and ugly, that was born of 2007 and secreted in blackness in the first Test when the South Africans made gross statements to Dave on the pitch, and again with the songs and masks, and now, with the press baying for blood.

In the coming days, Dave would apologise openly and unreservedly for his part in what transpired in South Africa, accepting his ban from cricket for a year and a lifetime ban from leadership positions, but I knew that wouldn't be enough, not then, or later.

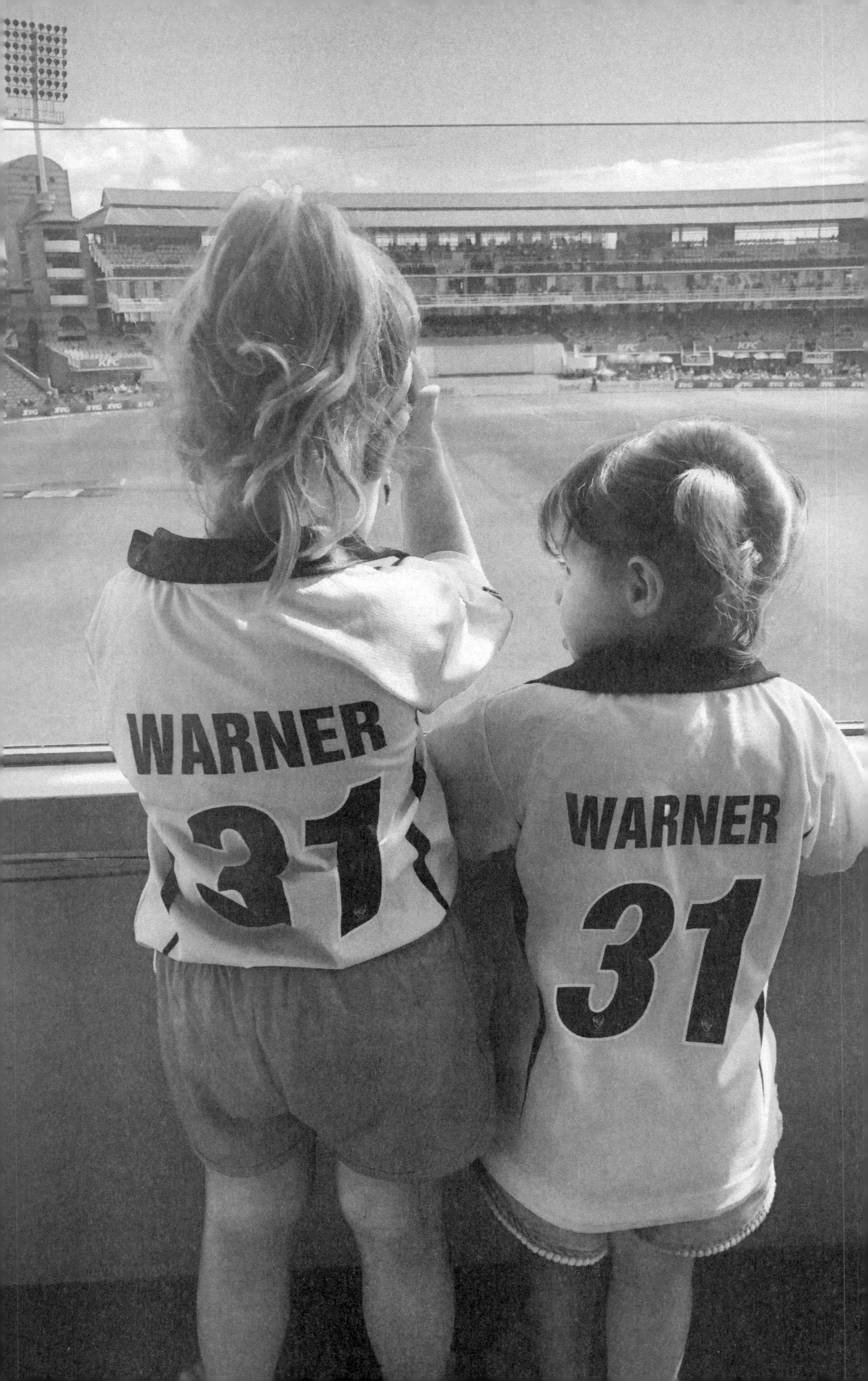
WARNER
31
WARNER
31

18

Rock Bottom

We spent three days in a gilded tower, at once comfortable and uncomfortable. Roxy had arranged a room for us in a hotel, overlooking the harbour, and when we arrived there were snacks and toys and activities for the kids, and a car that we could use.

Dave knew he'd have to front up to the media with a press conference, and he was of the understanding that he and Steve Smith would do one together. But by the time we'd arrived in Sydney, Steve had already given a statement and left the country for New York. Dave's instinct had originally been to speak when we arrived, after the long haul from Dubai, but he was advised to give it a few days, recharge and figure out exactly what line he wanted to toe.

When we arrived in Sydney, both Dave and I received calls from the owner of his IPL team, the SunRisers, Kalanithi Maran. He is such a lovely man, and really made the team a home for Dave. He called to tell Dave that he was looking forward to having Dave back in India in a few weeks' time, when the IPL was due to start again, and his wife called me to tell me that no one should go through what Dave was going through without support. She said she was there for us, and I thanked her. They are such a lovely family and I was so grateful for their support.

It helped Dave's mental state no end for him to know that there would be some cricket for him to play, and soon. He couldn't wait to get back on the pitch. None of us could. But first, we had to get through the press conference.

Dave's instinct is always to fight, and to tell the truth, and there's still a lot that hasn't been said about the ball-tampering incident, but this wasn't the time for that. He decided to set the press conference at the auditorium at the Sydney Football Stadium complex for the Wednesday after our return. In the days before we tried to maintain a relatively normal schedule for the kids, taking them to daycare, and preparing for what we knew was going to be a massive day in Dave's life.

At some point a photo had been taken of Dave in the window of our hotel room and had been published, so when the time came to head to the press conference, the hotel was inundated with media. Camera flashes battered the car as we left the hotel, and photographers chased us down the street, trying to get pictures each time the car stopped at a red light. My heart was pounding and I could feel my blood pressure soaring.

It was going to be even more stressful than I'd imagined.

I was in a state of immense anxiety. Dave had been fragile since we'd arrived back in Sydney, which is not something you could accuse him of being at any other time. He's normally so indomitable, up for any challenge. The stress on him was huge. As we were driven to the football stadium, I sat close and squeezed his hand, wishing that I could somehow shield him from what was coming. I wanted to support him as best I could, but I felt that old ball of guilt inside of me too.

Perhaps the most excruciating moment was when I had to leave Dave, as he took the podium with dozens of journalists and a bouquet of microphones in front of him. I kissed him on the cheek and left him, alone. It took every fibre of my being to walk away from him. My deep instinct was to stay with him at this time when he needed me most, but this was something Dave had to do on his own.

Dave gave his statement unreservedly apologising for his role in the incident and accepting his sanction and then, as tears streamed down his face, he apologised to me and the girls. I mouthed there was nothing to apologise for. It was destroying both of us, this pressure in the wake of the ball-tampering incident, but it wouldn't tear us apart.

Soon I was in tears as well. Roxy came and held me like the friend that she truly was.

It killed me, watching Dave expressing so much raw emotion. He's never that emotional and he never cracks. He could barely get his words out. Even I hadn't known how much this was affecting him, and how much he was suffering until he was up there on the podium.

That ball of guilt just grew and grew inside of me, especially as Dave's tears fell. This was all my fault. It all started in 2007, and now had become this – the whole of the country, damning and angry. Dave in tears. The prime minister chiming in, for Christ's sake, calling the incident a national disgrace. It was all my fault. It was all my fault. I had never said it, but I knew it and I felt it – this was all my fault.

We went out the back way to the car and took off, back to the hotel, before anyone could catch us. We were in the lift on the way back to our room when I found myself on the floor of the hotel's hallway. I'd collapsed and was sobbing. It was as though I was seeing it all from above, as though I was disembodied. I didn't mean to fall; I just did. I didn't mean to cry, I just did. I was saying that it was all my fault. It just came out. The words were mine, they were from deep inside me, but I hadn't chosen to say them.

'It's all my fault. It's all my fault.'

I had to be carried back into the hotel room. I hadn't eaten and had lost several kilograms that week. I was weak, I was stressed, I felt guilt and the physical and emotional pressures of pregnancy were mounting. I'd kept it all together, because I had to, and I really wanted to. I'd only ever wanted to support Dave, especially now when he needed it, but it had all become too much. My mind and body could only go so far.

I hadn't made any statements to the press, nor did I want to, but veteran journalist Phil 'Buzz' Rothfield of the *Daily Telegraph* was very keen on doing an interview with me at the time, and while I didn't have a relationship with him at the time, I was advised that a piece like this from Buzz could be helpful.

We spoke over the phone and I couldn't help but tell Buzz that I felt I was all to blame, and that the genesis of the whole incident was back in my past. I burst into tears over the phone and was again overwhelmed. Buzz was kind and understanding, which was a real comfort, but when I heard our exchange online and on the news the next day, the rawness and pain in my cracking voice was shocking to hear and it pushed me further into despair. It was a dark time for both Dave and me.

After the media attention died down Dave, the girls and I moved out of the hotel and back to Mum and Dad's place. I was glad to be back in my childhood home. Things had calmed down a little bit, and it was a place the girls and I would be comfortable and feel safe and supported while Dave was away playing in India with the IPL. Then Dave got the call from the SunRisers telling him that he wouldn't be going to India.

Dave wasn't allowed to play in the IPL, and therefore would not be paid his salary for the season. The decision was a very significant one for us. One of the things that kept Dave going was knowing that, after his return to Sydney from South Africa, and the pressure and the pain, he'd soon be back on the pitch, doing what he does best, what he was born to do. It was essential for his mental health, not to mention essential for keeping us afloat financially.

We were over-mortgaged. With our new block and the loan we'd taken out to build our new home and with Dave's IPL contract disappearing before our eyes, it looked like we would have no income for a year. I didn't know how we'd keep our heads above water.

The financial aspect was a lesser concern in those days, though. My primary concern was Dave's wellbeing, which I felt was precarious. He was vulnerable, and I wanted with my whole being to make sure that nothing hurt him when his armour was off, when his defences were down. I'd had my moments of weakness and pain and tears, but I was determined not to give in, so I steeled myself every day to be there and to be strong for Dave and the girls.

I believe in mind over matter, but as I discovered, there are limits to what you can just push through.

Perhaps a week or two after we'd moved back to Mum and Dad's place, I'd put the girls to bed and Dave was having a shower. I went into the bathroom, and sat on the toilet, and something strange happened. Something very, very sad. I could see blood, and I instantly knew what had happened.

I knew that I was no longer pregnant.

I stood up in shock for a moment. The pregnancy had meant so much to Dave and me during this harrowing time. It was the one thing that felt hopeful, and something that gave us perspective. Outside of the house and our family, where everyone had opinions and bile, there was a family bubble, where there was love, impenetrable and growing. But now this.

Dave jumped out of the shower and I think he knew what had happened just hearing my sobs. He held me and we cried, and in that moment we knew we'd arrived at rock bottom.

19

Turning Up

There's nothing like home, and the neighbourhood, and Mum and Dad. Especially Mum and Dad. Above all Mum and Dad. They were never going to be concerned with the media or public sentiment, no matter how loud things got outside. They only worried about us, and the girls.

I needed them: when Dave gave his statement, when the media interest was highest and when I miscarried, which didn't happen only once but twice, as I again fell pregnant shortly after the first miscarriage, but it was fated to last only a few weeks.

It was the place from which we could rebuild emotionally and also the place we could reassemble our lives, which had seemed to fall all around us. There was so much to do, and the first thing was just to keep going out – just to get coffee, drop the kids off at daycare and pick them up and, for me, to keep running.

There wasn't a lot that was positive coming out of the incident all those years ago in Clovelly, except that I learned one thing about being in the centre of a public-shaming episode – and that's if you keep turning up, you might start in the foreground but eventually you just end up in the background.

That didn't necessarily apply outside of our own neighbourhood and our everyday routine, but it did apply to the places we went every day. The first time you go to the café, or walk up and down your own street, people stare and they speak behind your back, but eventually they get used to your presence again and settle down. You're just living your life, and they are too. You can't hide in your own neighbourhood. If you rarely emerge, people will react every time. You'll never escape from those reactions. You just have to keep turning up. Sometimes it's hard to do and your instinct is to shut yourself in, but you've got to keep to your routine.

We tried to keep the kids' lives as normal as possible, so that made things a little easier. The media interest eventually died down. For a couple of months afterwards, Dave may have been stopped and snapped by a photographer or a journalist at the café down the road but, with nothing to say to them, a story with no new information and just an image of Dave in a cap with a muffin and coffee in hand didn't warrant space in the newspaper.

That was the first step to reclaiming our lives, feeling like we could just live in our own neighbourhood. That was only the first step, however. There were immediate financial concerns.

We were very much relying on Dave's IPL contract to keep paying our bills. We were in the middle of building a house and we had outgoing costs and mortgages, so we were going to go backwards financially. Dave and I sat down and did the numbers, and things didn't look good.

We could have sold our dream block, but I was adamant

that we didn't. It was more important than ever before that we maintain our connection and safeguard the dreams of our future in Maroubra. It was home, embedded with the precious family and friends who were our lifeline. And Dave had worked so hard, his whole life. He'd earned everything he had and if there was a way to keep the block and keep moving forward, that's what we were going to do.

I knew that there was always a way to keep going. We just had to find it. All of Dave's sponsors had dropped him, and his Cricket Australia and IPL contracts had also paused, so we had no money coming in at all. We had a construction loan already in place, so that we could continue building our place, but only pre-existing loans like that existed for us now.

We were going to go down the gurgler financially if Dave had to retire prematurely, but that wasn't something we could even entertain as a possibility. Cricket was, and still is, in Dave's bones. He's such a fighter, such a champion, and early retirement just felt wrong. He had so much cricket left in him. The sport needed him, and right now he needed the sport, too. If he was out there, smashing the bowling around somewhere, his headspace would be infinitely better.

Consolidating our position and downsizing, and entertaining the possibility of a future in which Dave didn't play professional cricket, was just wrong. We'd keep going, keep moving forward, and we'd assume Dave would see out this ban imposed on him and, at the other end of it, he'd go back into the teams and the form he'd been in previously.

In the meantime, however, we'd just do what we could to survive, day by day. We met all kinds of challenges and dealt with them accordingly; for instance, Dave was sponsored by a car company, which had given us a couple of cars to use. With those cars now reclaimed, we didn't have transportation and we couldn't afford to buy a car outright, or even secure a loan for one. Eventually we tackled that problem by going to the airport and renting a car, replacing that car with another after the maximum twenty-eight days that the rental places allowed.

Dave had to play cricket during the fallow period, and while all of the ICC-sanctioned tournaments and teams were off the menu, the unsanctioned secondary (but still professional) leagues were a possibility. The first port of call ended up being, of all places, Canada. Former Pakistani fast bowler Waqar Younis had been one of the coaches at the IPL side that Dave had been playing for, and had gone to Canada to coach a professional T20 side playing in the short Canadian league. Younis invited Dave over to Canada to captain his side, the Winnipeg Hawks.

After playing for a few weeks in Canada, Dave received an offer from a West Indian T20 side to replace an Australian in the team who had been called up to tour with the Australia A side. Dave flew out to St Lucia, one of the beautiful Caribbean islands close to the Bahamas, and there played for the St Lucia Zouks in the Caribbean Premier League.

With some money coming back in now, the girls and I had the opportunity to visit Dave in the Caribbean and it was amazing to be back watching him play. It was like watching an injured bird fly again, or a beached dolphin swim. This is simply what Dave was meant to do. When he came back to Sydney, Dave started to play some grade cricket for Randwick

Petersham Cricket Club, knowing that he'd need runs against acknowledged attacks to get back in the Test side, and the runs started to pile up. He really was hitting some excellent form and I knew it was going to be a bittersweet summer coming up, with the Australian team undoubtedly needing Dave's form but unable to use it because of the ban.

Despite the horror year we'd had, the grade-cricket period ended up being a lot of fun for all of us. The girls and I travelled all around Sydney and surrounds, hanging out with a picnic on the grass as we watched Dave play. One match that was especially fun was at Coogee Oval, just down the road from our place, and on a sportsground that Dad used to tend to when he worked for Randwick Council.

Steve Smith had also been playing grade cricket for Sutherland and when that side came to Randwick Petersham's home ground in Coogee, the prospect of Dave and Steve playing against each other was an enticing one for cricket fans. There was no animosity between the pair, but no one had seen the former test captain and vice-captain together on the same pitch since the incident in South Africa, so of course there was interest. Literally thousands of people turned up to the game, which was thrilling for the young players on both sides, who had never played in a game where there were so many spectators, camera crews and the intensity of high-level cricket.

As good as it was to see Dave out there in the field or at the crease, it was perhaps almost as gratifying watching him in the rooms and around the grounds with the younger players. Dave had become something of a veteran, and a mentor. He'd been around teams for his whole life, mostly as the star youngster, but now he had a different role. He really did want to give back to the game and appreciated that one of the ways he could do that was through mentoring.

He loved captaining teams. He could lead by example, guide young players and exercise the strategic muscles he'd developed over many, many years.

One of the aspects of the ban that didn't expire was the ban of ever having a leadership position in an Australian team again. This was devastating for Dave (and no doubt for Steve, too) as his leadership capabilities were growing and would only improve, but in this period his ambitions were limited to getting back to the Australian side, which he knew would be achieved by getting runs.

Dave was definitely getting the runs he needed, and sorely felt the pangs of missing out when spring took hold in Australia and the Indian side arrived for a one-day T20 and Test series. This would be the first Australian summer in a while in which he wouldn't be putting on the baggy green.

Dave's final international contract signed before the end of his ban was with a Bangladeshi T20 side, the Sylhet Sixers, who Dave captained and faced off against a number of other Bangladeshi sides, including the Comilla Victorians, a team that was captained by Steve Smith, and a team from Rangpur, the Riders, which featured in some footage that went viral as Dave, normally a left hander, batted as a right hander would while facing Chris Gayle's spin and smashing three consecutive sixes.

After the short Bangladeshi season ended, both Dave and Steve returned to Australia, where a Test series between Australia and India was about to begin.

Dave found it hard, watching that first Test against India in Australia on the television, for obvious reasons. It was made even more difficult by the fact that Australia's batting was not exemplary in that Test and that the Australian side was beaten at home by 30 or so runs.

I knew Dave wanted to get back into the Australian side for his own gratification and the resumption of his dreams, but I also know that he wanted to help. He wanted the Australian side to win and he knew that he would have been of great assistance in that endeavour.

The second Test was in Perth and, again, the Australian batting wasn't ideal. At the end of that Test, with two full innings, Australia was still without a century. The side had managed to win thanks to some excellent bowling, but the side needed more depth in their batting efforts. The side needed Dave.

Then the Boxing Day Test started, and with it all of the controversy started to build again. After play on the first day, Steve Smith and Cameron Bancroft sat down with Adam Gilchrist and gave what was advertised as 'tell all' interviews. Dave was asked to take part, but he declined. Smith and Bancroft spoke about the ball-tampering incident in South Africa, and overall the interviews were disappointing as the whole story was not told, or at least not in the version broadcasted.

After those stories were televised, pressure quickly built for Dave to also do an interview and we did talk about him telling his side of the story. The pressure only grew after the Boxing Day Test when Australia was humiliated, being scuttled in the first innings with no Australian batsman getting a score better than a couple of dozen runs, and Australia failing to get the Indians out in either innings.

The cameras returned. By then we'd moved back into our dream place in Maroubra and Dave was being photographed even when he was simply taking out the rubbish. There was again intense interest in Dave and his international career, which was due to resume after this series.

Dave's instinct was to tell the unencumbered truth, letting the cards fall where they may. He decided that wasn't the right course of action, however. Pride could wait. Right now the only important thing to do was to get back into the Australian side and back to the top of international cricket.

In January 2019, the Indian side left Australia having won both the one-day international and the Test series. A few weeks later, the Australian team went to India for a successful one-day international series and, in the wake of that series and in preparation for the integration back into the side of Dave and Steve Smith, the team and Dave and Steve were invited to travel to Dubai for a series of meetings and events looking at team culture.

These events were hosted by new Australian coach Justin Langer, who was someone Dave respected greatly, and when he returned home, he couldn't wait to get back on the pitch, playing for Australia.

I was excited for him and the year ahead. There was no international cricket immediately after the cessation of the ban, so the first games Dave was allowed to play in were in the IPL, which, I thought, was a perfect way to get back into the swing of things as he was so valued in India. Dave was always made to feel welcome in India and he was always very comfortable playing there.

I didn't travel with him this time, however, as I'd fallen pregnant again.

After the second miscarriage, I was adamant that we'd fall pregnant again before too long. We'd decided we wanted three children and it just felt wrong that both pregnancies had ended the way they had. It would probably be fair to use the word 'obsession' to describe the way I went about it.

I saw my doctor and after a raft of tests I was told that there was nothing physically wrong with me, and that the two miscarriages were just regular, bad-luck miseries. There was no reason not to try again, and so we did.

Again, I was relentless, endlessly doing pregnancy tests. I wanted our family to be complete. I wanted the 2018 incidents of South Africa and Sydney to be past us. I wanted for our lives to return to normal. When I did fall pregnant again, we were so happy, but also wary until, after weeks became months with no incident, we started to make preparations for the birth of our third baby.

We were into happy months again, with the cricket ban ending, me pregnant and the girls growing and content. The horror of South Africa, the cricket ban and the miscarriages had sometimes felt like a desperate, dark trend and I had been waiting for more calamity, but now that we were about to complete our family and Dave was about to play international cricket again, it truly felt we were getting our blessed life back on track.

20

Baby on Tour

It took a hell of a lot of organisation for the birth of our last child, which was going to happen in the UK while Dave was there on a monster tour of the country. First, the one-day team was going to compete in the ICC World Cup, which would run from May until July 2019, then there was to be some warm-up matches in preparation for an Ashes series of five Tests running through August and September.

Dave was to return to cricket with a series that was to take up close to five months of the year and there were two obligations that he would not miss. The first was the birth of our new baby. He just refused to; that's the kind of dad he is. Missing it was a non-starter. He also had to stay in the good graces of Cricket Australia.

It had been a hell of a year, and Dave knew there would be a lot of attention on his return to the Australian side. Previously, there had been some accommodations made for him, allowing him to spend more time with his family, but it was unlikely he'd get any leeway on this tour. He was going to have to be dotting i's and crossing t's for this season, not to mention having to make lots of runs for his team.

There was no shortage of people who wanted to see him fail, so we decided that we'd have our baby in England.

I flew to the UK thirty-five weeks pregnant, with two young kids in tow, at just about the limit of when you can fly safely with a baby in your belly. Dave had already been in the country for a few weeks, and I couldn't see him initially as the team was strictly enforcing a partner ban period, in which the wives and girlfriends were strictly forbidden from seeing the players.

Mum was going to be joining me when I gave birth, but in those first couple of weeks I was alone, staying in a hotel close to Dave's in Paddington in London, but not in it, and wrangling bags, kids and hospital appointments for the upcoming birth alone.

I'd planned everything I could in advance, but there are always unexpected trials and tribulations. The girls absolutely hated the daycare I'd found for them. It was so unexpected, as they normally loved daycare back home, and it completely derailed me. I couldn't bear to see them so teary starting their day, but they had to be in daycare because I had rafts of scans and tests to be done to be ready for the birth.

I was going to be induced at the Lindo Wing at St Mary's Hospital in London, which was where Princess Diana gave birth to her boys. That wasn't a consideration for me, though. Ivy and Indi had been delivered at the Royal Hospital for Women, a public teaching hospital in Randwick in Sydney, and both experiences had been excellent. We'd have been happy to go public for a third birth as well, but that wasn't an option for us in England. We had to go private, and the Lindo Wing was well regarded and also one of the more affordable options, even though it ended up being insanely expensive nonetheless.

While I was wrangling the girls and preparing for my induction date, Dave was cementing his way back into the Australian side. In his first six matches in the World Cup Dave had his two fifties, one not out, and two hundreds, with one of those being a very big ton against Bangladesh, which became the highest individual score of the tournament.

The birth was scheduled in a 7-day turnaround between matches near the end of the round. After a match against New Zealand, the team was to travel up to Manchester for their final knockout game against South Africa. There was a travel day and a rest day scheduled before training in Manchester, and Dave had been allowed to switch his travel and rest days, meaning he would be allowed to stay in London for the birth, and then catch the train up to Manchester the next day without missing any training.

The birth had some complications, but nothing particularly serious. I went into the hospital in the morning and before the sun had set we'd welcomed our third beautiful girl into our family. After Ivy and Indi we'd decided that we had to keep the 'I' theme going, and we both loved the name Isla, so Isla Rose she would be

Isla, Indi and Ivy. Those girls are our lives, our heartbeats. We couldn't have been happier welcoming that tiny little bundle of pink pudding into the world, and although there were moments when both Dave and I wondered what having a boy in our lives would be like, we were both simply ecstatic with the way things turned out. Dave and the girls, this was how it was going to be. I know it was very hard for Dave to leave us after only one night, wanting only to stay with us and our newborn, but such was the job. He caught the train up north, and I moved into an Airbnb with the new baby, the girls and Mum, who'd come over for a month to help me.

As was the tradition now, Dave scored a ton after the birth of his latest daughter up in Manchester.

After that match, the Australian team played the hosts, England, in a semi-final and lost pretty comprehensively. Following that match, Dave came back to stay with his newly expanded family for a little while, and we spent some lovely, quiet days in London together.

Shortly afterwards, Dave was back with the team, preparing for the Ashes series. The first Test was to be in Birmingham and that was, once again, a period in which the partners were not allowed to see the guys and, with a new baby in tow, it was a tough time for us.

This was Dave's first Test back since the ban, and I sorely wanted to be with him so, for each day of the Test, Mum looked after the baby, and the girls and I went and sat in the stands so I could watch Dave's return to Test cricket.

It wasn't the most successful Test for Dave, and it would prove to be a very trying series. In both innings, Dave's wicket was claimed by English quick bowler Stuart Broad for very few runs. It was a Test in which Steve Smith shone, returning to Test cricket with more than a hundred in both innings and effectively winning the match for Australia.

After that Test, a partner visiting period began and we moved into the players' hotel and were reunited with Dave, with a contingency plan in place should the baby prove to be unsettled and too much for us while Dave was playing.

I found it very strange, going back into the box with all of the other partners and the Cricket Australia officials. Besides a few players, in particular Usman Khawaja, Dave's childhood friend, not many people had been kind or considerate – nor honest and transparent when they had the chance – nor reached out to Dave when he was down.

We had been ostracised I think because many assumed we would never be back on the scene, but here we were. I had to work hard to make sure that I remained calm and non-confrontational in that period. I couldn't tell people how I really felt, which is what I normally do, and I did the best I could, which, if I'm being brutally honest, I probably didn't do particularly well. A lot of people thought the ban was going to be the end of Dave's cricket career and I wasn't capable of making small talk with them. It just wasn't in me.

Lord's and Leeds were, again, trying Tests for Dave. In London, Dave had had meagre scores in both innings, and in Leeds he had to fight extremely hard for his 61 in the first innings before being scuttled by Stuart Broad for a duck in the second innings. The London Test was drawn, with intermittent rain affecting multiple days of play and, despite scoring only 67 runs in the first innings, England went on to win the Test after a very impressive innings from Ben Stokes.

Then the series moved on to Manchester with the score tied at one a piece and, as strange as it had been for me to return to the box, I couldn't help wondering how strange it all must have been in the rooms.

*

I'd arranged an Airbnb in Manchester that appeared, online at least, to be a great-looking place with plenty of space, close to the cricket ground. It ended up being not quite what I'd expected.

When we arrived at the address – myself, two girls, one baby and also my friend Becky, who had flown over to spend some time with me and to help out after Mum had gone home – the driver, I could tell, was reluctant to leave us in this neighbourhood. It all seemed fine to me, but his reticence did put me off a little bit. There were people congregating around doorways and some homeless people too, but I figured that it was just the nature of big cities. I paid the driver, we took all the bags out of the car, and in we went.

We were staying on the third floor of the building, and with no lift, the two of us struggled carrying bags, girls and the baby up. We got there panting and were surprised to find that the door to the place was already open.

We pushed the bags into the apartment, I sat the girls on the lounge and, carrying the baby on my hip, I walked into the kitchen. There I found a man and, in front of him on the bench, a large quantity of drugs – pills, powder, weed. Loose, and also in small bags.

His eyes were wide as were mine. I was terrified and in the lengthening silence, I tried to figure out what to say. I ended up not saying anything. I just backed out to the lounge, told the girls we were leaving, and then started pushing the bags back towards the stairs. My adrenaline was spiking, and it was only when we were all outside did I really recognise what had happened. I suppose it was like being face to face with a potentially lethal wild animal. The danger was there and the danger was real, but in reality he was probably just as terrified as I was.

We managed to get back into a cab, but didn't know exactly where we should go. We couldn't go to Dave, and it looked like every hotel was full. Eventually a horrified and concerned Dave managed to book a place for us, and soon we were safely ensconced in our new accommodation, but on that day I learned there was only so much that could be planned for. Sometimes plans go awry.

We planned to stay for the fifth Test also, but after being trapped in the hotel because of the miserable weather we decided to leave before the Test started. It was time to head home with the girls. Dave was disappointed, but he understood.

The trip had been a huge one personally for both me and Dave – for me, giving birth to Isla while supporting Dave at work, and for Dave. After massive success in the one-day matches, scoring the second-most runs in the series, we'd hoped that Dave was back on track with his career, but the Test series had sorely tested him. Steve Smith had excelled throughout but Dave had struggled. He'd had meagre scores mostly, with Stuart Broad especially giving him trouble.

There were whispers, of course, that maybe Dave's temperament was no longer quite right for the Test side, but those whispers came from people whose opinions I had no time for at all. Dave's back was up against the wall after that series, but anyone who knows Dave knows that that's when he'll do something amazing.

*

In the lead-up to the Australian summer there was a lot of talk in the media about how it was time now for Dave to be dropped from the Australian Test side.

Eight of Dave's innings had been for fewer than 10 runs, with three of those being ducks. The conditions had been tough, with the ball swinging devilishly under grey skies while the Barmy Army chanted constantly about ball tampering.

According to the pundits, Dave was too hot-headed and not the right type of man for Test cricket. It was mindset, according to the experts. He could bat, and should continue to do so in the one-day and T20 matches, but perhaps this was the end of Dave's Test career.

When Dave got home, he was essentially told that he had to score a century playing for New South Wales to retain his spot in the Test side for the upcoming series against Pakistan, then he'd have to perform in that series to ensure he kept his spot. This was a short series, just two Tests after a T20 series, which meant there would only be limited opportunities to solidify his spot in the side, but I knew Dave would do everything he could to exploit those opportunities. We also knew the coach backed Dave. Dave and Justin Langer had a great relationship, and Langer had always had quiet faith in Dave having a bounce-back series in Australia.

What a bounce back it proved to be! Dave was at the crease for a little over 700 balls, for almost 500 runs, having been dismissed only once. It was amazing to see, but not surprising from my perspective. This was Dave through and through, tough, hard-working and above all tenacious. My heart swelled every moment he was at the crease.

The first Test was at the Gabba in Brisbane and, batting second, Dave, alongside Joe Burns and Marnus Labuschagne, set the Australians up for a crushing victory, with Dave scoring 154 runs. He wasn't required to bat in the second innings. The pressure was off a little bit going into the second Test in Adelaide, but Dave had no interest in taking his foot off the pedal.

The next Test in Adelaide was a pink-ball, day–night Test, which was a format Dave hadn't generally done well in. It was the end of November, but a freezing day to start that Test. Dave was opening the batting with Joe Burns, who was out in the first couple of overs, but almost from the first ball I could tell something special was going to happen. That's really the nature of Dave's batting: you can tell from the first over whether he is in the zone or not, and in this innings, you could tell that he was definitely in the zone.

His decision-making was amazing, his shot-making brilliant and every stroke dead and true. It was incredible to watch. At the end of the first day, Dave had already scored 166, all but guaranteeing an Australian win, but I could tell he was far from satisfied. During the day–night Tests, Dave and I stay at different hotels as his routine during those Tests and the kids' routine just does not work, but in the phone and text conversations we'd had that night, I could tell he really wanted to keep going the next day.

The next day started as all game days start: with Dave and I going for a morning walk. During that walk I could tell that he was going to be a danger on the pitch that day. He just seemed so calm and so focused.

When day two started, Dave picked up exactly where he had left off and just kept going and going and going. When he got to 200 he gave the little skip and a jump and the uppercut that he's known for, and when he got to 300 he did the same, except he added a little bow at the end of it.

That made me laugh. I knew what it meant. When Dave's batting, sometimes there are songs that repeat over and over in his head, and in this instance I knew he'd been listening to 'Rock-A-Bye Your Bear' by The Wiggles with the girls. That bow Dave made was what he would give to the girls when the song tells you to bow to your partner.

It was a lovely moment that was owned by the whole cricketing world, but was also owned only by Dave, me and the girls.

At 300, Dave was almost finished but not quite. One of the longest-standing records in Australian Test cricket was Don Bradman's 334 not out, the highest score by an Australian batsman until Matthew Hayden scored 380 in the early 2000s. Once Mark Taylor scored 334 in the '90s and declared, choosing not to surpass Don Bradman's mark. In

Adelaide, Dave decided to surpass the mark by one before carrying his bat.

The highest Test innings score ever was 400 runs scored by Brian Lara and, by chance, Lara was in Adelaide while Dave was batting. Dave would have loved to have gone on and try to take his spot atop the leader board but circumstances didn't allow it. Pakistan still needed to be bowled out twice to win the Test, so captain Tim Paine declared with Dave at 335 not out.

The Test was won easily, and Dave was named the player of the series. Later he was awarded the Allan Border Medal, which recognises the most outstanding male Australian cricketer of the year in all forms of the game. It was his third such medal, joining Test captains Ricky Ponting and Michael Clarke as the only cricketers who had been awarded the medal more than twice, with Steve Smith joining them the following year when he too received the medal for a third time.

Dave had wanted an Allan Border medal for each of the girls, and now he had that.

You can just never count Dave out, and if you do, you'll be doing so at your own peril.

21

A Role of My Own

Until the controversy in South Africa, I'd been working at Channel Nine intermittently on the panel show *Sports Sunday* and I'd been loving it. The show was born of the legendary *Nine's Wide World of Sports* Sunday show and discussed all kinds of sport, Australian and overseas. Working on that show gave me something to look forward to.

It wasn't much, and I didn't do it every week, but it was mine. I loved being a mum and a wife, and I understood that the nature of the cricket schedule and our lives meant that I had to travel and build my life around someone else's dreams, but there were times when I wanted something for myself. Dave was always so helpful and supportive, and when we came back from South Africa he would have supported me going back to *Sports Sunday*, but I didn't feel it was the right time for me to be out there, after the controversy and while Dave was completing his ban, so I told Nine I was going to be sitting out for a while. They were great, telling me the door was open whenever I wanted to come back.

It's funny, but in the wake of the South Africa controversy, I received a lot of offers, from TV and elsewhere. My profile had been raised and there were lots of opportunities, but I turned everything down. It wasn't the right time and it wasn't the right decision until Dave was back where he should be, ensconced atop the batting order in the Australian side.

Then, after the English tour, I did start to think that if the right thing came up in terms of work, I'd consider it. Roxy was sending me offers regularly but they weren't things I wanted to do. While I'd taken part in *It Takes Two* with Anthony Callea when I was much younger, it really wasn't my style anymore to do shows like *Dancing with the Stars*. I was keen to do something for myself, but the right offer with the right timing hadn't come.

Then Roxy sent me a link to a British show, telling me that I was being considered for the Australian-celebrity version. When I clicked the link, the video showed something that I instantly connected with. The British show was called *SAS: Who Dares Wins* and in it, a group of civilians was taken to the British countryside for an amended version of the UK Joint Special Forces Selection course, which looked absolutely brutal. It looked cold, exhausting, depleting … and definitely something I wanted to try.

I told Roxy I was interested. She said she didn't think the money was going to be much, but I told her I didn't care, I just wanted to be on the show.

She accepted the offer on my behalf, and then the moment of truth came – her call about scheduling. I'd only be able to do the show if it was shot in a period when Dave was home, and Dave really wasn't home that often. They sent over the dates and there were only a few days' overlap between when Dave was going to be overseas and when I was supposed to be shooting, and for those days Mum would be able to look after the girls. I started to get really excited about doing the show.

I didn't want to do the show for money or profile, or even for it to be a goal to try to achieve, although that was something I knew I'd respond to. I wanted to do it because I wanted to test what my mettle really was. I knew I was resilient and mentally strong, especially in the wake of South Africa, but I wanted to know for myself exactly what my reserves were – mentally and physically.

The episodes of the British show that I'd watched were all about resilience. Athleticism and endurance were undoubtedly a big part of it, but that wasn't really what decided success or failure. The way participants exited the show was at their own request, and the way they stayed in the competition was simply because they kept going.

I wanted to see if I could keep going when things were really tough, really exhausting, really stressful. When I told Dave about the show he thought I'd do really well, except for one thing – my fear of heights. Ever since I was a little girl, I couldn't even go on the most benign rides at a carnival, but I told him I thought I'd be able to confront it if I had to, drawing on a well of resilience that I thought I had in me.

The truth was, I didn't know what was inside of me and I really wanted to know what was there. I also wanted to know what my mind and body could do now after I'd had my third child.

I signed up to do the show, which was going to be called *SAS Australia*, only a few months after Isla was born, and I was still quite weak. Isla was to be our third and final child and I wanted to reclaim my body. This show would give me a reason to get fit and strong, which is what felt like my most natural state to be in.

I was a member of a gym in Surry Hills, in Sydney's inner east, and I told one of the trainers what I was planning to do. He introduced me to another trainer who was absolutely the perfect person to help me prepare.

Kev Toonen had been in the military for more than a decade, and he'd been a high-performance trainer for the Special Air Service Regiment (SASR), Australia's premier warfighting military unit. He'd also been part of the SASR's brutal selection course, which was the closest thing in Australia to what the show would be attempting to emulate.

Kev started putting me through my paces straight away. I needed fitness and strength and he put me onto an intense training program that focused on just that, with cardio and weights included. But that wasn't the end of it. He also had me doing specific things that he thought the 'directing staff' or DS, those conducting SASR selection and also running the show's course, would make me do.

Some of it seemed insane and impossible. I remember one session vividly in which he handed me a weighted bar, telling me that it couldn't touch the floor. The bar didn't seem particularly heavy when I started, easily doing lifts, lunges and squats, but near the end I swear that little piece of metal weighed 100 kilograms.

There were a lot of times when I was training that I felt I couldn't go on, but I suppose that's what the training was for. As I trained I became much fitter and much stronger in a way that I hadn't been when I was training as a professional Ironwoman.

Previously I'd been training in a very specific way for a specific purpose, but now I was becoming more rounded in the kinds of exercises I was doing. For instance, I'd barely ever been able to do a chin-up before, as that kind of strength just wasn't needed in Ironwoman events, but after working with Kev I got to the point where I could bang out sets of twelve or fifteen unassisted.

Kev also had me pack marching, and that was something initially I didn't think I'd be able to do. That involved carrying a thirty-kilogram pack for quite long distances – up to twenty kilometres – something he said he thought I'd be doing a lot of on the show.

I thought perhaps we'd do some work with a weighted vest interspersed with a little training with an actual pack, but Kev told me that's not how that kind of training worked. The point of pack marches is that you can carry a pack full of essential equipment. You can't distribute the weight for training ease. You can't distribute the weight in front and back. You can't walk in a controlled environment like a cool gym on the treadmill; you just have to put thirty kilograms in a pack and go for a bloody long walk. So that's exactly what I did.

Kev gave me a camouflage pack, and I put thirty kilograms of rice inside of it, slapped Dave's wraparound Oakleys on my face, and started to walk the ten kilometres from Maroubra to the gym in Surry Hills and back again with the pack on.

I worked hard before heading to New Zealand, where the filming was taking place, and when I arrived there, I was absolutely pumped. Bring it on, I thought.. I was ready. Then I started hearing about this new disease, a bit like SARS, called the coronavirus. Like SARS, I expected it to be a big deal, but a big deal for someone else. I didn't think it would affect my life and my family's, but of course it affected everyone's life and everyone's family all the way around the world.

We'd been given a date on which the show was supposed to start and in preparation for that we'd been taken from our hotel rooms – hooded – to shoot promotional videos, but as the shoot date came close, it was pushed back, and then pushed back again, as the producers scrambled to accommodate the changing biosecurity situation.

Those days soon became a week, and we were only allowed to leave our room for a few hours at a time, to ensure that we wouldn't bump into the other candidates, none of whose identities I knew except for Roxy, who had told me that she'd also signed up to do the show.

Eventually we were all called into a meeting room together, and there I found that a number of people I already knew a little bit were to be part of the show, including Shannan Ponton from the TV show *The Biggest Loser*, comedian Merrick Watts, swimmer James Magnussen, and model and TV host Erin McNaught. Only we were told we weren't going to be on the show anymore – or not for a while, anyway. The border between New Zealand and Australia was about to be slammed closed, and tightly, and no one knew when it would be opened again. We went away with the message that there was a good likelihood the show would proceed at a later date. We were told to keep training. Some people did, some didn't. I tried, but we all soon learned what COVID was like.

*

I don't think I was the only person, nor were we the only family, who appreciated the slowdown of life that the early parts of the pandemic enforced in many parts of Australia.

Dave was home and so was I. We were with the girls every day. Every day Dave was playing with the kids, teaching them, joking with them and connecting without counting the days until he was packing his bags again. I think it was lovely for all of us.

Mum developed an obsession with sourdough and made bread every single day. At about three or four in the afternoon, Dave and I would slow down from the slowdown and have a glass of wine. It was really lovely, despite the terrible restrictions that we knew were wreaking havoc on people everywhere.

Dave and I trained together too, every day. At the start of the pandemic I ordered some gym equipment and some mats, and we made a little gym at the bottom of our newly built house that we'd only recently moved into. We were each other's motivation and we stayed fit. Which is not to say we stayed thin!

There was a period in which I was eating a loaf of bread every day, not to mention a little wine every afternoon. Dave was in a similar boat, and it was the thing that prompted us to start running together, going from our place, past Matraville, where Dave grew up, then to La Perouse and back again. It was a good fifteen- to twenty-kilometre run, and when we ran we were alone, but together, running just for running's sake.

The COVID period was almost a glimpse of what life would be like when Dave retired from cricket. He was home; we were together. He'd work and I would also when the time came, but we'd be more of a normal family, which wasn't necessarily something we dreamed about, but something the COVID period proved would be quite wonderful.

The finish line wasn't there yet, though. Dave had fought damn hard to cement his place back in the Australian team and there were still big things in his career that he wanted to do. When cricket resumed, as it was supposed to with Australia's tour of England scheduled in August, he was going to be right in the thick of it.

In June, I got a call that *SAS Australia* had been resurrected and while the border between Australia and New Zealand was still closed, a plan had been developed to shoot the show in the New South Wales Snowy Mountains in August. The dates worked out perfectly. I'd be able to shoot the show, and when I returned, Dave would be due to leave for England for the next Test series, which was allowed to proceed under strict COVID protocols.

I went back to the specific training that Kev had tailored for me, and I also did some boxing training, which, we were told, would come into play at some point in the show.

When August came around, I thought I was ready for the show physically and mentally, and when we started shooting, I thanked my lucky stars for every minute I had spent preparing.

*

When we arrived on site in Berridale and began shooting the show, there were familiar cast members from the last attempt at shooting, including Roxy, who I was immediately pitted against in a boxing match, after which Roxy left the show. There were also people I hadn't met before, such as Schapelle Corby, who was well known as a convicted drug trafficker, actor Firass Dirani, and the impressive Sabrina Frederick, an AFLW player for Richmond Football Club in Melbourne.

I was instantly judgemental when introduced to Schapelle, but as I got to know her, my attitude changed. She's a very resilient woman, and someone with a surprisingly optimistic outlook. We were paired together for some of the trials and while Schapelle struggled with some of the physical stuff, she refused to quit and never stopped trying. We were paired together in the abseiling and I had to goad her up the mountain as I could tell she was far more fearful of heights than I was. She did it slowly, but managed to get up and down the mountain, something I thought she wouldn't be able to do at all.

Then we had to take our packs up and down an incline and we were last by a mile as she was really not very fit, but I never left her, even as the directing staff were screaming in my face. At the end I was carrying my pack and dragging her, and I didn't quit, but she didn't either. I was proud of her.

Afterwards she and I sat on a rocky outcrop and had a really in-depth conversation about what life's like for her. I found parts of her story really resonated with me. When she'd returned to Australia from prison in Bali, she'd struggled to be out in public, worried about what people were thinking about her and the assumptions they were making. I'd made assumptions about her, myself, and I of all people should have known better.

On the third day, Schapelle took herself out of the competition but, honestly, I was impressed she went as far as she had.

The evening after Schapelle withdrew, there was a bit of disharmony within our group as many people believed Firass Dirani was responsible for her quitting, and she had been someone people had started to really like. I didn't think it was helpful to attack Firass, however, so I took on something of a mother-hen role, trying to mediate arguments between some of the younger candidates like Firass and Shane Warne's son, Jackson. I filled up water bottles and made sure people's socks were dry, and intervened in arguments – honestly, it wasn't too different to being at home, except for the cold and the exercise!

Twice during the series I was called in for interrogation by the *SAS* directing staff, Ant Middleton and Jason Fox (Foxy). Ant is a British adventurer, and former soldier and marine who's also written books on his life experiences and mental fitness, but with a chequered past of his own, and Foxy is also an ex-British soldier and adventurer. In each instance I knew they might try and bring up the incidents of 2007 and also more recently in South Africa – after all, I was part of a reality television show, and reality shows thrive on drama.

When I sat down in front of Ant and Foxy, my priors got the better of me. I assumed we were going to be adversarial, and that they'd be yelling at me about things that had happened in the past, and things that I may be embarrassed about. I was frazzled, with my defences up and ready to fight. Ant and Foxy were unsettlingly cool.

Ant asked where all my aggression came from. I had no answer, though. He was just asking benign questions and I had already erected a front.

And then Foxy picked me instinctively, telling me that he thought I was doing the show because I knew I'd be asked tough questions while I was tired and exhausted, and that I wanted to know how I'd perform in such moments of extreme discomfort and confrontation. To test what I could take, not only physically, but mentally and emotionally as well.

It was really impressive. He'd got me in one, and the exchange that followed afterwards was something I'll never forget.

Foxy said that one of the most enlightened things to do was to let my walls down and be vulnerable.

I told him I didn't know how to do that – I was scared that if I let my guard down and was less aggressive, then I may end up exposed. Then he asked me if that was such a bad thing … and I had nothing to say.

Emotions were gathering like storm clouds inside of me and I tried not to cry, because I knew a lot of people, including my critics, would be watching the show, but my eyes welled up; it was as if all the pressure that had been building up for years was dissipating.

I'd only been known in public as an ambitious, hard-faced person, and it felt like that was a façade that I had to maintain, but now things were different. I knew the producers were going to run the footage of that interview and that afterwards I wouldn't be able to pretend in public that nothing bothered me – that the scandals, real or imagined, were just water off a duck's back. People would know afterwards that they could hurt me – that they could get to me – and although that was something that I'd tried to avoid, now I realised I no longer cared.

It felt so good to offload and relieve the pressure without judgement.

Had I not had that interview and my time on that show, I don't think I would have written my story. I don't think I would have been able to bare myself in the way I've been able to. In that moment I think I became a completely different person.

Before going into the show I'd made a promise to myself that I'd do everything we were asked to do, and to never voluntarily quit. When I started, I kept just reinforcing that promise in my mind, and after the interview with Ant and Foxy, that promise honestly just became easier and easier to keep, as I really started to trust and admire them. I knew they weren't going to ask me, or any of us, to do anything that was dangerous – just difficult, and difficult I could handle.

I wanted to do everything we were asked, and as the days dragged on, the hardest things weren't actually the challenges but the little things like keeping our feet warm and dry, battling with little infections and fungi, and getting our Bergens – our backpacks – in order.

After ten days, I think the producers and the directing staff were surprised at how many contestants were still left on the course, and that they weren't necessarily the people they thought would be. Footballers Nick Cummins and Sabrina Frederick were still on the course, but so too were Merrick Watts, Firass and me.

I'd been impressed with Firass, who was a bit mouthy, but also a great athlete and someone with lots of perseverance. Contestants turned on him and, after one incident, every other person on the show decided that they wanted him gone, which was something that could only be done with a unanimous vote from all the contestants.

I didn't want that. Firass is a good person, he was just a little immature, and I didn't think he should go, so I fought for him and that kept him in the show. Firass and his situation reminded me of Dave, and how people had turned on him as a pack, and I didn't like that mentality, that piling on. You don't turn your back on people if they're your people. I was adamant he should stay and Firass continued.

We'd worked as a unit, unexpectedly, and on day ten we were expelled together, which did feel quite arbitrary to me. While I was a bit annoyed at the way in which I was leaving the show, I went home very satisfied with my performance and my experience.

What I'd discovered was that I knew my body and mind were capable of so much more than I'd realised and that felt good, and I'd also learned a big lesson about the importance of being vulnerable and opening up, too.

But honestly, the best thing I got out of being on *SAS Australia* was the response I received from people who watched the show. For me it was transformational.

I know a lot of people who have been on these kinds of shows have been quite upset about the way they were represented, or how they were edited, but for every frame of the show that I appeared in, it was 100 per cent me. Not only that, it was the me that I never show anyone in public, nor even in my private life very much.

I think the show showed why I am the way I am in public, or used to be anyway – why I put up a front, why I'm sometimes a little short, a little abrupt, a little prickly. Not only that, I think the show helped me learn how to deal with difficult or uncomfortable situations.

Previously in those kinds of situations, I always saw them as confrontations and I would just shut up shop emotionally and prepare to fight, but the show taught me that difficult situations are just challenges. They aren't even necessarily uncomfortable, they're just things to be worked through, and that there's always a way out or a way to be negotiated. This too shall pass.

So in that way, the show taught me how to be comfortable in uncomfortable situations and above all, that's what I took away from my experience. It's something I've thought about often while in the box at the cricket. Since the events of South Africa, I've often been uncomfortable in the box, hearing in my mind what I think are the thoughts of the other people sitting near me.

It made me uncomfortable and, I can imagine, it made others uncomfortable too. It probably created something of a feedback loop as well, where there may have been a little bit of pre-existing ill-feeling that was amplified by my oversized response to it.

The publicity from the show was overwhelmingly positive. I'd never been in the public glare for such positive reasons before. I'd won an Ironwoman event and that had been publicised somewhat, but previously the things that people really paid attention to had been negative. The show had been heavily promoted and people had generally only said nice things to me about it. It seemed it had reframed people's attitudes about me and the things they connected me with, like the Clovelly incident, or what happened in South Africa. People would stop me in the street – people I didn't know – to tell me that they'd either underestimated or misunderstood me. It was hugely gratifying and the response gave me so much confidence – in myself, who I was, and what I was capable of.

I would do that show a hundred more times if they asked me to.

*

SAS: *Australia* also helped me go forward to do some of the things I'd always wanted to do professionally.

I've always loved sport, and have always liked talking about sport, but I wasn't confident about my opinions. Even when I was a professional athlete, there was always a voice in my head telling me that my opinion wasn't valuable, that I was just considered for opportunities because of my sporting achievements, or because I look a certain way. That voice was also in my head after I met Dave, a voice telling me that people assumed that my opinions were just Dave's.

I did a lot of radio during and after *SAS Australia* aired, and I became more confident with each interview. What I was talking about was my experience, and it was true. They were my thoughts, my opinions and people seemed interested and responded well. Even friends said that on the radio, and during the show, they saw a different side of me. A side that was more accessible and open.

After I did an interview with Triple M radio in Sydney, the producers asked me if I'd like to fill in as Lawrence Mooney's co-host of *Moonman in the Morning*, a highly rated breakfast show, while the regular co-host Jess Eva was a contestant on *I'm a Celebrity Get Me Out of Here*.

It felt great to be in that radio environment. More than any other radio station, Triple M felt like a place where my point of view was accepted. It was sports-oriented, it was fun, it was perhaps a little blokey, and these were all aspects of my personality. I loved it.

Then I was offered a twelve-week stint at 2GB, doing the *Wide World of Sports* radio show, and I think that before *SAS Australia* this kind of opportunity would neither have been offered nor accepted. There was no place to hide on this show. Where previously I'd been reactive, talking about the show I'd just participated in and a little about my life and history, with *Wide World of Sports* I was expressing my thoughts and opinions on all kinds of things, with no place to hide.

I was ready for it, and I loved it. My co-host Mark Levy recognised how green I still was on the microphone, and he coached me through the first few weeks, with the most important lesson being to own what I was saying. He told me that when I had an opinion that was honestly held, it didn't matter if there was a tiny little ripple of backlash – I didn't need to be scared of it, and I didn't have to catastrophise, and it didn't mean I didn't know what I was talking about either. If I had an opinion, I should own it, Mark taught me. Universal approval was for dictators and chocolate makers.

What I wanted, above all, was to be considered seriously, not just as someone who was part of a media scandal, or someone who was married to a cricketer. When I received an offer to be part of Channel Seven's commentary team for the Tokyo Olympics, working from Sydney, I felt like I'd finally reached the escape velocity required to get beyond the orbit of my past.

They asked me to do the commentary on the open-water swimming event, and also the men's and women's triathlon alongside Dave Culbert, a former Olympic track and field finalist and Commonwealth Games medallist and commentator. No one watched the Olympics to hear commentary about the tactics of open-water swimming from someone involved in a scandal fifteen years ago – they want to hear from someone who knows what they're talking about, and it was again so gratifying to know that my expertise and experience was being taken seriously.

Then another offer came in. I was asked to do the Channel Ten television commentary for the upcoming Ironman and Ironwoman national series.

I was ecstatic. It felt like I was going back home.

*

To be honest I felt more pressure doing the commentary for the Ironman and Ironwoman series than for the Olympics. I suppose that was because when I normally did media, I didn't have a really intimate sense of the audience, but when I was doing the surf lifesaving commentary, I knew the audience well – *really* well – and that made me nervous.

But I was also just so at home with the culture, the tactics, the sport itself. Beach and surf lifesaving racing was deeply embedded in the core of my being and I understood the races and the athletes better than anything else.

The surf lifesaving commentary was such a big part of my life when I was a girl. It's the way I first really understood the sport, when I was tiny little thing with Dad at the club in Maroubra, watching the races on a Sunday afternoon. The commentary was in my head when I was training as a girl too, fantasising about how the commentators were stunned by my actions. 'Falzon has caught that wave!' or 'Falzon powers to the front!'

Nothing annoyed me more, when I was in the series, than the commentators not understanding the sport well – something that happened often when swimming commentators were called in to do the lifesaving commentary.

I wanted to do it justice, and I knew I *could* do it justice. I suppose it's not up to me to say whether I managed that or not, but I was so proud of my commentary and interviews. Some were even with girls who I had actually competed against on the back stretch of my career.

It was just lovely to be on the beach again, among the carnival atmosphere of the series. Of course, it was so different to cricket with its money and exposure and sponsorship and huge crowds, but there was something so very pure about being back in surf lifesaving. I was impressed with the professionalism and skill of the athletes, and I even impressed myself that I was once in their number.

After that season ended I was offered another gig, which I still have today. Triple M Sydney was resurrecting their weekly sports show *Dead Set Legends*, and they wanted me to be part of their new panel. It was such a case of the right thing coming along at the right time.

I was ready to talk. I was comfortable on air now, and felt more like a professional than a blow-in. I've watched a hell of a lot of sport in my life, and now I had an excuse to watch even more. I also was now happy to be talking about sport, something I really know about.

I've always been very honest, but I can imagine even a few years ago I would have been wary of having a view contrary to the prevailing wisdom, but I don't feel like that anymore. When there's a controversy or a scandal, I can often see things from the other side.

I still believe some things are right and others are wrong, but I think you're in a far better position to discern between the two when you understand that the people involved on both sides of every confrontation or transgression have their own motivations. Sometimes those motivations are black and craven, and sometimes they're pure white and innocent, but in most instances those motivations are a shade of grey and the people involved on both sides are living, breathing humans who feel hurt and pain just like everyone else.

*

I love to work, and hope to work even more in the future. Currently I have a number of media gigs in television and radio and they're the things that maintain me in the back end of Dave's playing career.

As much as I love being a mum and a wife, and as much as I'm dedicated to being there to support Dave's career and travelling with him as much as I can, I love that I now have an emerging career in my area of expertise. It gives my weeks and months structure and meaning that isn't owned by someone else's life and career. I think my career will also be useful in the future, when Dave finally hangs up his batting gloves.

Dave will always be involved in cricket, I think, and I reckon that if he isn't, the game will be poorer for it. He has a unique perspective and has an amazing mind for the game. He will be a coach or commentator or administrator, and he'll do an amazing job, of that I have no doubt. In fact he's looking forward to joining the Fox Cricket's commentary team over the coming year, and on retirement as well. I just want him to be able to do what he wants to do, when he wants to do it.

I want Dave to be able to take a year off or more if he likes, and for me to be able to pick up the slack.

Dave's had an incredible career, and has had incredible opportunities, but he's sacrificed a lot, especially since the girls were born. Some dads don't really want to do school pick-ups, or go to Oztag training or coach kids cricket, or play silly games and dance for entire rainy afternoons, but Dave isn't one of those dads. I want Dave to be able to just live that dad life, and enjoy himself for as long as he wants.

Very often Dave has to do his parenting on FaceTime. It hurts him, I know that, but there are still more things that he wants to do in cricket. He's still hungry.

22

Beginnings and Endings

It was magic, being back on the water with my arms aching, my lungs burning and a ski scything through the waves, with the lowering sun in front of me. I wasn't enjoying myself, though, and the reason was that between me and the sunset were other paddlers, who were faster than me.

One of the North Bondi Surf Life Saving Club legends and coaches, former Olympian Jimmy Walker, had been doing some handyman work in our house, and he asked if I was still doing much exercise. I was, I said – I was doing a lot.

When Dave was in town, I'd be doing everything he did, so I was essentially still training like a professional athlete. We ran a lot together. When Dave's program asked for long distance, that's what I'd be doing. When he was doing fartlek training, or sprints, or mid-distance sets, I'd be running alongside him, as best I could anyway. I could keep up with Dave on the longer distances, but he's a beast in a sprint. Off the track, we'd be in the gym together but working on different regimes, with Dave doing exercises that were usually specific to batting, and I'd be doing a more general-purpose workout designed by my trainer.

When Dave was away, I kept my exercise frequency up with a mix of cardio and weights with my trainer Jono Castano. When Dave and I worked out together, we did so as a couple, spending that time as bonding time. And when I worked out alone, I did it to keep my head where it needed to be. Without it, there were few opportunities to talk to an adult and expel negative thoughts that may have collected in my head.

Then Jimmy asked me whether I was doing any paddling and I told him no. He asked me why, and I had no answer.

Why *wasn't* I doing any paddling? North Bondi was only a short drive away, and I loved the atmosphere and camaraderie of afternoon paddling training. When Jimmy came by, Dave was about to go away for four months, and with the older girls now in school we wouldn't be travelling with him. I thought maybe a paddle was exactly what I needed.

In the first few sessions, I was very frustrated with my speed on the craft, and also my understanding of the ocean. It had been eight or so years since I'd been on a ski, and the time off the water showed. Some girls whom I'd been training against when I'd been an Ironwoman were still in the water, and either they'd improved greatly or I'd slowed down a lot.

Of course, it was probably a mix of the two. Of course, I wasn't going to be able to walk away from a sport at a professional level and come back at the same level. Of course, of course.

I just couldn't quite manage my expectations, though. In my mind I was still an Ironwoman. There was something about being back on the craft and being back on the water that triggered a drive, a motivation and, ultimately, a frustration.

For the first few sessions on the water, I was coming back onto the beach angry with myself because I wasn't beating the girls I wanted to beat. It's embarrassing to admit that. I was now a mother of three, and someone who hadn't been in the sport for the best part of a decade, and I was beating myself up that girls in their twenties were beating me.

What I am proud to say is that I kept paddling and kept turning up, and eventually I got over the egotistical hump. When that happened, I started to really enjoy myself. And not only that, my speed started to improve as well.

When I was asked to commentate in the Ironwoman series, including the Australian titles on the Gold Coast, I figured that perhaps I could compete in the Masters category that was happening in the days before the open events. It ended up being a wonderful experience: competition undertaken in a very healthy spirit.

I competed in a lot of events, including some soft-sand running races I hadn't participated in since I was a kid, pacing myself through a two-kilometre soft sand run and some 80-metre sprint races. I did well too, winning some team golds, but the thing I was proudest of was that the tough, ultra-competitive girl in me didn't come out. We all raced as best we could, having trained as best we could, with most of us having other lives and other concerns. Afterwards we all went out for drinks and talked about our families.

It was a great experience, and one that I'll do again, although it's coming up again very soon and I haven't even really started training yet. We'll see.

*

A little while ago, my eldest daughter, Ivy, came to me with her iPad with a video from YouTube she wanted to show me. It was a news report from 2007, and as soon as I saw the external shot of the Clovelly Hotel I knew exactly what it was. It was a shock.

Ivy has developed an independent curiosity that Dave and I both love, but she's only eight and there are some things she won't yet understand. Some of those things relate to her parents and their past.

I'd already told Ivy not to google Dave or me, and when I found she had, coming up with a news report about the 2007 incident, I was instinctively upset. It was a useful a reminder that some psychic wounds never completely heal.

I know I'll have to talk to Ivy soon, about myself and my history, and about Dave's history also. It frightens me, though. She thinks that her mum and dad are like superheroes, and I like her thinking only positively of us. It breaks my heart to think that she may judge me in the way other people have. I don't think she will, but it's a fear that's keeping me from sitting down with her and explaining what that YouTube video is. I'll have to do it soon, but I can't do it just yet. Not yet.

We can never ignore our pasts, because they're not just ours. They intertwine with other people's pasts as well as with history. We can't ignore the past, we can only learn from it.

As I write it's the summer of 2022/2023 and Dave is back in the news again. There had been talk of the ban that stopped Dave from being in a leadership position in an Australian team being overturned. This was something Dave was amenable to, as he thought he could bring something to one of the sides, whether that's T20, one-day or Test cricket.

There was to be an internal review of the decision, as per the terms of the original ban, and Dave was happy to submit to questioning in private. Then it was announced the process was to be public, and Dave decided he didn't want to be involved anymore. Some saw this for what it was, which was Dave protecting his family and choosing not to be involved in a process that he saw as unfair. Others who didn't understand Dave, nor ever cared to, saw the decision differently, saying that Dave was just looking out for Dave.

I don't know whether the man who verbally attacked me in Adelaide in the December Test against the West Indies was part of the second group, but it wouldn't surprise me if he was.

Adelaide is one of the only Australian grounds where, in the lunch break, the kids and I can walk over from the box to where the players are to catch up briefly between sessions. It's something the girls love to do, especially Ivy. It requires us to go through the public areas, and we usually don't get any grief. Not usually.

The yelling came from a group of men in their twenties. Only one man was shouting at me, but there was a group snickering as he did. He called me a slut. He mentioned the 2007 incident and yelled out obscenities. Before I could even think about what I was doing, I was marching towards the group of men, with the girls in tow.

I was shaking but I was composed. I asked them who had shouted at me. They smirked but said nothing. I asked them if they were proud of themselves. Again they smirked and said nothing. I asked them if they thought that was an okay thing to say to a mother with her daughters in tow. Yet again, they smirked and said nothing.

We were on the concourse and there were lots of people around. They didn't say anything, not any of them. I was so disappointed in these men, and also in all the people around who had heard what had been shouted, but did nothing and said nothing.

I walked away shaken and angry that the girls had been there for this confrontation, but I also knew the moment would be useful for them. You have to stand up for yourself, and you have to stand up for what's right.

I could have walked away and pretended that nothing had been said, but something *had* been said. I'd heard it and my girls had too. If I'd just walked away, nothing would change. Given that it was 2022 and I was still being called repulsive names over an incident from 15 years earlier, perhaps nothing changes anyway.

My girls will be ready for whatever world they step into as adults. I'm working hard as a mum towards that goal, and Dave's doing the same too as their father, sharing that with his role as a professional cricketer, but we know that we're closer to the end of that road. Life will change when Dave retires from cricket, but neither of us want the end to come prematurely.

I find it hard to watch the cricket live when Dave is playing now, because I know how much it means to him. I've been like that since the 2019 Ashes series in the UK on Dave's return to the Test side, when Stuart Broad kept taking his wicket. I talk to someone else while he's batting and only once he's at about 20 runs or so can I start paying attention. I block my ears because I don't want to hear the appeals. Ivy is a nervous wreck, too, when Dave is at the crease. We were both on the edge of our seats during the Boxing Day Test against South Africa in Melbourne, which marked Dave's 100th Test. When Dave's back is against the wall it always brings out his best performance, and in the morning of that game, he was eerily calm and I knew he was going to do something really special – and he did, with a staggering double century in scorching 37-degree heat. But I always tell Ivy that, regardless of whether he's out for a duck or gets a ton, he's still Daddy and will always be Daddy.

Mummy will always be Mummy, too.

It's strange to write a memoir when it feels like a new life is about to begin, but for a new life to start I suppose it must replace an old one. In part I wrote this book for my girls, so that one day they'll be able to read it and understand the details of my story without interference or influence, and to show them that, as women, no matter how hard things get – and it does for women, in the world we live in – that they just need to keep going, keep breathing. That tough times pass, but that in order to get through those tough times you need to find something for yourself that will create a sense of safety and resilience, and to surround yourself with people who know you and who love you. For a long time, I felt that all I could do was to run away from my problems, when all I really needed to do was run back towards myself, breathe and allow myself to be loved. Now I'm the happiest I've ever been and I wouldn't change anything for the world. My life to this point has been ups and downs, forever learning who I am, and while there will undoubtedly be more ups and more downs, I don't think there's too much more to learn about who I am.

I will change over the years of course, but whatever may come I will always know who Candice is. I am Mum to my girls, and I forever will be. I am wife to Dave, and forever will be. I am a daughter and a sister, to parents and brothers, and forever will be. I am an athlete, a commentator and the woman who will take you to task should you call her names in public.

I most certainly know myself, and may you all be so lucky to know who you are, too.

ACKNOWLEDGEMENTS

First of all, I want to thank Mum and Dad, Kerry and Mickey Falzon, for being the best parents a girl could ever have, and for their ever-present and tireless, loving support; and also to Tim and Pat for being the best brothers in the world.

To the love of my life, Dave, I thank you from the bottom of my heart for all that you do for me and with me – I couldn't have wished for a more supportive and loving husband. You're a dream come true. I also want to thank my daughters, Ivy Mae, Indi Rae and Isla Rose for their boundless love and energy – I'm so glad to be your Mum!

Thanks to Llara, Naomi, Kelly and all my female friends and fellow competitors, athletes and commentators. I'm so glad to have you in my life. Thanks too, to Paul Tonich and Rick Turner, for believing in me and knowing what I was capable of.

Huge thanks to Sarah Wagner at TSA Talent – your support and friendship has meant the world to me over the years. Many thanks to Ben McKelvey, who helped me tell my story – it was so wonderful working with you. Thanks also to my publisher, Roberta Ivers, and Jim Demetriou, Helen Littleton, Shannon Kelly, Kate Butler, Lucy Inglis and Alice Wood at HarperCollins Australia for all your hard work on my book, along with the amazing sales team, including

Karen-Marie Griffiths, Sean Cotcher, Kerry Armstrong, Kate Huggins, Anne Walsh and Hillary Albertson, and all the field sales managers around the country. Many thanks to Hazel Lam, Senior Designer at HarperCollins, who designed my beautiful book, and also thanks to the talented team behind the cover photography and styling – Alana Landsberry, Kelly Bowman and Jessica Jade.

Many thanks too, to Harvie Allison; GM Photographics; Stephen Chu; Kirk Powell; and Getty Images, including Matt Roberts and Chris McGrath, for their wonderful photographs.

SURF LIFESAVING MEDALS
AND AWARDS

NIPPERS

1998
NSW State Championships
2nd Under 13 Ironwoman

1999
NSW State Championships
1st Under 14 Ironwoman
1st Under 14 Board Race

SENIOR COMPETITION

2000
Australian Championships
2nd Under 16 Ironwoman
3rd Under 16 Board Race

2001
NSW State Championships
1st Under 16 Ironwoman

Australian Championships
2nd Under 16 Board Race

2002
NSW State Championships
2nd Open Board Rescue
3rd Open Taplin Relay

Australian Championships
3rd Open Taplin Relay

2003
NSW State Championships
3rd Open Board Rescue
3rd Open Board Relay

2004
NSW State Championships
1st Open Board Race
3rd Open Taplin Relay

2005
NSW State Championships
3rd Open Taplin Relay

Australian Championships
2nd Open Taplin Relay

2006
NSW State Championships
3rd Open Surf Teams

2008
NSW State Championships
1st Open Board Race
1st Open Board Rescue
2nd Open Ironwoman

Australian Championships
1st Open Surf Teams

2009

WA State Championships
1st Open Taplin Relay
1st Open Surf Teams
1st Open Board Relay
2nd Open Ironwoman
2nd Open Single Ski
2nd Open Board Rescue
3rd Open Ski Relay

Australian Championships
1st Open Board Relay
1st Open Surf Teams
2nd Open Rescue Tube Rescue

2010

WA State Championships
1st Open Ironwoman
1st Open Board Rescue
1st Open Rescue Tube Rescue
1st Open Surf Teams
1st Open Taplin Relay
2nd Open Surf Race
2nd Open Board Relay
2nd Restricted Surf Race
3rd Open Board Race

2011

NSW State Championships
1st Open Surf Belt
1st Open Ski Relay
1st Open Surf Teams
1st Taplin Relay
2nd Open Ironwoman
2nd Open Board Relay
2nd Open Board Rescue
2nd Open Rescue Tube Rescue

Australian Championships
1st Open Taplin Relay
3rd Open Ski Relay

2012

NSW State Championships
1st Open Double Ski
1st Open Surf Teams
1st Open Rescue Tube Rescue
1st Taplin Relay
2nd Open Ski Relay
2nd Open Board Relay

Australian Championships
1st Taplin Relay
1st Ski Relay
1st Double Ski

World Championships
1st Open Rescue Tube Rescue
1st Open Taplin Relay

2013

NSW State Championships
1st Open Ironwoman
1st Open Taplin Relay
1st Open Surf Teams
1st Open Board Rescue
1st Open Board Relay
2nd Open Board Race
2nd Open Ski Relay
2nd Open Rescue Tube Rescue

Australian Championships
1st Open Ski Relay
1st Open Double Ski
1st Open Board Rescue
1st Open Rescue Tube Rescue
2nd Open Taplin Relay
2nd Open Surf Teams

CAPTIONS AND CREDITS

Page 16 – 3 years old, with Dad (Mickey) at the beach.

Page 28 – A young Nipper.

Page 43 – Ironwoman under-14s, South Maroubra. © **Stephen Chu**

Page 44 – 15 years old, on my way in the professional series.

Page 57 – 17 years old, in a surf race.

Page 58 – In the surf, in my element.

Page 72 – Racing in the pool for Endeavour High School. © **Stephen Chu**

Page 96 – Surf skis, on the beach.

Page 117 – With Llara in Fiji.

Page 118 – Mooloolaba Beach, Queensland.

Page 144 – Winning the Taplin Relay, Kurrawa. © **Harvie Allison Photography**

Page 165 – With Naomi Flood, double ski winners. © **Harvie Allison Photography**

Page 166 – With my brother Patty at the City2Surf.

Page 181 – An early shot with Dave.

Page 182 – With Dave at the 2013 Ashes.

Page 193 – With Mum (Kerry) in Greece, 2014.

Page 194 – Engaged!

Page 200 – With baby Ivy at the cricket.

Page 210 – With Mum and Dad on my wedding day. **Photograph by GM Photographics.**

Page 222 – With Dave, Ivy and Isla, 2016.

Page 237 – Celebrating my finish of the Gold Coast marathon with Ivy.

Page 238 – Dave wrote my and the girls' names on his hand wrapping, Durban, South Africa.

Page 262 – Ivy and Indi, Cape Town, South Africa.

Page 278 – Ivy, Isla and Indi, my three girls.

Page 290 – Training for *SAS Australia*.

Page 312 – Back on the ski. © **Kirk Powell**

Pages 321 and 322 – Running strong. © **Kirk Powell**